Transnational Cinema

Transnational Cinema

An Introduction

Steven Rawle

 macmillan
international
HIGHER EDUCATION

palgrave

First published 2018 by
PALGRAVE

Palgrave in the UK is an imprint of Macmillan Publishers Limited, registered in England, company number 785998, of 4 Crinan Street, London, N1 9XW.

Palgrave® and Macmillan® are registered trademarks in the United States, the United Kingdom, Europe and other countries.

ISBN 978–1–137–53013–4 hardback
ISBN 978–1–137–53012–7 paperback

A catalogue record for this book is available from the British Library.

A catalog record for this book is available from the Library of Congress.

Contents

List of figures

Acknowledgements

This book has been the product of a number of years of research and teaching. Therefore, there are many people to thank. Firstly, I'd like to thank all the students at York St John University who have studied transnational cinema in some form over most of the last decade with me, students of film and TV production, media production and film studies – their discussions, insights and critiques of films and ideas around transnational cinema have had an immeasurable impact on the text. Many colleagues have also contributed along the way; perhaps most strongly Martin Hall, with whom I have been teaching transnational cinema for four years, and our many ponderings about the subject have found their way here in many regards. Furthermore, I'd like to thank the heads of department who have given me the opportunity to teach this subject and to support my research time in preparing the manuscript (especially after breaking my arm in a cycling accident meant my plans were thrown into some disarray), Jenny Kean and Keith McDonald. Thanks should also go to Dan Crawforth, Andy Platts, Kevin Gash, Alan Clarke, Maria Rovisco and Wayne Johnson for supporting and providing moments of discussion along the way. There are also many more friends and colleagues to thank who have contributed ideas in their research, many of whom have been cited throughout the book – without their work, this book certainly wouldn't exist. Our meetings at conferences have significantly impacted my own understanding of the subject – there isn't space enough here to thank everyone individually, so general thanks go out to them all here, and for their contributions throughout the text. Special thanks go to Iain Robert Smith, who lent me a pre-publication copy of the manuscript of *The Hollywood Meme*. There are several people to thank at Palgrave: Lloyd Langman, who helped initiate the project, and Jenna Steventon, who saw it to fruition, along with Nicola Cattini. The editorial team at Palgrave were beyond patient as the book fell behind schedule. The readers for the proposal and draft manuscript were diligent and critical, and helped shape the final manuscript in significant ways, and I'm grateful for their contributions.

Finally, the book is dedicated to Lorna, for her unwavering love, support, patience and willingness to let me fill her home with piles of books and copies of odd films.

The book is secondarily dedicated to our cats, Connie and Clyde, not for their support, but for their dogged ability to lie on my keyboard at the most inconvenient times. Fortunately, none of their 'writing' made it to print.

Introduction

On 23 June 2016, the United Kingdom held a referendum regarding its membership of the European Union. With a high turnout, 71.8 per cent, just under 52 per cent of voters voted to leave. The leave campaign's aim was to 'Take Back Control', of borders, and of immigration. In many regards, the vote was read as a protest against globalisation and free movement of labour, in opposition to supranational organisations such as the EU. The campaign, which took place alongside the political rise of Donald Trump in the US and its comparable slogans about 'Making America Great Again', refocused attentions on nationalism, border protectionism, human migration and globalisation. The prominence of these issues at the time of writing make this book timely in the ways in which transnational cinema engages with many of them. Fundamentally, transnationalism is concerned with flows of people and objects across borders, between and above nations. At a time when borders have been more porous than ever, the intensified focus on nationalism restates the prominence of nation-states in popular consciousness, even as our lives are impacted by technologies and economies that easily transcend borders, and our reliance on consumer items, food, clothing, energy and culture that are products of multinational industries. This means we engage with transnational capitalism whenever we put the kettle on, reach for our Chinese-assembled phone or wear a T-shirt made in a Bangladeshi factory.

Transnational cinema has emerged as a critical focus in this era of globalisation, although many studies, as we'll see, have argued that cinema has always been a transnational medium that has persistently crossed boundaries and cultures. Films travel around the world, as do film crews, with relative ease, often courted by local governments that welcome the inward investment. As Dudley Andrew perceptively pointed out: 'Borders are thresholds as much as walls' (2011, p, 1,008). Transnationalism helps us to understand how the national relates to the global in several ways, as we'll see. More recently, transnational film studies has emerged as an academic discipline. The *Transnational Cinemas* journal was launched in 2010, its aim 'to break down traditional geographical divisions' and consider how global film cultures are changing, creating new industrial formations necessitating fresh methods of textual analysis. In 2012, the Society for Cinema and Media Studies approved the formation of a scholarly interest group (SIG) dedicated to transnational cinemas, with the goal of bringing together scholars to work collaboratively towards more concrete theorisation of cinematic transnationalism. Four years later, the two co-founders of the SIG, Austin Fisher and Iain Robert Smith, coordinated a critical roundtable on issues relating to transnational cinemas, published in *Frames Cinema Journal* (2016). They brought together ten key scholars (most of whom we'll encounter later in the book) and asked them to respond to a series of questions about how they conceptualise transnational cinema. There was no specific consensus view, although each of the ten scholars in some way used the term to problematise the concept of nation. Lucy Mazdon perhaps articulates this position best when she contends that 'Transnational cinema should not be reduced to international co-productions or an accumulation of national cinemas. Understanding cinema as transnational means being aware of its porosity, its intersections with others (including the national), its indeterminacy and its contingency' (Fisher & Smith, 2016). Where there is consensus in the roundtable is about the pluralism and polycentrism, to use Lúcia Nagib's term, of methods in relation to the study of transnational cinemas. As we'll see through our journeys across borders in this book, understanding how cinema is transnational can take numerous forms, from the empirical examination of production histories to archival research and historiography, as well as textual analysis. Since it is a comparative method, it poses a few challenges for us: we need to interrogate our own cultural position, as well as tackle the multilingualism of researching films across different cultures. Shifting from a mono-cultural point of view to multi-cultural polycentric outlooks invites us to challenge how we see the world, especially if we view the world through the point of view of western privilege. As Sonia Livingstone (2013) has argued, cross-national study can help us see our own nations from the point of view of an outsider, while facilitating an insider's understanding of others. Tim Bergfelder reminds us of this in the *Frames Cinema Journal* roundtable, that 'transnational cinema ... puts higher demands on students because it forces them to negotiate at least two different cultures (if not languages)' (Fisher & Smith, 2016). And, as Ruth Doughty and Deborah Shaw (2016) have noted, the study of transnational cinema can often take us out of our comfort zones, linguistically and culturally, showing us images of the global dispossessed to shed light on our own western privilege and allowing us to see film outside Euro-American frameworks from around the world, in many different languages. Yet, as this book demonstrates, and as the curricula of many university courses in world and transnational cinema also show, space and time is limited, and choices have to be made about which areas to focus on (Doughty and Shaw say this is to *sample* the world rather than teach it), and this means, in one sense, stepping back into our specialist areas but then going outside them, to show a broader canon than just those from a European or American context, and to work toward a de-westernised film studies.

This book is intended as a primer on concepts, theories and aspects of transnational cinema. It is not intended to be all-encompassing or definitive regarding all the films we could consider as transnational – as Andrew argues, what is most important is 'Displacement, not coverage' (2011, p. 1,000) – but a gateway to further study. The case studies have been chosen because they have been subject to exploration by scholars of national and transnational cinema, and because they help us to understand core aspects of theories and concepts in the discipline.

The book's primary focus is the exploration of modes of transnational analysis, including the ways in which we can view how cinema has become a medium for engaging with questions of transnational experience, and how cinema itself is transnational. The opening chapter asks why we have come to studies of transnational cinema only recently, and why we aren't thinking in terms of a 'world cinema'. It looks at the broad theorisation of transnational cinemas, and how we envision the centre/margins models of world cinema. The next two chapters consider what we might think of as 'classic' approaches to national cinemas, looking firstly at ways in which cinema has engaged with the narratives of the 'imagined communities' of nations and the knowledge associated with national myths and identities. Chapter 3 looks more specifically at Third and postcolonial cinemas, those often considered to be engaged in struggle with or in opposition to cinemas of the First World. By looking at these issues relating to national cinemas we'll develop a viewpoint that can later articulate how transnational cinemas engage with the national and how they go beyond and above issues relating to nation. Subsequent chapters consider how cinema has become transnational or how it has engaged with transnationalism, exploring the ways in which border-crossing is implicated in questions of identity and inequality, as well as how borders are imagined in transnational films. Chapter 6 goes on to consider cinema's transnational modes of production that facilitate the flow of creative individuals and capital around the globe. Finally, in Chapters 7 and 8 we'll look at how cultural material crosses borders in remakes and genres where material is appropriated and localised as it flows around the world.

Within each chapter, you'll find case studies of selected films, some from within the established canon of film studies, some from outside, that model concepts and ideas as they can be applied to your own analyses of transnational cinema. These, along with lists of further reading and viewing, should act as gateways for your own application of this book's ideas and concepts, to hopefully stimulate your own research and exploration.

CHAPTER 1

World or Transnational Cinema?

Browse any film store, in the actual or virtual world, and you'll normally find a section, alongside genres like action, horror and science fiction, that's devoted to 'world cinema'. Normally, this section is very neatly or clearly laid out, or browsable, by major film-producing countries, such as France, Germany, or Japan. However, some might be more problematically labelled by area or continent, such as Africa, the Middle East, or Scandinavia. Often the simple designation of cinemas by their country of origin (usually by their predominant language) can mask the complexities of production, funding, and the reception and consumption of films, let alone their engagement with issues of identity and subjectivity. What we generally won't find in the 'world cinema' section are films in the English language, from the UK, the US and Canada. These films will sit more prominently in the main section, usually arranged by genre – they won't be designated by their nationality. They will occupy a more mainstream position, while the films from other areas are situated as more marginal, even if produced in popular genres, for their arthouse appeal.

World cinema remains a relevant category for many film viewers, despite how porous borders have become as globalisation has intensified. Alongside the growth of transnational film studies, we still see the primacy of national cinemas as categories that promote and classify films. But, in these times marked by increased global connectivity, transnational cinema comes to stand as a signifier of a world in which people, capital, ideas and technologies circulate much more freely than they have done previously. Thinking about cinema as a series of transnationally connected industries and as an artform that reflects the experience of individuals and social groups within a transnational system can help us better understand this world and how it operates. This first chapter will frame some of the core issues in the book around the shift in film studies from thinking about the 'us' and 'them' binaries of world or national cinemas to thinking in terms of the transnational. It will unpack some key discourses that define the ways in which world cinema has come to be considered under globalisation.

Why transnational cinema now?

The term 'transnational' has been adopted more and more by film studies recently to discuss films that can't be explained or analysed only in relation to a single national context. As such, the term has come to be applied to cinemas dating back to the inception of cinema, as co-productions developed, individuals moved around the world to make films, or where films were distributed globally. Silent cinema was a transnational phenomenon. Films didn't need to be dubbed or subtitled, and intertitles could easily be changed. Filmmakers were already moving around the world to make films: Alfred Hitchcock served his apprenticeship at UFA in Germany before returning to the UK to direct films like *The Lodger: A Story of the London Fog* (1927). With him he took the expressionist style that had been popular in Germany in the early 1920s. Later, of course, Hitchcock produced films in the US, making him a transnational filmmaker. Some of the movements described under the term 'transnational cinema' are often as old as cinema itself, as is 'transnational', with its earliest uses dating back to the 1910s and 1920s to describe hyphenate or migrant identities: trans-nationalities.

In *Flexible Citizenship: The Cultural Logics of Transnationality* (1999), Aihwa Ong defines *transnationality* as a 'condition of cultural interconnectedness and mobility across space', something which has been 'intensified under late capitalism'. *Transnationalism* she describes as 'the cultural specificities of global processes, tracing the multiplicity of the uses and conceptions of "culture"' (p. 4). Ong's definitions here help us to understand how we might refer to the transnational as a way of talking about the movement of people, capital and culture across borders in an era of globalisation, of 'human practices and cultural logics'. Transnationality 'alludes to the *trans*versal, the *trans*actional, the *trans*lational, and the *trans*gressive aspects of contemporary behaviour and imagination that are incited, enabled and regulated by the changing logics of states and capitalism' (p. 4). As conceptual terms, 'transnationality' and 'transnationalism' (just as we might distinguish between postmodernity and postmodernism) provide a range of means for considering how culture is affected by the changing dynamics of national boundaries, migration, economic globalisation and the flow of cultural material.

The term transnational has been described by Daniela Berghahn and Claudia Sternberg as 'a generic category that comprises different aspects of film production, distribution and consumption which *transcend* national film cultures' (2010, p. 22; emphasis added). This is an important argument in that transnational cinema does not replace thinking about national cinemas, but supplements it. National cinemas remain an important and relevant emphasis in film cultures, as our example of the film store evidences, but the 'trans-' prefix denotes thinking about how cinema crosses and transcends national boundaries, just as individuals, capital, films and culture do. As Sonia Livingstone has remarked, it 'has become imperative to examine the transnational flows of media technologies, formats and specific texts, the rise of powerful institutional networks and media conglomerates and the practices of interpretative communities within and across national borders' (2013, p. 417). Hence the study of transnational cinema grapples with a range of both hegemonic, culturally dominant forms and counter-hegemonic, marginal ones.

In the introduction to their collection *Transnational Cinema: A Film Reader* (2006), Elizabeth Ezra and Terry Rowden state that:

> The global circulation of money, commodities, information, and human beings is giving rise to films whose aesthetic and narrative dynamics, and even the modes of emotional identification they elicit, reflect the impact of advanced capitalism and new media technologies as components of an increasingly interconnected world-system. The transnational comprises both globalization – in cinematic terms, Hollywood's domination of world film markets – and the counterhegemonic responses of filmmakers from former colonial and Third World countries. (p. 1)

While Hollywood has always had a stronghold on most of the world's media markets, aside from a few, like India or South Korea, its dominance has often been considered a form of cultural imperialism where its outside influence is considered a threat to the local film culture. Andrew Higson, however, has viewed this as limiting, the national seen only in a binary opposition between 'them' and 'us':

> The movement of films across borders may introduce exotic elements to the 'indigenous' culture. One response to this is the anxious concern about the effects of cultural imperialism, a concern that the local culture will be infected, even destroyed by the foreign invader. A contrary response is that the introduction of exotic elements may well have a liberating or democratising effect on the local culture, expanding the cultural repertoire. A third possibility is that the foreign commodity will not be treated as exotic by the local audience, but will be interpreted according to an 'indigenous' frame of reference; that is, it will be metaphorically translated into a local idiom. (2006, p. 19)

The 'foreign' influence therefore may not be seen simply as an 'invader' but subject to localisation. In terms of cultural expression, films can be remade locally, as they routinely have been in Turkey, India and Hong Kong, as discussed in Chapter 7, or appropriated and re-read subject to local customs and subjectivities. As Koichi Iwabuchi has noted in his book *Recentering Globalization: Popular Culture and Japanese Transnationalism* (2002), Japanese and Taiwanese youngsters are likely to see an American brand like McDonald's through their own indigenous frame, and not as 'American'; in this sense transnational commodities can often take on a culturally odourless quality which makes them more likely to be subsumed by a process of localisation (p. 46). Hence they become integrated into a local frame of reference, even though they are transnational products, or even products seen as representing a strong sense of national specificity such as the hamburger (infused with a strong American odour, yet named after a town in Germany).

However, to see transnational flows of culture in these terms can be problematic. Such flows are often uneven and hierarchised. As Iwabuchi argues, Japan can see itself as part of Asia, albeit superior to it, but also subject to strong cultural influence from the US. Likewise, many American films and television programmes are often shot across national boundaries; sometimes these films use international locations to stand in for American ones, such as Toronto with its strong resemblance to several cities in the US. This is frequently a consequence of budgetary necessity, since filmmaking in Canada is often cheaper than in the US, and favourable tax incentives exist to encourage filmmakers to shoot outside the US. Other films, such as the Bourne or Bond films, are shot around the world, something which brings investment to the countries featured, but their content is generally rooted in typically American or western hegemonic concerns about terrorism or cold war politics. However, although these films bring investment into other countries, this is often at the expense of local forms of expression and subjectivity, as the focus of the narrative remains the white male protagonist, with some local characters provided only for supporting purposes. Consequently, these flows tend to return to the top of their respective hierarchies.

In the introduction to the first edition of the *Transnational Cinemas* journal, Deborah Shaw and Armida De La Garza (2010) articulated 15 different categories or themes relating to the study of cinema's transnationalism, each of which we will explore at different points throughout this book:

1. Modes of production, distribution and exhibition
2. Co-productions and collaborative networks
3. New technologies and changing patterns of consumption
4. Transnational film theories
5. Migration, journeying and other forms of border-crossing
6. Exilic and diasporic film-making
7. Film and language
8. Questions of authorship and stardom

9. Cross-fertilization and cultural exchange
10. Indigenous cinema and video and the cinemas of ethnic minorities
11. Cultural policy
12. The ethics of transnationalism
13. Historical transnational practices
14. Interrelationships between local, national and the global
15. Transnational and postcolonial politics (2010, p. 4).

The breadth of themes in the list outlined by Shaw and De La Garza demon-strate the complexities in the study of transnational cinemas, where a singular approach, they argue, would fall into 'an essentialist trap' in which complexity is elided in favour of 'flattened' and 'over-simplified answers' (p. 3). There is no single condition of transnationalism for cinema. Shaw later revisited this list in an article entitled 'Deconstructing and Reconstructing "Transnational Cinema"' (2013) in which she revises some of the terminol-ogy, but also introduces some new categories (these are italicised):

1. Transnational modes of production, distribution and exhibition
2. *Transnational modes of narration*
3. *Cinema of globalisation*
4. *Films with multiple locations*
5. Exilic and diasporic filmmaking
6. Film and cultural exchange
7. Transnational influences
8. *Transnational critical approaches*
9. Transnational viewing practices
10. Transregional/transcommunity films
11. Transnational stars
12. Transnational directors
13. The ethics of transnationalism
14. Transnational collaborative networks
15. *National films* (p. 52).

Perhaps most interestingly, Shaw adds 'national films' to this list. This final category emphasises the continuing relevance of national cinema for a transnational frame of interpretation and study, that the national retains its prominence in terms of cultural policy, identity, economics and ideology. The imagined communities of nation-states remain prominent in ideologi-cally constructed discourses around immigration, national identity, religion and regional politics. The UK's relationship with the European Union has repeatedly engaged with conceptions of nationhood and sovereignty, espe-cially in media reporting about the relationship, its renegotiation or its end, and those discourses continue to have a relationship with cinema that is reflected on the screen.

All of the categories mentioned by Shaw and De La Garza span the range of themes and practices that engage with the flow of individuals (exilic and diasporic filmmaking; transnational stars and directors; questions of authorship and stardom), the circulation of texts and their influences (cultural exchange; transnational influences; modes of production, distribution and exhibition), and texts that engage with the condition of living in a transnationally interconnected world (the cinema of globalisation; stories of migration, journeying and other forms of border-crossing; and the transnational modes of narration that express the condition of living as a transnational subject). These two lists therefore give us a broad set of core concepts through which we can explore the range of expressions, on industrial, individual and political levels, that span the field of transnational film studies.

Challenging the centrist model

World cinema has been a problematic term, one that continues to circulate in film cultures. The national cinemas it describes can be transnational in nature, although that doesn't necessarily mean that transnational cinema is considered the same thing. Indeed, as Chris Berry has pointed out, for '"transnational cinema"... to have any value, it needs to be more than just another way of saying "international cinema" or "world cinema"' (2010, p. 112), and there needs to be clear difference in what those terms articulate. World cinema is often seen through a lens of Otherness. The term often relates to cinemas not in the English language, and therefore generally subtitled. It has also often been used as a term to refer to a cinema characterised by humanist realism, such as that of Italian Neorealist films following the Second World War, or those from Iran or Senegal. What is often not included in the term 'world cinema' is Hollywood, against which all world cinemas are considered to struggle, resist and/or oppose. While Hollywood might be highly transnational, border-crossing in practice and in its influences, it has traditionally been posited as outside, even above, world cinema, and as such has been the way in which value is assigned to world cinemas. This constructs a binary opposition between Hollywood and the rest of the world, a dominant centre against a struggling Othered periphery.

This viewpoint has been challenged. In her book chapter, 'Towards a Positive Definition of World Cinema,' Lúcia Nagib problematises the binaristic conception of world cinema as split between the cinema of Hollywood and all other cinemas; while world cinema might seem an 'all-encompassing, democratic vocation', its conceptualisation has tended to be 'restrictive and negative, as "non-Hollywood cinema"' (2006, p. 30). Consequently, Nagib argues, the dominant form of Hollywood cinema has been conceived as a method of assessing the value of a world cinema that sees Hollywood as a means of 'viewing world cinema as "alternative" and "different"' (p. 31). 'A truly encompassing and democratic approach,' she concludes, 'has to get rid of the binary system as a whole' (p. 33), escaping the them-and-Other approach to the understanding, categorisation and evaluation of world cinemas as a homogenised block. She proposes 'a method in which Hollywood and the West would cease to be the centre of film history ... [so that] once the idea of a single centre is eliminated, nothing needs to be excluded from the world cinema map, not even Hollywood' (p. 34). This inclusive approach would be 'polycentric' in the sense that it would be pluralistic rather than binaristic, posing no us-and-them scenario so typical of Othered art forms. Finally, Nagib gives us a series of points for discussion:

- World cinema is simply the cinema of the world. It has no centre. It is not the other, but it is us. It has no beginning and no end, but is a global process. World cinema, as the world itself, is circulation.
- World cinema is not a discipline, but a method, a way of cutting across film history according to waves of relevant films and movements, thus creating flexible geographies.
- As a positive, inclusive, democratic concept, world cinema allows all sorts of theoretical approaches, provided they are not based on the binary perspective. (p. 35)

Nagib's call for a positive definition of world cinema aims to see it recuperated from the margins of cultural expression, as defined by its opposition to Hollywood since the early twentieth century. Such a move would see norms set via a more inclusive, democratic methodology, especially as film history is concerned. The focus on flexible geographies allows us to understand the flow of influence and ideas in the history of global cinema as more interconnected and diverse than simple binaries of cultural imperialism and resistance. Therefore, one might not see the New German Cinema of the 1960s and 1970s simply as a rejection of the norms set by a dominant Hollywood system, but through its relationship with the Third Cinema films of Glauber Rocha and Brazil's *Cinema Novo*. Seeing these channels of flow as more open and inclusive can help us understand how transnational cinemas are connected, not from a Hollywood centre outward, but in multidirectional and polycentric directions.

That is not say that this move away from a centre/margins model has been unchallenged. In a later introduction to the book *Theorizing World Cinema*, Nagib, with Chris Perriam and Rajinder Dudrah, defines an 'important part of the conversation between transnational and world cinema [as] the restitution to the former of a radical potential that the latter embodies, but whose negative definition in opposition to the mainstream has all too often elided' (2012, p. xxiv). Whereas world cinema 'includes and takes forward radical elements of filmmaking and film critique, including the questioning of imposed ideas of national cinemas', transnational cinemas can be more conservative by nature. The major centres of global filmmaking – Los Angeles, Mexico City, Bombay and Hong Kong – they allege, might incorporate mechanisms relating to transnational modes of production or identification, but their expression can often be seen as less challenging, more hegemonic in nature: 'they almost certainly have not been consistently interstitial, alternative, resistant or troubling of the status quo' (p. xxiv). So, while a world cinema will tend to be more radical, a mainstream transnationalism may not be interstitial (as coming from a space in-between borders or states), challenging or opposed to ideological norms relating to nation or to politics.

This view is one echoed by John Hess and Patricia R. Zimmerman in their manifesto for transnational documentaries. They draw a distinction between corporatist and adversarial transnationalisms. In the corporatist sense, there is movement towards homogenisation and deterritorialisation, although that deconstruction of the territory is one that reconstructs a space that is a product of globalised capital. Within this matrix, 'racial, gender, and sexual identities are to be dematerialized, depoliticized, declawed and corporalized into new, further segmented markets for the new accelerated capital growth. The conflicts that mark and define these ... are neutralized within commodity fetishism' (2006, p. 99). The media landscape of the late twentieth and early twenty-first centuries, of MTV, Disney/ABC, Sony-Columbia, has appropriated the radical oppositional politics of race, sexuality and gender into advertising campaigns, alongside the depoliticisation of rap music and courting of gay audiences. Capital's fluid, state-less travel online controls and minimises difference by making the globally disenfranchised invisible or abject; Hess and Zimmerman's examples include: AIDS patients without access to affordable healthcare; immigrant sweatshop workers; victims of genocide in Europe and Africa; ethnic communities in the US.

Adversarial transnationalism therefore 'wrenches the notion of the transnational away from its corporatist location, moving it instead into the disruptive realms of bodies, people, movements and representational practices that dislodge corporate influence by creating new places for social justice on a global scale' (p. 99). Since the epochal shifts of the end of the twentieth century, with the fall of the Berlin Wall, the Tian'anmen Square protests in China and the first Gulf War, that marked a restructuring of capitalism and global politics, Hess and Zimmerman identify not only a growth of a different kind of documentary, but also an explicit need for one; one that opposes the traditional relationship between nation and documentary first seen in the work of John Grierson and the GPO film unit in Britain in the 1930s. These necessary documentary films, such as *Handsworth Songs* (John Akomfrah and Black Audio Collective, 1986) and *Obsessive Becoming* (Daniel Reeves, 1995), for Hess and Zimmerman, employ alternative representational strategies to interrogate the notion of nation through their engagement with history, power, diasporic identities and the transgression of borders, both actual and metaphysical. Such films, they argue, 'refuse the fragmentation, isolation and nationalism that is the corollary of corporatist transnationalism by looking for and imagining new social and aesthetic alliances ... They are acts of refusal and hope' (p. 105). As this shows, we can see more than one kind of transnationalism: a type that adopts the strategies of corporatist transnationalism, the more conservative mode that Nagib, Perriam and Dudrah demonstrated, and the more adversarial type called for as a necessity by Hess and Zimmerman.

World cinema at the margins

Challenges such as these to the construction of a binary way of seeing the separation between a hegemonic, often western, cinema and the rest of the world viewed as being at the fringes of view, contest the Eurocentrism of viewing world cinema in oppositional terms. Eurocentric viewpoints proliferate globally, not just in Europe but in cultures described as neo-European, such as in North America or Australia. In their seminal text, *Unthinking Eurocentrism: Multiculturalism and the Media* (1994), Ella Shohat and Robert Stam argue that:

> [So] embedded is Eurocentrism in everyday life, so pervasive, that it often goes unnoticed. The centuries of axiomatic European domination inform the general culture, the everyday language, and the media, engendering a fictitious sense of the innate superiority of European-derived cultures and people. (p. 1)

The tendency to see world cinema through the lens of a method that assigns value to texts, movements and national cinemas only through their difference from the hegemonic norms of Hollywood echoes Shohat and Stam's point that opponents of multiculturalism represent a 'procrustean forcing of cultural heterogeneity into a single paradigmatic perspective in which Europe is seen as the unique source of meaning' (pp. 1–2). Europe is therefore offered as an originator of civilisation, through which all others can be measured and assigned value. This is like the ways in which an English-language western cinema can be posited as a Eurocentric overarching criterion of value

through which all other cinemas can be measured in opposition or in relation. The corporatist transnationalism of Hess and Zimmerman is one such
way of retaining a Eurocentric focus on the colonisation of people and territories, to depoliticise and integrate them into a pre-existing homogenising
subjectivity, excluded as Other or defined by lack, or through a 'mania for
hierarchy' that sees marginalised groups as inferior (Shohat and Stam, 1994,
p. 23). This retains colonialist discourses that expel those outside hegemonic
norms to the margins, just as world cinemas are banished to the periphery
in traditional ways of thinking about national cinemas.

Shohat and Stam suggest a shift from monocentric Eurocentrism to a form
of polycentric multiculturalism. 'Within a polycentric vision,' they argue:

> the world has many dynamic cultural locations, many possible vantage
> points. The emphasis in 'polycentrism,' for us, is not on spatial or primary
> points of origin but on fields of power, energy, and struggle. The 'poly,' for
> us, does not refer to a finite list of centers of power but rather introduces
> a systematic principle of differentiation, relationality, and linkage. No
> single community or part of the world, whatever its economic or political
> power, is epistemologically privileged. (p. 48)

In many ways, this call for a multiple, hybrid and pluralist manner of seeing
the world is echoed in Nagib's view of world cinema as having no centre,
'positive, inclusive, democratic' without Otherness. To see a world cinema
as having Otherness or being Other is to posit a norm against which those
criteria are defined, which would be to retain a Eurocentric way of seeing and
therefore to epistemologically privilege a community or part of the world,
even if that part of the world might be defined as loosely as 'the west'.

Drawing on Shohat and Stam's ground-breaking work, Dina Iordanova,
David Martin-Jones and Belén Vidal have argued, in their collection *Cinema
at the Periphery*, that 'the relationship between center and periphery is no
longer necessarily a straightforward, hierarchical one, where the center seeks
to subsume its margins' (2010, pp. 6–7). In the age of globalisation and the
political upheavals of the late twentieth century mentioned by Hess and
Zimmerman, the oppositional geography of centre and margin, like that of
Nagib's argument, becomes less relevant as transnational forms of cinema
and storytelling emerge. Central to their book's project is the understanding
that:

> many new films from the periphery subvert traditional hierarchies of loca-
> tion, as they come from, and/or are set in, places traditionally deemed
> remote, dependent, subaltern, minor, small or insular. Their key themes
> and narratives are defined by a growing awareness of instability or change,

by homelessness or incessant journeying and border crossing, counteracting the certainty of fixed coordinates. (Iordanova, et al., 2010, p. 7)

This final point is an important one for considering some of the key themes of transnational cinema, which is often marked (as Shaw and De La Garza mentioned) by homelessness, journeying and border-crossing. Marginal cinemas of Scotland, New Zealand, Quebec and Aboriginal Australian filmmaking provide a polycentric and flexible conception that go beyond the dichotomous homogenising of 'the rest' in a way that causes the editors to ask (polemically) if the periphery might now constitute a new centre (Iordanova, et al., 2010, p. 17).

Iordanova also offers an overview of a transnational mode of distribution that is hybrid, often unofficial and diasporic, that might be driving towards a model that displaces the traditional centre of world cinema. Traditionally, Iordanova points out, global distribution has been difficult to measure, whereas it has been easy to track Hollywood box office grosses through trade papers like *Variety* or *Screen International* or latterly with tracking websites like the Amazon-owned *Box Office Mojo*, which has only partial international data. She points to research that has shown that Hollywood controls 'less than 70 per cent of the international market' (Iordanova, 2010, p. 29), while global audiences might now be 'more susceptible to new, alternative models that may come from elsewhere', challenging the presumed longevity of the Hollywood hegemony and bringing us 'a more flexible vision of the future' (p. 30). Non-Hollywood films are facilitated by a set of transnational channels that straddle official and unofficial distribution to offer films to audiences in ways that challenge perceived hierarchies. The festival network forms an official channel that offers non-Hollywood films exposure to distribution and exhibition by supporting different kinds of filmmaking, such as the Berlin Film Festival's support of Fatih Akin's *Head On* (*Gegen die Wand*, 2004) that brought focus to the Turkish-German filmmaker's exploration of diasporic Turkish communities in Germany, or festivals that cater to diasporic audiences like the annual Polish Film Festival in Los Angeles. Local distribution of films to diasporic audiences, such as that offering Indian films to British-Indian and South Asian audiences in England, also broadens the range of films available, both officially in cinemas and unofficially through the ease of importing DVDs via the internet over the last 15 years. Likewise, internet streaming and downloading has facilitated the expansion of film distribution, again through both official and unofficial methods, with platforms including Netflix offering a range of films that cover global genres such as anime, martial arts, Bollywood or films from Nigeria, colloquially known as Nollywood, such as *October 1* (Kunle Afolayan, 2014) or *Onye Ozi* (Obi Emelonye, 2013). Access to such films remains limited through such platforms; through unofficial channels the range expands, with peer-to-peer sharing or YouTube's selection of segmented and whole classic films, via which the swiftness of exchange is generally much faster than through official channels. This is something to which we'll return in Chapter 8, but is important to highlight at this stage, as, for Iordanova, the growth of decentred or hybrid channels for transnational distribution offers a flexible way of considering the growth of global hubs and distribution networks that challenge the centrist model that promoted the supremacy of the Hollywood model. This enables the movement of films across borders in ways unseen even 20 years ago.

Hybridity has become an important focus for thinking about how transnational cinema engages with border-crossing and the ways in which culture engages with globalisation, such as the challenge to 'the west' and 'the rest' opposition posited by Koichi Iwabuchi, following Stuart Hall's argument regarding post-colonial hybridity in 'When was the Post-colonial? Thinking at the Limit' (Hall, 1996, p. 247):

> [Hybridity] fruitfully displaces our conception of clearly demarcated national/cultural boundaries, which have been based upon a binary opposition between 'us' and 'them,' 'the West' and 'the Rest,' and the colonizer and the colonized, with a postcolonial perspective that 'oblige(s) us to re-read the binaries as forms of transculturation, of cultural translation, destined to trouble the here/there cultural binaries forever'. (Iwabuchi, 2002, p. 51)

Once more we encounter ways in which the transnational has been conceived as a concept that destabilises former binaries and the neat borders between nations and identities that Eurocentrism constructed so problematically. Iwabuchi's analysis of the ways in which Japanese cultural products move and are localised around East Asia demonstrates how 'global cultural flows have decentred the power structure *and* vitalized local practices of appropriation and consumption of foreign cultural products and meanings' (p. 35). Thus there is no longer a top-down flow to the ways in which cultural products and their meanings circulate around the world – this need not be thought of as a process of cultural imperialism, but a process of localisation through which cultural products are indigenised. As Iwabuchi demonstrates:

> Transnationally circulated images and commodities ... tend to become culturally odorless in the sense that origins are subsumed by the local transculturation process. By appropriating, hybridizing, indigenizing, and consuming images and commodities of 'foreign' origin in multiple unforeseen ways, even American culture is conceived as 'ours' in many places. (p. 46)

Processes of hybridisation and appropriation localise products across borders, just as film remakes might do (something we'll explore in more detail in Chapter 7), so that those texts and images become odourless. For Iwabuchi, it is the lack of culturally specific odour or sensibility, as seen in the lack of ethnicity in the design of anime and manga characters, that allows for this rewriting of the text to happen in the moment of transculturation as the text or product travels across global cultural flows.

The notion of 'global cultural flows' upon which Iwabuchi draws comes most strongly from the work of Arjun Appadurai. In his article, 'Disjuncture and Difference in the Global Cultural Economy' (1990), Appadurai argues that the 'new global cultural economy has to be understood as a complex, overlapping, disjunctive order, which cannot any longer be understood in terms of existing center-periphery models' (p. 296). While this centre/margins argument has been discussed earlier in the chapter, Appadurai's foundational contribution to the theoretical background of this subject can't be understated. His overarching contention was that the global economy at the time he wrote his article was becoming complicated by 'fundamental disjunctures' and disconnections between economics, culture and politics. To further explore the disjunctures between these areas, Appadurai proposed looking at the issue through five facets of 'global cultural flow':

- *Ethnoscapes*: the people whose movement across borders reflects the shifting boundaries of the world that are challenging the politics of and relationships between nations: 'tourists, immigrants, refugees, exiles, guestworkers and other moving groups and persons' (p. 297);
- *Mediascapes*: the spread of the electronic means by which images of the world can be disseminated and produced, as well as the images created by such technologies across a range of genres: documentary, fictional, news, print, cinema;
- *Technoscapes*: the global distribution of technologies across borders and industries;
- *Finanscapes*: flows of global capital, electronic and actual;
- *Ideoscapes*: like mediascapes, an interrelated series of images in the service of ideologies of nation, or in opposition to such ideologies.

Each of the aspects that categorise cultural flow is subject to a 'fluid, irregular' formation (p. 297), and the push towards deterritorialisation creates fertile grounds for the disjunctures between the different aspects of cultural flow to be exploited. For instance, films are made for, and about, diasporic communities, as Appadurai argues is the case with Mira Nair's *India Cabaret* (1985), a documentary about a group of women who work in a strip club in Mumbai. The film examines the disjuncture between the everyday respectability of the women's daytime roles and the scandalous immorality of their nighttime personas as dancers and prostitutes. For Appadurai, it is telling that some of women are economic migrants from the southern, and less cosmopolitan, area of Kerala:

> These tragedies of displacement could certainly be replayed in a more detailed analysis of the relations between the Japanese and German sex tours to Thailand and the tragedies of the sex trade in Bangkok, and in other similar loops which tie together fantasies about the other, the conveniences and seductions of travel, the economics of global trade and the brutal mobility fantasies that dominate gender politics in many parts of Asia and the world at large. (p. 303)

This conjunction of *mediascape* and *ideoscape* in Nair's film and in the related politics of the global sex trade that intersect in the deterritorialised global cultural economy demonstrate the complications and consequences of the disjunctures between the different dimensions of cultural flows. So, while Iwabuchi uses the term to describe the ways in which Japanese or Taiwanese youngsters might adopt or relate to a potentially foreign product as 'local', this doesn't mean that the transculturation of products across cultural flows is leading us into utopian territory, nor ultimately an equal playing field. As Iwabuchi himself argues, it 'does not mean that the United States has lost its cultural hegemony' (p. 41). And likewise, discussing the common practice of Hollywood remaking films from Japan and South Korea, Gary Xu has stated that 'Hollywoodization is irreversible' (2007, p. 158). He argues that there is an '[o]veremphasis on multidirectional ... flows of cultural production ... If all cultural productions were interconnected, deterritorialized, and freely exchanged, then Hollywood would have been dispersed and would have lost its special interests deeply rooted in American hegemony'. The 'biggest irony is that the more transnational national cinemas become, the more dominant Hollywood is' (p. 151).

During this section of the introductory chapter, we've looked at ways in which the centrist/marginal model in world cinema is challenged as we shift towards notions of transnational cinema. Historically, the relationship between 'the west' and 'the rest' has been defined as a binary, with difference from a hegemonic norm demarcated by Eurocentric or Hollywood standards against which all other cinemas or film movements draw their value. As we've seen, there are different ways of considering the meaning of the centre and the margins, and how hybridity and polycentrism are changing the way we (can) think about cinemas at the periphery or the movement of texts, products and people within cultural flows. The section ends with a note of caution, however, that while there is a struggle to recognise a changing system, this doesn't mean that the current system has no centre or that Hollywood doesn't retain a prominent place with that system, despite a shift away from binaries towards hybridity; the terrain is still uneven and cultural flows are unequal. This is something to which we'll return throughout the book as we consider how power relations are reconsidered or reconfigured in transnational cinema.

'Below-global/above-national'

The final section of this chapter considers some of the ways in which the study of world, nation and transnational cinemas are interconnected. Although the consideration of transnational cinema is a fairly recent development in film studies, it doesn't automatically overwrite other modes of analysis; that is to say that it does not do away with thinking about cinema at the level of nation and national cultural policy, nor how it expresses aspects of national identity or local concerns. As Nataša Ďurovičová has remarked, in the preface to the important edited collection *World Cinemas, Transnational Perspectives* (2010a), transnational is an 'intermediate and open term' that 'acknowledges the persistent agency of the state' while 'the prefix "trans-" implies relations of unevenness and mobility' (Ďurovičová, 2010a, p. x). She identifies two broad methodologies through which the transnational can be located: the first is geographical, charting the border-crossing that has become a political factor of emerging globalisation (such as that discussed by Appadurai) in which mismatched or unequal spaces are brought into one another's spheres of influence and negotiation; the second is a historical approach, locating narratives that position the transnational as 'below-global/above-national' (p. x). Since 'global' denotes a totality, the analysis takes place at the level of the supranational; like the 'trans-' prefix, the 'supra-' prefix also denotes an organisation that goes above or beyond the level of the national. The sub-global, supranational level of analysis that Ďurovičová describes assigns important agency to the national as a component of transnational analysis; therefore we'll begin the next chapter with an overview of approaches to national cinema. We'll see how modes of analysis that consider the nation have developed into more transnational modes that explore the 'contact zones' of world cinema, as Kathleen Newman calls them, in relation to cultural exchange between national cinemas. Like other critics we've examined in this chapter, Newman positions the transnational interactions between different zones as a way of 'moving beyond any tendency to reduce the centers and peripheries of present-day capitalism to the past familiar binary of cultural imperialism' (2010, p. 9). Like so many of the other commentators in this chapter, Newman is aware of previous discourses of nation and subjectivity that come from binaristic Eurocentric points of view. Thinking in terms of transnational cinema can explore the fluidity and polycentrism of world cinema's system with multiple centres, its unidirectional but imbalanced lines of flow, and the ways in which globalisation has shaped it. Therefore:

> What is now at stake in film studies is the question of how motion pictures register, at formal level of narrative, broad and long-term social transformations, that is, changes in the capitalist world-economy at the regional and global scales and over multiple decades. While this is a question of recognizing ongoing inequalities and how they may articulate one with another, it also must be a question of how film registers, and therefore serves as evidence of, equality among and between peoples over and against the hierarchies of capitalism. (p. 9)

Once again, Newman returns us to questions of power and imbalance and how cinema represents and engages with these questions of inequality that have emerged because of changes in the global economy. As we'll see throughout the book, this has been imagined in a few ways, not just at a formal level of narrative, but in terms of industrial organisation, as well as in the transnational stories that filmmakers choose to tell.

Similarly, Will Higbee and Song Hwee Lim's article in the first issue of *Transnational Cinemas* journal, entitled 'Concepts of Transnational Cinema: Towards a Critical Transnationalism in Film Studies' (2010), reiterates these points, albeit with an important warning, in their suggestion that:

> the term 'transnational cinema' appears to be used and applied with increasing frequency as both a descriptive and conceptual marker, it also tends, for the most part, to be taken as a given – as shorthand for an international or supranational mode of film production whose impact and reach lies beyond the bounds of the national. The danger here is that the national simply becomes displaced or negated in such analysis, as if it ceases to exist, when in fact the national continues to exert the force of its presence even within transnational film-making practices. Moreover, the term 'transnational' is, on occasion, used simply to indicate international co-production or collaboration between technical and artistic personnel from across the world, without any real consideration of what the aesthetic, political or economic implications of such transnational collaboration might mean – employing a difference that, we might say, makes no difference at all. (p. 10)

Ultimately, 'transnational' is a term whose use we must be wary about. As has been demonstrated repeatedly during this chapter's introduction to the discourses of transnational and world cinema, the value in engaging with notions of transnational cinema in film studies is its ability to interrogate questions of power, inequality and ideological negotiation across borders that can function not only on a global basis, but within nations and between nation-states in more regional and continental formations. As Higbee and Lim note here, the deployment of the term in film studies has the 'potential to obscure the question of imbalances of power (political, economic and ideological) in this transnational exchange' (p. 9) rather than to engage fully with them as a descriptive, rather than critical, term.

The final issues to draw from Higbee and Lim's overview of approaches to transnational cinema are the three strands of transnational analysis that they identify in ongoing work about concepts of transnational cinema in film studies. Synthesising work to date, they define three themes of analysis that we will pick up in a variety of ways throughout the rest of the book:

1.   The analysis of the movement of films and filmmakers across borders in terms of production, distribution and exhibition;
2.   The development of regional cinemas, 'examining film cultures/national cinemas which invest in a shared cultural heritage and/or geo-political boundary';
3.   'Work on diasporic, exilic and postcolonial cinemas, which aims, through its analysis of the cinematic representation of cultural identity, to challenge the western (neocolonial) construct of nation and national culture and, by extension, national cinema as stable and Eurocentric in its ideological norms as well as its narrative and aesthetic formations' (p. 9).

In each approach, they argue, there are drawbacks and limitations. In the first, the consideration of films' movement across borders, their adoption by local audiences, and the flow of individuals in production, broader questions of inequality and disparity might be elided in favour of questions of production and localisation, whereby important political questions of difference go answered. Whereas the approach to the national might be 'limiting,' using Andrew Higson's term (2006), such a method has the danger of making the notion of the transnational 'no difference at all'. The second approach, one that might be used to explore issues relating to Scandinavian cinema, may not significantly benefit from being considered transnational, where a term such as supranational might sufficiently demonstrate how a regional cinema functions at a level above the national. The final method, which draws strongly on the work of Hamid Naficy (2001) and Laura Marks (2000) (both of whom we'll encounter later, particularly in Chapter 5), engages with the political questions of difference and cultural identity potentially overlooked by the first, but can, Higbee and Lim argue, tend to focus only on cinemas on the margins, such as the Maghrebi-French or Algerian émigré cinemas that examine the place of migrant communities *within* France (*cinéma beur*), and therefore the experience of displaced or migrant communities positioned somewhere between home and host communities within nations. We will return to these three themes throughout the book, although it's important to note that each has potential drawbacks and limitations, and the study of transnational cinema can fall into the trap of potentially minimising the significance of questions of difference and inequality that recur time and again in the study of national, world and transnational cinemas. Finally, however, as Higbee and Lim note:

> a critical transnationalism does not ghettoize transnational film-making in interstitial and marginal spaces but rather interrogates how these film-making activities negotiate with the national on all levels – from cultural policy to financial sources, from the multiculturalism of difference to how it reconfigures the nation's image of itself. (p. 18)

The concept of transnational cinema therefore allows us to view the spectrum of ways the national interacts with the transnational, from local concerns to more global ones, and with the place of the nation-state in an increasingly borderless world. We'll look at these issues from a series of perspectives across the rest of the book.

Discussion questions:

- How useful do you think terms like national, world and transnational cinemas are in considering contemporary cinema?
- In what ways might the terms be too broad?
- What kind of difficulties do you think we might encounter when studying cinemas across borders?
- How much do you think we should try to 'think globally' and see beyond mono-cultural points of view?

CHAPTER 2

The National Cinema Paradigm

Let's go back to the film store we visited at the beginning of the last chapter. Despite the ways in which we've come to understand cinema as a much more cross-cultural and transnational formation than previously considered, we still see the primacy of nation for classifying a great number of the films from around the world. For British and American films, we'll most likely see them grouped together by genre rather than by language or national origin. The exception might be for films targeted at diasporic audiences, films from India for the diasporic South Asian audience in the UK or those whose primary audience will be Spanish-speaking in the US. Already, therefore, we're starting to see some of the diversity of national cinema cultures. However, those cultures are generally dominated by Hollywood products. This, therefore, begs the question of what this means for a national cinema. How do we understand what makes a national cinema? Is it an industry? Is it about the content of films? Genres? Or is it really about what audiences are watching? Do nations have one single cinema culture or many? Throughout this chapter, we'll look at some of the ways in which national cinemas have been theorised and defined, as well as some the problems of analysing cinema from this perspective. Along the way, case studies will draw attention to classic examples of national cinema, films that draw on national myths, histories and politics, and how those films begin to expose some of the limits of concepts of national cinema.

The concept of national cinema

As a starting point, note down the first things that come into your head in response to the following questions:

- What does a French film look like?
- What is the main genre in British cinema?
- What are the key themes of Brazilian cinema?
- What do you think about when you think of Japanese cinema?
- What is Senegalese cinema like?

Now, it's possible that when you thought about French cinema, you wrote down that the film would be in black and white, stylish, cynical maybe, artistic, political, and in many respects this would correspond with the image of the *nouvelle vague* from the 1960s; maybe you thought about the films of Gaspar Noé, such as *Irréversible* (2002), or Mathieu Kassovitz's *La Haine* (1995), popular arthouse hits. The cool art cinema of the 1960s often stands as a metonym of French cinema, or we think of an art cinema in its classical sense of resisting conventional norms of form and content, something which can often obscure a view of popular comedies, musicals and dramas, many of which don't receive wide international distribution.

When you thought about British film genres, did you think about the period dramas of Jane Austen or Charles Dickens adaptations? Perhaps you wrote down the gangster film, or the heritage horror of Hammer. Kitchen sink dramas? The romantic comedies of Richard Curtis, like *Four Weddings and a Funeral* (Mike Newell, 1994)? Maybe you simply wrote 'Bond'. In many respects, each would be correct, and have accounted for many popular films at the British and worldwide box office. What you answered will have depended on where you're from and how you're exposed to British cinema, as well as your image of Britishness. This would even include where you're from in the British Isles: did your notion of a British cinema account for any films in Welsh, or Scots Gaelic? How many of these examples depend on an image of white Britishness? Did class account for anything in your decisions? Again, when we look beyond the surface, we see a broad image of the nation through its cinema, culturally, socially and politically, many of which are absent from a popular imagination of Britain. Industrially, also, how many of these films are financed by British money and how much is produced by the Hollywood studio system? The Bond films, as we'll see in a later chapter, are produced in Britain by an American company with a Japanese owner. Meanwhile, through the British Film Institute's cultural test, which is linked to a production tax break, many Hollywood films are classified British, often with key British personnel, facilities and technologies, despite not featuring any identifiably British content, including *Gravity* (Alfonso Cuarón, 2013) and *Star Wars: Episode VII: The Force Awakens* (JJ Abrams, 2015, Figure 2.1). This is something to which we'll return in Chapter 6.

For your responses to Brazilian and Japanese cinemas, you might have a limited knowledge of key themes and films. You could think all Brazilian films are about poverty, taking a cue from *City of God* (*Cidade de Deus*, Fernando Meirelles and Kátia Lund, 2002), while you might perceive all Japanese cinema as weird and crazy, like Takashi Miike's *The Happiness of the Katakuris* (*Katakuri-ke no Kōfuku*, 2001). Often this is due to the choices

Figure 2.1 Major Hollywood productions elsewhere now enjoy national film status due to their production locations, such as *Star Wars: Episode VII: The Force Awakens* (JJ Abrams, 2015) (Lucasfilm/Disney)

distributors make in particular countries to promote images of that other country or of a limited range of cinema that is imported. For cinephiles, this might mean having only an incomplete view of that cinema, unless, as cult fans often do, they actively seek out a broader range of films, purchasing or downloading online. Sometimes this is difficult to do, for reasons of limitations of language, as not all films are sold with subtitles (or have fans to share subtitling duties, which is often the case with Japanese anime), so audiences are reliant on distributors to pay for subtitling, and therefore can access only a small amount of cinema outside their primary language. Finally, it's entirely possible that you've never seen a Senegalese film, although if you have, it might only have come from a very small pool of *auteur*s.

What we're getting at here is that when we think about national cinemas, we can sometimes stereotype those cinemas, something which often creates or relies upon a limited image of the nation in question. By delving further into the notion of national cinemas, we can explore why we might have those reactions and challenge the idea of singular notions of nation, nationhood or culture. Few nations are monocultural, and dominant ideologies change with time, so it's important to historicise the development of national myths and narratives that support nationalism at any time, and cinema is one of the ways we understand that nationalism.

Andrew Higson's seminal article, 'The Concept of National Cinema', first published in the journal *Screen* in 1989, gives us several ways in which we might understand and classify a national cinema. 'To identify a national cinema,' he argues, 'is first of all to specify a coherence and unity; it is to proclaim a unique identity and a stable set of meanings' (2002, p. 133). As we saw in the small exercise above, that can often be a difficult thing to establish; stability and coherence will often be determined with the absence of multiplicity – the loss of polycentrism. As Higson continues:

> The process of identification is thus invariably a hegemonising, mythologising process, involving both the production and assignation of a particular set of meanings, and the attempt to contain, or present the potential proliferation of meanings. At the same time, the concept of a national cinema has almost invariably been mobilised as a strategy of cultural (and economic) resistance; a means of asserting national autonomy in the face of (usually) Hollywood's international domination. (p. 133)

Following Paul Willemen, Higson refers to this as a form of 'internal cultural colonialism' (p. 139). As we saw Shohat and Stam argue in the last chapter, this kind of homogenising viewpoint comes at the exclusion of diversity from that hegemonic image or 'set of meanings', 'wherein the interests of one particular social group are represented as in the collective or national interest' (Higson, 2002, p. 139). Higson's promotion of this process as an almost given (signified above by his repeated use of 'invariably') is particularly focused on defining a theoretical method predominantly through an image of British cinema and its attempts to ward off the threat of Hollywood. In some cases, this led to quota legislation, firstly *The Cinematograph Film Act* (1927), which set quotas for the amount of screen time allotted to British films. In 1927, this was initially 5 per cent; by 1936 that had risen to 20 per cent. While this is an example of an institutional move to support a national film industry in the face of threat from overseas, it was also an attempt to ensure that films that showed a demonstrably British character were present on-screen. This led to a rise in the production of what became known as 'quota quickies', low-cost films produced to fulfil the quota. Other countries have used quota systems to maintain the flow of local product and support the development of a national cinema industry. In South Korea, a screen quota system was instigated in 1966. After this time, screens in South Korea were legally required to show locally produced films for a minimum of 90 days per year. In 1981, this was raised to 165, and relaxed to 146 four years later, a figure that stood until 2006 (Yecies, 2007). During the time of the quota, it was been challenged regularly by the Motion Picture Export Association of America (MPEA), and the subsequent cut to 73 days came as a result of pressure from trade negotiations with the United States. 2006 had been a record-breaking year for South Korean cinema, with locally produced films accounting for a 64 per cent market share of domestic box office. Following this, the share for American-produced films began to increase steadily.

Higson's article gives us a range of ways for understanding what constitutes a national cinema. On one level, a national cinema is an industry, owned, funded, controlled and regulated through a series of national institutions. As we've seen above, sometimes governments legislate to support the growth of a national film industry, to ensure employment and export revenue. However, this is not to say that a film industry is unified or homogenised – it is often a series of interconnected media industries and institutions (including funding bodies, regulatory institutions, censors, independent production companies, studios, visual effects companies, edit houses, and many freelance practitioners, from writers to electricians). The second way of understanding a national cinema is through its contribution to the dissemination of a national cultural identity. Primarily, this focuses on the content and subject matter of films, how nation is represented, its dominant themes and traditions: 'the ways in which cinema inserts itself alongside other cultural practices, and the ways in which it draws on the existing cultural histories and cultural traditions of the producing nation' (2002, p. 138). As a form of internalised colonialism, the promotion of cultural histories and traditions aims towards a minimisation of difference, homogenisation and consensus amongst the audience. This is not to say that all films will contribute to a unified image, although supplementary discourses in other media, such as television or print journalism, or in state apparatuses such as school curricula, might work to construct that unified image. As Jeffrey Richards has argued in his book *Films and British National Identity: From Dickens to Dad's Army* (1997), there is 'always a dominant ideology, a dominant image; otherwise there would be nothing to contest or negotiate with' (p. 2).

Higson's multiple approaches also consider the composition of a national cinema audience and their consumption habits. The complexity of understanding a national film culture includes exploring 'the range of films in circulation within a nation state', including films produced by that nation, but also by other nations, including Hollywood; 'the range of sociologically specific audiences for different types of film', the cine-literacy of different audiences and their socio-economic identities, to understand the diversity of consumption habits for a national cinema audience; and 'the range of and relation between discourses about film circulating within that cultural and social formation' and the ways in which audiences relate to particular discourses of art and entertainment. Specifically, Higson here is interested in 'the *use* of films (sounds, images, narratives, fantasies)', understanding the point of consumption rather than the moment of production, producing an *evidenced* audience member, rather than the notional 'I' of most purportedly objective film criticism, and critique of their experience of film within a national film culture (2002, pp. 140–141). Since Higson's article was published, there have been many studies that put into practice his call for more audience studies and a better understanding of audiences' use of film texts. Importantly for our understanding of national cinema, Higson's conclusion already highlights the impurity of notions of national cinema. While he acknowledges that national cinemas are often a result of institutional regulation and legislation in the constitution of a national film *industry*, he shifts thinking towards considering the constitution of a national film *culture* that is less insular than national attempts to intervene on a level of production and exhibition, and more encompassing of international trends in cinema. While this protects Hollywood's dominant place in most cinema markets, it helps us better understand the diversity of audiences, whereas we need other approaches to understand the diversity of a national film industry's output, both hegemonic and counter-hegemonic.

National cinemas and Hollywood

In a slightly later article, entitled 'Reconceptualising National Cinema/s' (originally published in the *Quarterly Review of Film and Video* in 1993), Stephen Crofts offers a range of options for theorising different varieties of national cinema. Like Higson, he is conscious of the hybrid status of the nation-state and the increasing reliance on transnational connections, locally and regionally, that muddy the waters. Foreshadowing much of the theorising of transnational cinemas, Crofts acknowledges the 'unequal distribution of power across axes of nation as well as class, gender, ethnicity, etc.' and that 'In the context of the relations of unequal economic and cultural exchange obtaining between Hollywood and (other) national cinemas, the generation and/or survival of indigenous genres is a gauge of the strength and dynamism of a national cinema' (2006, pp. 55–56). For Crofts, then, the question of national cinemas is largely one of opposition to or a relationship with Hollywood. He lists seven categories or types of national cinema that largely come to be defined by their proximity with Hollywood:

1. Cinemas which differ from Hollywood, but do not compete directly, by targeting a distinct, specialist market sector;
2. Those which differ, do not compete directly *but* do directly *critique* Hollywood;
3. European and Third World entertainment cinemas which struggle against Hollywood with limited or no success;
4. Cinemas which ignore Hollywood, an accomplishment managed by few;
5. Anglophone cinemas which try to beat Hollywood at its own game;

6. Cinemas which work within a wholly state-controlled and often substantially state subsidised industry; and,
7. Regional or national cinemas whose culture and/or language take their distance from the nation-states which enclose them. (pp. 44–45)

These categories are 'highly permeable', though. As Crofts shows us, certain cinemas might straddle different categories. For him, French cinema crosses the first and third varieties with some films falling into the second. These would include the films of the *nouvelle vague*, or of the 1970s Jean-Luc Godard, whose more radical political experimentation, influenced by the New Left, reached a different audience to that of Hollywood, or explicitly critiqued it, or struggled against that paradigm, sometimes with public funding. Of course, since Crofts' article was first published, things have changed in French cinema. A company like Luc Besson's EuropaCorp would sit comfortably within the fifth category, as many of its films seek to play the Hollywood game, making anglophone films that use typically mainstream strategies, such as genre and stardom, to compete in the international marketplace. Now located in Saint-Denis on the outskirts of Paris and founded in 1997, EuropaCorp has been responsible for some major international hits that model Hollywood methods. While its first film, Gary Oldman's 1997 British kitchen sink drama *Nil by Mouth*, remained firmly within traditional national cinema models (a relatively typical European co-production strategy), later films have been in the Hollywood mould, such as the *Taken* (Pierre Morel, 2008, Oliver Megaton, 2012 and 2015, and TV series from 2017) and *Transporter* series (Corey Yuen, 2002, Louis Letterrier, 2005, Oliver Megaton, 2008 and Camille Delamarre, 2015, as well as a TV series, 2012–2014), and *District 13* (*Banlieue 13*, Pierre Morel, 2014, Figure 2.2), its sequel (Patrick Alessandrin, 2009), and English-language

Figure 2.2 EuropaCorp's blend of spectacular action and genre cinema is highly transnational, such as the Parkour-styled *Banlieue 13* (Pierre Morel, 2014) (EuropaCorp/TF1 Films Production/Canal+)

Figure 2.3 EuropaCorp's transnational strategies extend to its English language remakes, such as *Brick Mansions* (Camille Delamarre, 2014) (EuropaCorp/Brick Mansions Productions Inc/Canal+/D8/Ciné+/Transfilm/Téléfilm Canada)

remake, *Brick Mansions* (Camille Delamarre, 2014, Figure 2.3). The films feature recognisable stars, such as Liam Neeson and Jason Statham, and are generally produced in English. In many respects, a company such as EuropaCorp, built upon the success of Besson's earlier international hits, such as *The Big Blue* (*La Grande Bleu*, 1988), *La Femme Nikita* (1990), *Léon: The Professional* (1994), and *The Fifth Element* (1997), which themselves straddle the first and fifth of Crofts' categories, demonstrate how fluid national cinema categories can be and how limiting thinking only in terms of the national can become. While EuropaCorp are located primarily in France, it works in conjunction with companies in Hollywood, Canada and China, as a production company that both exploits and benefits from the fluidity of globalisation. However, that's not to say that a company like EuropaCorp can only be explained in relation to the fifth of Crofts' categories. It does still produce films in the first mode, such as *L'amour dure trois ans* (*Love Lasts Three Years*, Frédéric Beigbeder, 2011) a co-production with other companies in France that doesn't attempt to compete with Hollywood in anglophone markets. A romantic comedy starring Gaspard Proust and Louise Bourgoin, the film showed little outside France (it had no British or American cinema release); despite the prominence being given to transnational cinemas, it's important to remember that films that target local audiences are still produced, even by transnational companies such as EuropaCorp.

As Crofts notes, there are few cinemas that successfully ignore Hollywood. The examples that he discusses have dated, such as his reference to Hong Kong cinema. Since the 1997 handover to China, the Hong Kong film industry has faltered, producing less films, while foreign imports have increased. This decline began in the 1990s following Hong Kong's return to Chinese control, as a Special Administrative Region (under the 'one country, two cultures' policy) the region has seen a growth in co-productions with the mainland and a shift in the kinds of films being produced (see Chu, 2010). In some regards, this conceives of Hong Kong as part of a Chinese national cinema (a point to which we'll return to Chapter 6), but also demonstrates earlier limitations of the national cinema model: as Poshek Fu and David Desser have argued, 'Hong Kong presents a theoretical conundrum' since it was 'a Chinese community under British rule, a cinema without a nation, a local cinema with international appeal' (2000, p. 5). It is only following the return to China that, as Meaghan Morris has pointed out, Hong Kong becomes 'no longer exactly a cinema *without* a nation' that is 'no longer unequivocally local', if it was even local in the first place 'given the aggressive export drive of its major studios and producers, the formative tension between Cantonese and Mandarin-language filmmaking in its past, and its increasingly multi-glossic orientation today' (2005, p. 10). Bliss Cua Lim, in her book *Translating Time: Cinema, the Fantastic, and Temporal Critique* (2009), has perhaps described this theoretical conundrum most clearly:

> A national cinema paradigm rooted in the auteurist model of the postwar European new waves remains poorly suited to Hong Kong cinema, whose own new wave was not an art cinema but an innovative form of commercial filmmaking that viewed Hollywood less as an object of critique than a partner and rival to Hong Kong cinema. The national cinema model typically works on a contrastive principle of difference from Hollywood, but in the case of Hong Kong cinema, the prominent other against which to demarcate cultural and stylistic distinction is not Hollywood but other Chinese cinemas. Despite its intransigence to national cinema paradigms, however, Hong Kong cinema as an object of cinephilia and critical study has produced a *national cinema effect*. (p. 188)

This *national cinema effect* exposes the constructed nature of national cinemas demonstrated in Crofts' approach to the subject. Even cinemas that don't stand in opposition to or critique of Hollywood are defined in that binary approach. The Eurocentrism of the approach to this *national cinema effect* is to reduce national cinemas to the sum of their relationship with Hollywood. While some transnational filmmaking aims to imitate or exploit Hollywood trends, such as the EuropaCorp example, others are more concerned with local and regional relationships, such as the prominence of Hong Kong films in Taiwan or the Philippines, that stimulate translocal trends in neighbouring regions, such as the horror films explored by Lim in her book.

For Crofts, the dominant models of national cinema are the European-model art cinemas, Third Cinema (which we'll encounter in the next chapter), and the commercial cinemas of the Third World and Europe. The dominant European-style art film emerges from the elitism of a bourgeois nationalism, crucially built upon concerns for cultural and literary traditions and quality filmmaking. As Crofts notes, this is a model that is generally difficult to impose onto many cinemas around the world, his key example being India, where only Satyajit Ray's films, such as *The Apu Trilogy* (*Pather Panchali*, 1955, *Aparajito*, 1956 and *Apur Sansar*, 1959), rely on conventional art cinema forms of realist style and subject matter that are shared with neorealist cinema, such as *Bicycle Thieves* (*Ladri di Biciclette*, Vittorio De Sica, 1948). Indeed, India is a difficult cinema to classify as a national industry in itself. While it demonstrates the hallmarks of a cinema that ignores Hollywood (although it also remakes Hollywood films and capitalises on its generic trends), it can't easily be classified as *national* cinema. During the year from April 2013 to the end of May 2014, the Central Board of Film Classification in India certified just under 2,000 films. This included films in 35 different languages, and across nines centres of film production. Filmmaking in India is highly regionalised. Although the term Bollywood is used to classify a national Indian cinema, it only accounts for around a third of all Indian film production. The majority of films produced in Mumbai (the home of Bollywood cinema) are in the Hindi language, while other areas cater to regional populations and languages, such as: Tollywood, comprising the Bengali cinema based in Tollygunge in Kolkata, and the Telugu cinema based in Hyderabad; Kollywood, the Tamil cinema in Chennai; and Pollywood, the Punjabi cinema (while Delhi is the largest Indian city in the Punjabi region, most Punjabi films are produced in Mumbai, although Punjabi language films have also been produced in Lahore in Pakistan (Lollywood) as the region straddles two countries). This again produces a conundrum for thinking of a unified national cinema, where Bollywood often stands metonymically as a signifier of an Indian cinema, one that cannot be simply defined by a single language or type of film. Like the Hong Kong cinema, it produces a national cinema effect that conceives of a unified national cinema. This is a much more pronounced effect than that described by Higson in the case of British cinema. However, it likewise points to the problematic nature of the national cinema paradigm that conceives of the nation as a stable and unified entity, whereas what counts as a national cinema can be more fragmented and outward looking than the inward-looking gaze of nationalism and its 'imagined communities'.

Case study: *Bicycle Thieves* (*Ladri di Biciclette*, Vittorio De Sica, 1948)

The classic auteurist-realist mode of national cinema is well emphasised by the Italian neorealist movement that emerged following the Second World War. Italian neorealism was a short-lived and loosely connected set of films that shared a common set of traits, both stylistically and thematically: an avoidance of studio filming aesthetics; natural lighting; seemingly accidental *mise en scène*; a lack of dramatic or analytical editing or montage; location filming; non-professional actors; and an overall non-interventionist, documentary-style approach to filmmaking. Writing in 1948, the influential French critic André Bazin praised the 'ethic of objectivity' that it shared with literary reportage (2002, p. 60). The movement's subject matter focused on the everyday, ordinary working-class individuals toiling following the end of fascism and German occupation. The turn towards realism was a rejection of the qualities of the films made in the 1930s under Mussolini, where the *Telefoni Bianchi* (white telephone) comedies focused on the glossy and aspirational lives of the bourgeois middle classes. The white telephone came to stand as a symbol of the consumerism of the era. The filmmakers of the neorealist moment took their inspiration from elsewhere. As Mark Shiel has remarked, their inspiration came from 'leftist politics, especially the agendas of the Italian Communist Party (PCI) and Socialist Party (PSI)', and the desire to reconstruct a better Italy after fascism, despite a dominant conservative ideology led by the Catholic Church (2006, p. 2).

As an example of a national cinema, Italian neorealism has exerted a long shadow over subsequent Italian cinema. As we'll see with the example of *Bicycle Thieves*, it was conceived as a cinema of social and political protest, an alternative to the dominant popular cinema, in Hollywood and in Italy, but importantly it grew out a specific socio-historical moment in Italy, one that, as Laura Ruberto and Kristi Wilson have pointed out, showed 'how a national identity could be shaped and/or redefined by cinema' by filmmakers in a particular moment. However, they also note that 'national cinema can be seen as an insidious and isolationist concept, one that collapses many forms of identity into a hegemonic vision of culture' (2007, p. 3). So, while Italian neorealism might have been a popular and influential form (as is demonstrated by the chapters in Ruberto and Wilson's collection, *Italian Neorealism and Global Cinema*, that show the legacy of neorealism beyond Italy, in Hong Kong, Brazil, India, even in America), it was short-lived and narrow, despite the prominence paid to it by critics, filmmakers and scholars.

Shiel notes that there is a consensus view that there are only seven 'pure' neorealist films: *Rome, Open City* (*Roma, città aperta*, Roberto Rossellini, 1945), *Paisà* (Rossellini, 1946), *Shoeshine* (*Scioscià*, Vittorio De Sica, 1946),

Germany Year Zero (*Germania anno zero*, Rossellini, 1947), *La Terra Trema* (Luchino Visconti, 1948), *Umberto D* (De Sica, 1952) and *Bicycle Thieves*. By the time the 1950s came, there was a lot of discussion about a 'crisis of neorealism', as Italian filmmakers explored the form and took it in different directions – by the 1960s, Italian cinema was known internationally through the films of Federico Fellini, and their self-reflexive magical realism, and the Spaghetti Westerns of Sergio Leone, although neorealism continued to have a pull in the ways in which Italian national cinema was conceived.

De Sica's *Bicycle Thieves* demonstrates many of the aspects shared by the neorealist films and reveals the ways in which a national cinema might be thought of as resistant to dominant cinema trends. Perhaps the best known of the classic neorealist films, the film is about the downtrodden and unemployed Antonio Ricci (played by former factory worker Lamberto Maggiorani) who is eventually offered work as a bill-poster. He has just one problem: he has pawned his bicycle, and he must have one for the job. His wife pawns their best bed linen to get the bike back from the pawnbroker. But, on his first day, the bicycle is stolen. Forced to look for the bicycle himself after the police prove unhelpful, Ricci wanders the streets with his son Bruno (Enzo Staiola, who De Sica cast after seeing him watching production on the street) desperately seeking the thief. They look through markets, around Rome's streets and homes until, believing they have found the thief, Ricci himself is treated like a criminal for abusing the man he suspects is the thief. Bazin commented that the film had 'not enough material ... even for a news item: the whole story would not deserve two lines in a stray-dog column' (1972a, p. 50). Its story, for Bazin, was anti-dramatic, its focus on the objective portrayal of the struggles of the working classes, something that led him to call it:

> the only valid Communist film of the whole past decade precisely because it has meaning even when you have abstracted its social significance ... [, that] in the world where this workman lives, the poor must steal from each other in order to survive. (p. 51)

This formed the thematic core of neorealism. As Cesare Zavattini, the film's screenwriter, argued in an important piece that theorised Italian neorealism, entitled 'Some Ideas on the Cinema' (it had no formal manifesto, unlike other film movements):

> neorealism can and must face poverty. We have begun with poverty for the simple reason that it is one of the most pivotal realities of our time, and I challenge anyone to prove the contrary. To believe, or to pretend

to believe, that by making half a dozen films on poverty we have finished with the problem, would be a great mistake. (2000, p. 146)

Zavattini here demonstrates the commitment to leftist, humanist politics that define the film, and the neorealist movement, something which has had lengthy resonance for later filmmakers. Politically, Ricci is pitted against several institutions – the church is unhelpful, as are the police. Carlo Celli has argued that the film represents a melodrama in which the villain is 'the society of reconstruction Rome' (2004, p. 48), precisely because of the film's critique of the post-war society in which different social and political institutions are either indifferent to Ricci's plight, or are unable to help. Even sport is implicated, as Ricci's final downfall comes amongst the crowds outside a football match; as Celli describes, sport held a restorative, mediating power in Italy immediately following the war, but this offers little solace for Ricci.

The film demonstrates many of the stylistic traits of neorealist cinema: the main actors had little or no experience, while the film is generally shot in medium to long shots, with few close-ups, and was shot entirely on location around Rome. Location shooting at the time was largely a necessity – Rome's largest studio, Cinecittà, had been bombed during the war, and served as a refugee camp for a couple of years afterwards. The ending offers no clear resolution or solution to the problem: Ricci doesn't find his bicycle and turns to crime in desperation – seen through the previously admiring eyes of his son, this moment reinforces the hopelessness of their situation and the uncertain moment for the Italian people. As Zavattini noted in the face of criticism over the lack of closure in neorealist films: 'they remain unresolved from a practical point of view simply because "this is reality"' (2000, p. 147). The almost scientific commitment to reality (as designated by the roots of the term neorealism) is demonstrated throughout the film in its style and narrative structure, where it wanders rather than is driven by action, despite its occasional forays into melodrama, something Bazin noted was highly indicative of Italian cinema, and something the film could not resist entirely. The film rejects excessive stylisation or ornamentation. However, one of its key moments critiques Hollywood spectacle. At the time Ricci's bicycle is stolen, he's putting up posters of Rita Hayworth. The signifier of Hollywood glamour is in stark contrast to that of Ricci's plight – when we first see him, he's literally sat on the ground in the dirt (Figure 2.4) – and juxtaposes the reality of post-war Rome. It forms a moment in which the film is critical of Hollywood cinema and the fantasies that it offers. De Sica was no stranger to the glamour of cinema – he had been a prominent leading man in the 1930s in Italian comedies. Here, just as Zavattini was in his article on neorealism, the film critiques mainstream cinema, thereby demonstrating its resistant political stance.

Figure 2.4 In a long shot, Antonio sits in the dirt of Rome's semi-rural landscape when we first meet him in *Bicycle Thieves* (Vittorio De Sica, 1948) (Produzioni De Sica – S.A./Arrow Films)

Bicycle Thieves in some respects is a metonym for the neorealist cinema. Its stylistic and thematic features emblematise the features that constitute a classic of European *auteur*-realist national cinema. As a very popular international film – it has been re-released many times, including by prestige distributors such as The Criterion Collection that promote auteurist art cinema – it promotes a reading of the film as a distinctly national expression, one that was common in Italian cinema at the time (despite the argument that only seven neorealist films were ever made across seven years between 1945 and 1952), and has come to be a defining example of Italian cinema ever since, partly due to the film's recirculation and popularity in art cinema discourses. However, it also demonstrates a way in which we might see national cinema as monocultural, as particular expressions are promoted over others, and how a national cinema might be promoted as less than the sum of its parts, or through limited readings.

Recommended viewing:

Rome, Open City (*Roma, città aperta*, Roberto Rossellini, 1945)
Paisà (Rossellini, 1946)
Germany Year Zero (*Germania anno zero*, Rossellini, 1947)
Bitter Rice (*Riso amaro*, Giuseppe De Santis, 1949)
La Strada (Federico Fellini, 1954)

Mamma Roma (Pier Paolo Pasolini, 1962)
Gomorrah (Matteo Garrone, 2008)

Recommended further reading:

On Italian cinema, neorealism and after:

Barattoni, Luca (2012), *Italian Post-Neorealist Cinema*. Edinburgh: Edinburgh University Press.

Bayman, Louis, and Sergio Rigoletto (2013), *Popular Italian Cinema*. London: Palgrave Macmillan.

Bertellini, Giorgio (2004), *The Cinema of Italy*. London: Wallflower.

Bondanella, Peter, ed. (2013), *The Italian Cinema Book*. London: British Film Institute.

Ricci, Steven (2008), *Cinema and Fascism: Italian Film and Society, 1922–1943*. Berkeley and London: University of California Press.

Rocchio, Vincent F. (1999), *Cinema of Anxiety: A Psychoanalysis of Italian Neorealism*. Austin: University of Texas Press.

On the international influence of neorealism:

Giovacchini, Saverio, and Robert Sklar, eds (2012), *Global Neorealism: The Transnational History of a Film Style*. Jackson: University Press of Mississippi.

Jie, Lu (2014), 'Walking on the Margins: From Italian Neorealism to Contemporary Chinese Sixth Generation', *Journal of Italian Cinema & Media Studies* 2(3): pp. 317–333.

Martin-Jones, David, and Soledad Montañez (2007), '*Bicycle Thieves* or *Thieves on Bicycles*? *El Baño del Papa* (2007)', *Studies in Hispanic Cinemas* 4(3): pp. 183–198.

Pollacchi, Elena (2014), 'Spaces and Bodies: The Legacy of Italian Cinema in Contemporary Chinese Film-making', *Journal of Italian Cinema & Media Studies* 2(1): pp. 7–21.

Zhong, Huang (2014), 'The Bicycle Towards the Pantheon: A Comparative Analysis of *Beijing Bicycle* and *Bicycle Thieves*', *Journal of Italian Cinema & Media Studies* 2(3): pp. 351–362.

Case study: *The Apple* (*Sib*, Samira Makhmalbaf, 1998)

The legacy and influence of Italian neorealism can be seen throughout many national cinema movements. Realism has long been associated with politically motivated cinema, with its ambiguous motivations, character-driven narratives and wandering narrative structures that often place characters at the behest of social and political forces that they are unable to control, or even comprehend. In *Bicycle Thieves*, Ricci is powerless against the forces that led to the theft of this bicycle and later against the institutional forces of reconstruction Italy that make it impossible for him to find it without turning to crime himself. That this is witnessed by his son who, through innocent observant eyes, comes to understand his father as simply human is also highly significant. The trope of the child or childhood has been a common feature of neorealist and realist cinema in many worldwide national cinemas. One film that shares this focus is Iranian Samira Makhmalbaf's debut feature *The Apple*.

Directed when Makhmalbaf was 17 years old, *The Apple* tells the story of a family in Tehran who come under scrutiny when neighbours report to the authorities that their twin daughters, Massoumeh (Massoumeh Naderi) and Zahra (Zahra Naderi) have been virtually imprisoned by their father (Ghorban Ali Naderi), don't go to school, and are unclean. When social workers call, they discover the girls are barely able to talk, and have limited understanding of the world beyond their small yard. Their mother is blind and fearful for her own safety and theirs, as is their father, who is unemployed and poor, relying on handouts from neighbours to buy food. Initially, we see the father choose to tutor his daughters himself – their only viable future is as married women, and he attempts to teach them how to cook rice – but when the social worker returns and a neighbour's son climbs over the wall to help her into the house, she's disappointed to find the girls still locked in and the father absent. When he returns, she locks him in the house and sends the children out to play. Borrowing a hacksaw from one of their neighbours, she tells him to saw his way out through the bars to look for the girls. Meanwhile, the twins explore their neighbourhood, encountering children at play, buying ice cream and being teased by a boy who dangles an apple in front of them.

The film goes beyond neorealist techniques, blending reality with fiction. The central cast are all non-professionals – the two girls and the father play themselves. At the beginning of the film, we watch the girls being taken into state care, questioned and cleaned up. The sequence is clearly shot on video and looks strongly like documentary footage. It demonstrates little by way of intervention from the filmmakers, is roughly cut and, as the family leave the building, the light is overexposed and their bodies lose shape in the daylight (Figure 2.5). When they return home, the film is shot on celluloid, and uses some more conventional techniques, such as shot-reverse-shot editing, although there are also many long takes, as in the final sequence, where the same boy who dangled an apple in front of Massoumeh and Zahra does the same thing to their mother, wandering out in the alley in search of her family who have left to buy a watch. In blurring fiction and reality, Makhmalbaf mixes scripted scenes with interviews with the father. The social worker and neighbours act effectively as interviewers to get across his story, his perceived need to protect his daughters (he likens them to flowers who will wither in the sunlight of male attention), and his dismay and anger at the attention his family's story is receiving, from neighbours and from the local press (we see a shot of an article about them). The self-reflexive realism of the quasi-documentary technique is not unheard of in films of this kind, and we'll come to its relationship with Iranian cinema in just a moment.

Figure 2.5 The quasi-documentary style of *The Apple* (Samira Makhmalbaf, 1998) demonstrates little intervention from the filmmaker, including the use of video and over-exposure (Hubert Bals Fund/MK2 Productions/ Makhmalbaf Productions)

As mentioned above, *The Apple* was Makhmalbaf's first feature as a director. It was scripted in collaboration with her father, Mohsen Makhmalbaf. Also a major Iranian filmmaker, Mohsen Makhmalbaf's films exhibit some of the same techniques as those of his daughter, the similar blending of reality and fiction in films such as *Actor* (*Honarpisheh*, 1993), and the engagement with the plight of individuals and groups struggling against oppression, including *The Cyclist* (*Bicycleran*, 1989), about an Afghan refugee forced to ride a bicycle in a circle for a week to raise money for medical treatment for his wife. As a teenager, he had been a member of a militant political group fighting against the regime of Mohammad Reza Pahlavi, the Shah of Iran at the time. When he was 17, he was convicted of the attempted murder of a soldier by stabbing. Too young to be hanged, he spent five years in jail, and was released following the 1979 Iranian Revolution, which turned Iran into an Islamic Republic under the rule of Ayatollah Khomeini. Afterwards, he became a prominent artist, writer and film director. Since 2009, he has lived in exile in Paris, following his criticism of the re-election of Mahmoud Ahmadinejad, with his support for reform movements in Iran. For his daughter, the political issues are quite different. As Hamid Dabashi has shown, Samira Makhmalbaf's generation is post-ideological – it didn't identify with any specific ideology, unlike her father's. The 1997 election of Mohammad Khatami, a reforming president, who had previously been the Minister for Culture, had been backed by a strong youth movement: 'They were fed up with ideological slogans and political demagoguery, the logic of their material need for change far exceeding their patience for ideological rhetoric' (Dabashi, 2001, p. 268). For Dabashi, *The Apple* reflects this generational belief in its lack of blame. Like *Bicycle Thieves*, the film has an ambiguous ending, although its meaning is clear: the girls' mother, her face covered (as it is for the majority of the film), wanders lost into the street in search of her family. The little boy who teased the girls dangles the apple in front of her, and she attempts unsuccessfully to grab at it, just as her daughters had done (Figure 2.6). Makhmalbaf leaves the shot to linger, with whispered dialogue overheard, and ends with a freeze-frame, just as she grabs at the apple. The image reflects the disenfranchisement of women in Iran, their imprisonment within rigid gender roles and severe limits on their liberty. Yet, the film claims 'no one is to blame'. The problem is identified, but the film has no villain, no ideological pedagogy behind it. Dabashi refers to something that he was told by Mohsen Makhmalbaf just as the original story emerged in 1997: 'It is the story of our nation ... We have all been kept in a cave by our fathers. We can't even look at the sun.' (p. 269) The metaphor of the sun is turned into a signifier of women's oppression – the father quotes from a little book, *Advice for Fathers*: 'a girl is just like a flower, and the sun is like the man who is not related to her. Should the sun cast its light on the flower, the flower will wither.' At the beginning of the film, we see the girls water a flower through the bars of their home, and the sun shines down on them, visually representing this advice for fathers, the dogma he and his wife so willingly force on their daughters.

Figure 2.6 *The Apple's* final shot signals an ideological statement about women's gender roles in Iran (Samira Makhmalbaf, 1998) (Hubert Bals Fund/MK2 Productions/Makhmalbaf Productions)

When the two girls are first pushed out of the home to play, they have difficulty, and there is a continual (unfulfilled) unease for the viewer about what might befall these two youngsters in Tehran. At first, they buy ice cream from a young boy, but they misunderstand the transaction and, when they try to return the melted ice cream, an overlooking neighbour lends them money to pay him. When the other boy teases them with the apple, he pulls it out of their grasp, and then leads them to a grocer's shop. Again, they have no money, and return home, where their father lends them money to buy some apples. Subsequently, they find themselves playing hopscotch with two other girls. Massoumeh and Zahra are both unknowing of the rules, they skip outside the lines; Massoumeh hits one of the girls in the face with one of her apples, twice, and calms the girls' complaints, first with an apology and then by sharing their apples. Finally, they accompany the two other girls to a watch seller to buy a watch that they believe sounds like a train – one of the girls is enamoured by watches and clocks as material objects. When the girls need money to buy a watch, they return home to find their father locked in and attempting to saw himself free. The social worker gives them the key, and Massoumeh tries desperately and emotionally for some time to unlock the door (in one of the film's most moving scenes) and free the older generation from their own imprisonment. After many attempts, she does so, and this echoes the elder Makhmalbaf's comments that they 'have all been kept in a cave by their fathers'. At this point the father and daughters leave with the other girls and the social worker back to the watch seller, leaving the mother bewildered in the dark. The liberation of the girls, and the father, without harm or 'withering' is an overt critique of the oppression women suffer in countries such as Iran, and its production at a time of optimism politically puts its national meaning in focus. It's here too that we can see the enduring legacy of neorealism, although that must be understood in a more local context, where other filmmakers have used similar techniques. One particular example is Abbas Kiarostami, whose films, such as *Close-up* (*Klūzāp, nemā-ye nazdīk*, 1990), which is based on the true story of a man who pretended to be Mohsen Makhmalbaf, and *A Taste of Cherry* (*Ta'm-e gīlās*, 1997) have used a similar blending of reality and fiction to examine the nature of fiction and documentary.

The Apple was a critical success, and screened at the Cannes Film Festival in 1998 (the previous festival's *Palme D'Or* had been won by Kiarostami). Film festivals are important outlets for films such as this, read through the lens of national cinemas. This can sometimes lead to a prominent place for films that are critical of their nation's political regimes, such as might be the case for films from countries like China, Chile or Iran, from filmmakers within the country or from those in exile (like Kiarostami and Mohsen Makhmalbaf). As Hamid Naficy has shown in his multi-volume history of

Iranian cinema, this can bring criticism from audiences, filmmakers and politicians. He notes that the selection of critical films like *The Apple* by major film festivals in the west are seen in a few ways. Films that are critical, and therefore most likely to be chosen by film festivals, can be seen internally as validating an 'export culture' to bring investment from foreign sources, but also as a signifier of a 'soft war' against the Islamic Republic (Naficy also notes that this dark image of Iran might also be a product of the country's censorship of free expression). For exiled or diasporic audiences, there might be two reactions: the films might be validating in their humanism, or they might be criticised for not representing 'their Iran'. As Naficy notes:

> spectators felt ashamed of these movies, for the 'burden of representation' that they themselves had placed on them was too much. No single Iranian film could represent the entirety of Iranian 'national culture.' Since rarely a small body of films is able to fulfil this high expectation, there will always be criticism of their national representation when movies cross national boundaries. (2012, p. 253)

This demonstrates one difficulty of the 'burden of representation' in national cinema models, where only a small percentage of a nation's film output might be taken to represent the whole country's culture and political zeitgeist, or where film festivals favour programming that promotes certain representations at particular moments in time. This looks ahead to some of the problems relating to transnational cinema, where films cross borders with such ease, but often at the expense of their specific national contexts and meanings, or with this 'burden' that connects films to specific readings, rightly or wrongly.

Recommended viewing:

Close-up (*Klūzāp, nemā-ye nazdīk*, Abbas Kiarostami, 1990)
Taste of Cherry (*Ta'm-e gīlās*, Abbas Kiarostami, 1997)
Blackboards (*Takhté siah*, Samira Makhmalbaf, 2000)
Kandahar (*Safar e Ghandehar*, Mohsen Makhmalbaf, 2001)
Offside (Jafar Panahi, 2006)
Persepolis (Vincent Paronnaud, Marjane Satrapi, 2007)
A Separation (*Jodaeiye Nader az Simin*, Asghar Farhadi, 2011)

Recommended further reading:

Aquino, Rowena Santos (2010), 'The Collective Performance of Female Youth in The Apple (1998)', *Red Feather Journal* 1(2): pp. 26–40.

Chaudhuri, Shohini and Howard Finn (2003), 'The Open Image: Poetic Realism and the New Iranian Cinema', *Screen* 44(1): pp. 38–57.

Esfandairy, Shahab (2012), *Iranian Cinema and Globalization: National, Transnational, and Islamic Dimensions*. Bristol and Chicago: Intellect.

Naficy, Hamid (1994), 'Veiled Vision/Powerful Presences: Women in Post-revolutionary Iranian Cinema', in eds Rose Issa and Sheila Whitaker, *Life and Art: The New Iranian Cinema*. London: BFI, pp. 44–66.

—— (2011, 2012), *Social History of Iranian Cinema*, 4 vols. Durham and London: Duke University Press.

—— (2012) 'Neorealism Iranian Style', in eds Saverio Giovacchini and Robert Sklar, *Global Neorealism: The Transnational History of a Film Style*. Jackson: University Press of Mississippi, pp. 226–239.

Sheibani, Khatereh (2011), *The Poetics of Iranian Cinema: Aesthetics, Modernity and Film After the Revolution*. London and New York: IB Tauris.

Şerban, Silviu, and Anita Grigoriu (2014), 'Feminism in Post-revolutionary Iranian Cinema', *Journal of Research in Gender Studies* 4(2): pp. 967–978.

Tapper, Richard, ed. (2002), *New Iranian Cinema: Politics, Representation and Identity*. London: IB Tauris.

Weinberger, Stephen (2007), 'Neorealism, Iranian Style', *Iranian Studies* 40(1): pp. 5–16.

Cinema and the 'national narrative'

In a much-cited text on nationalism, Benedict Anderson refers to nations as 'imagined communities'. He argues that nationalism and nationhood are 'cultural artefacts of a particular kind' that emerged in the late eighteenth century (1991, p. 4). They are 'imagined as a *community*, because, regardless of the actual inequality and exploitation that may prevail in each, the nation is always conceived as a deep, horizontal comradeship' (p. 7). The nation, Anderson argues, was constructed through a number of discursive means, including the development of a national print language, as well as through the construction of a particular kind of time that Walter Benjamin described as 'homogeneous, empty time', an objective, shared time 'measured by clock and calendar' (p. 24). Time within the nation became shared and linear, as did its history. Through this we begin to move towards what David Martin-Jones explores in cinema as 'national narratives'.

Martin-Jones's examination of the ways in which national identity is narrated temporally through cinema draws not so much on Anderson (although Anderson's work has been a common reference point for many theorists, including Higson and Crofts, to discuss the ways in which nation is constructed through cinema), but on Homi K. Bhabha's critique of Anderson's work in *Nation and Narration*. Bhabha contends that Anderson's notion of the shared linearity of national time:

> works like the plot of a realist novel. The steady onward clocking of calendrical time, in Anderson's words, gives the imagined worlds of the nation a sociological solidity; it links together diverse acts and actors on the national stage who are entirely unaware of each other. (Bhabha, 1990, p. 308)

Bhabha's postcolonial reading of Anderson's work notes that the 'meanwhile' observed by Anderson, also drawn from Benjamin, in the daily lives of the nation's people disappears in favour of the narration of linearity and solidity. Instead, Bhabha contends that the nation is narrated in a double-time, a double-writing. There are two competing fields of time – the present is progressive while its origins are rooted in a past that is timeless. The national narrative is therefore constantly in the process of being written (performed) and rewritten (as a pedagogical discourse). The push towards nationhood, the root of the imagined community, is one that is totalising (erasing difference) and essentialising (that it has always been that way). The dominant narrative attempts to reclaim any counter or progressive ones (to overwrite the performance with the pedagogical):

> Counter-narratives of the nation that continually evoke and erase its totalizing boundaries – both actual and conceptual – disturb those ideological manoeuvres through which 'imagined communities' are given essentialist identities. For the political unity of the nation consists in the continual displacement of its irredeemably plural modern space, bounded by different, even hostile nations, into a signifying space that is archaic and mythical, paradoxically representing the nation's territoriality, in the patriotic, atavistic temporality of Traditionalism. Quite simply, the difference of space returns as the Sameness of time, turning Territory into Tradition, turning the People into One. (p. 300)

The double-writing of the national narrative is continually threatened (disturbed) by counter or minor voices and narratives that run in parallel with or in a different direction from the mythic origin story of the nation. Time and progress must move forward in an Enlightenment-style narrative, but this creates a disjunction between what the nation could become and what it should be (concepts at the root of many attempts to 'make the nation great again' or to go 'back to basics'), something that is resituated again in the creation of a new origin story that fits the present moment. Martin-Jones defines this in terms developed from the French philosopher Gilles Deleuze, of a deterritorialisation of the nation's narrative followed by a reterritorialisation of it:

This process of de- and reterritorialisation of national identity is perhaps easiest to consider in terms of a series of recognitions, or perhaps appropriations, of previously marginal minorities into the mainstream. Take postwar Britain for instance. The sixty years since the end of the Second World War have seen the accepted face of national identity deterritorialise, and then reterritorialise to incorporate (to a greater or lesser degree) feminism, queer sexualities, postcolonial histories, post-industrial identities, and more recently, the devolved identities of Scotland, Wales and England. (Martin-Jones, 2006, p. 35)

Martin-Jones uses Deleuze's distinction between the movement-image ('the straight line') and time-image ('the labyrinth') to discuss the ways in which cinema has negotiated crisis moments in national identity. Without taking a lengthy digression into Deleuze's film-philosophy in *Cinema 1* (2001) and *Cinema 2* (2000), we can summarise that the movement-image offers an edited, but linear, image of time in which a situation is altered through action into an altered or changed situation, whereas the time-image gives us a non-linear image of time which forks or splinters into multiple potential or virtual parts. The classic form of the movement-image is generally associated with the narrative of the classical Hollywood cinema, whereas the time-image is connected with the post-war European art cinema, particularly that of Alain Resnais such as *Last Year at Marienbad* (*L'année dernière à Marienbad*, 1961). Martin-Jones argues:

films with non-linear narrative time schemes might initially appear to express the crisis of truth of the postwar time-image that actually use narrative time to renegotiate the 'national self-concept' in the face of major postwar 'events' and movements such as globalisation. (2006, p. 44)

One of his key examples, Tom Tykwer's *Run Lola Run (Lola Rennt*, 1998), demonstrates how this occurs in its parallel narrative. The boyfriend of Lola (Franka Potente), Manni (Moritz Bleibtreu), is a courier for a violent mobster, and he calls her to say he's lost the payment for a delivery he's made, giving Lola 20 minutes to find the money and return it to him. The film replays this narrative three times, as an 'either/either/or' scenario with three different outcomes (one in which Lola dies, another in which Manni does, and a final one in which neither of them dies, but in which they

find the money twice over). Martin-Jones argues, despite Tykwer's suggestion that the film could have been set in any major global city, that the
film's use of multimedia and technology specifically offers a contemporary
image of post-wall Berlin, as a 'rewired [city that] can connect Eastern and
Western Europe, and Europe and the rest of the world' (p. 106). Although,
despite stressing a 'new form of national identity over the old', he suggests
that it retains 'the linearity of the national narrative': the transformed city
offers the potential for a new contemporary identity to be forged, released
from the nation's split past. Mixing the experimentation of the European
auteurist art cinema and the popular action film, the hybridity of the film
also suggests a continuity with older traditions, along with the globalising
pull of post-wall Europe and the transformations that have spanned it. The
non-linear, labyrinthine play of the film's either/either/or structure gives
way to the reterritorialising of the 'one "right" conclusion' in which 'all
other possibilities are rendered "wrong"' to maintain 'a coherent image of
national identity' (p. 113). This would include the performativity of the
central character, whose gendered agency is minimised by the game, and
the revelation of the 'right' conclusion and the maintenance of a traditional identity, despite the appearance otherwise during the film's labyrinthine trio of possible stories (Figure 2.7). The potential deterritorialised,
globalised city is reterritorialised within a coherent, continuous national
narrative that preserves previous traditions in a reclaimed straight line of
national cinema history.

Figure 2.7 *Run Lola Run* (Tom Tykwer, 1998): Lola's either/either/or choices are
represented in the narrative structure and, visually, by this crossroads *mise-en-
abîme* (X-Filme Creative Pool/Westdeutscher Rundfunk (WDR)/Arte)

Case study: *Blind Chance* (*Przypadek*, Krzysztof Kieślowski, 1987)

Unlike *Run Lola Run*, another of Martin-Jones's examples, Kieślowski's *Blind Chance* offers no 'correct' restorative ending. With 'a different set of historical circumstances to those of recently reunified Germany, the same formal structure yields a very different outcome' (Martin-Jones, 2006, p. 223). Part of a Polish 'cinema of moral anxiety', *Blind Chance* concerns the life of Witek Długosz (Bogusław Linda), a young man studying to be a doctor in Łódź. The film opens with an extreme close-up of Witek screaming, and the camera pushing down his throat as he cries out (Figure 2.8). This is an event we'll only ascribe meaning to at the end of the film, although we might consider it as being an expression of Witek's existential crisis at the most crucial moment of the film. A brief montage of Witek's formative years build up to the point of crisis in his life: the death of his father, which throws his world into chaos, as his father confesses on his deathbed that Witek is no longer obligated to become a doctor (he tells him he 'you don't have to do anything'). Witek takes a leave of absence from his studies and catches a train to Warsaw. At this moment, the film takes three different forks in the narrative. In the first version, Witek briefly bumps first into an old lady and then a vagrant who's fortunate enough to pick up a coin dropped by the woman that means he can buy a beer. He buys a student ticket and runs to the platform. The bumps (like those in *Run Lola Run*) precipitate different outcomes. This first time, he catches the train, on which he meets Werner, a committed Communist, and he becomes a Party member and advocate. Witek quickly becomes disillusioned, and betrayed into naming his girlfriend as a dissident. This sequence ends with him about to board a plane for Paris. In the second iteration, he fails to catch the train, having collided with the vagrant hard enough to make him drop his beer. He gets into a fight with a guard on the platform and is imprisoned. During his incarceration, he falls in with a group of religious dissidents. Baptised in the Catholic Church, he comes into conflict with the state when trying to gain a passport for his flight to Paris. They offer him the opportunity to travel, on the condition he informs on anti-Communist sympathisers in France. He refuses, but when the headquarters of his faction are raided, he's suspected by his peers. In the final version, the shortest of the three, Witek fails to collide with the vagrant, but again misses the train. On the platform, he meets Olga, and they begin a relationship. He returns to his studies and practises medicine. When Olga becomes pregnant, they get married, and have a son. This time, he resists engaging in politics, refusing to sign a petition in support of the Dean's son, who is accused of spreading contraband literature. Witek is then asked by the Dean to travel to Libya to deliver talks on his behalf. When he books his flight, he's due to connect through Paris.

Figure 2.8 *Blind Chance's* (Krzysztof Kieślowski, 1987) opening shot offers an ambiguous glimpse of Witek's existential crisis and Poland's 'moral anxiety' (P.P. Film Polski)

He kisses Olga goodbye at the train station with his son, and she tells him she's pregnant with a daughter. When he arrives at the airport he passes by some of characters we've seen in the other two segments, as the narratives converge at this point. The plane taxis to take off, but when it does it explodes and crashes. We can only interpret its opening shot as the pain felt as the plane explodes. Unlike *Run Lola Run*, and *Sliding Doors* (Peter Howitt, 1998), with which it shares the either/or possibility of catching a train or not, there is no restorative ending, despite the obviously happy circumstances in which Witek leaves Olga. This suggests the inevitability of the violence of the ending in the Polish national narrative.

While the film was produced in 1981, it wasn't screened in Poland until 1987, having been banned. There is no attempt to produce a 'coherent image of national identity' in the film's image of a totalitarian Poland that one character remarks is 'disintegrating'. Witek's life criss-crosses the country's national narrative: he points out that he was born during the June 1956 uprising in Poznań (while his mother and twin brother died during childbirth); his great grandparents took part in the 1863 January Uprising (against the Russian Empire's attempt to conscript young Polish men); his grandfather served in the 1920 Polish-Soviet war; his father fought against the German invasion in September 1939, while a childhood friend was forced out of the country to Denmark during the 1968 anti-Semitic purges. Despite this, as Paul Coates argues, *Blind Chance*:

is profoundly subversive of ideas of destiny ... In the process, it subverts the black-and-white notions of character that were so prevalent in a deeply politicised Poland polarised between 'them' and 'us'. In each of his first two lives, Witek is the victim of society's stereotypical division into martyrs and traitors. (2005, p. 193)

Kieślowski avoids the double-writing of history in this narrative. The third option, which Coates speculates is the truest of the three, is the most conventional, as well as the one that brings closure to the opening shot, suturing shut the ambiguity of its initial refusal to give it meaning. What is deterritorialised remains so, there is no reterritorialisation of the national narrative in this film.

Where there was reterritorialisation of a national narrative was in the reception of the film following its six-year banning. The film was released in a very different political climate in Poland. The Solidarity (Solidarność) trade union led by Lech Wałęsa had been founded in 1980, and the film was written prior to the institution of a period of martial law that lasted from December 1981 until July 1983. During that time, the leaders of Solidarity were imprisoned and the union went underground. When the film was released, the political climate had worsened as the Soviet Union, under Mikhail Gorbachev, reformed. This led some critics to see the film as something of a historical relic, a marker of a previous time, while others hailed the film's philosophical treatise on fate and destiny (see Haltof, 2004). So, while the film commented upon history, it was itself overtaken by the country's historical narrative, causing it to reflect on a previous period in history, although it can also be seen as a further statement by the *auteur* (typical of *auteur*-driven approaches to national cinema and questions of quality), one that he later explored as a transnational filmmaker, in his *Three Colours* trilogy, based on the principles reflected in the French tricolour, of freedom (*liberté*), equality (*égalité*) and brotherhood (*fraternité*): *Blue* (1993), *White* (1994) and *Red* (1994).

Recommended viewing:

Illumination (*Iluminacja*, Krzysztof Zanussi, 1973)
Camouflage (*Barwy ochronne*, Krzysztof Zanussi, 1977)
Man of Marble (*Człowiek z marmuru*, Andrzej Wajda, 1977)
Top Dog (*Wodzirej*, Feliks Falk, 1977)
Camera Buff (*Amator*, Krzysztof Kieślowski, 1979)
Provincial Actors (*Aktorzy prowincjonalni*, Agnieszka Holland, 1979)
Interrogation (*Przesluchanie*, Ryszard Bugajski, 1982)

Recommended further reading:

Bradatan, Costica (2008), 'Transcendence and History in Krzysztof Kieslowski's *Blind Chance*', *East European Politics & Societies* 22(2): pp. 425–446.

Falkowska, Janina (1995), '"The Political" in the Films of Andrzej Wajda and Krzysztof Kieślowski', *Cinema Journal* 34(2): pp. 37–50.

Haltof, Marek (2002), *Polish National Cinema*. New York and Oxford: Berghahn.

—— (2004), *The Cinema of Krzysztof Kieślowski: Variations on Destiny and Chance*. London & New York: Wallflower.

Insdorf, Annette (1999), *Double Lives, Second Chances: The Cinema of Krzysztof Kieślowski*. New York: Hyperion.

Jagielski, Sebastian (2013), '"I Like Taboo": Queering the Cinema of Krzysztof Zanussi', *Studies in Eastern European Cinema* 4(2): pp. 143–159.

Lubelski, Tadeusz (1999), 'From *Personnel* to *No End*: Kieślowski's Political Feature Films', in ed. Paul Coates, *Lucid Dreams: The Films of Krzysztof Kieślowski*. Wiltshire: Flicks, pp. 54–76.

Mazierska, Ewa (2015), 'The Ideal and Reality of Work in the 1970s Films of Krzysztof Kieślowski', *Studies in Eastern European Cinema* 6(1): pp. 64–81.

Mazierska, Ewa, and Michael Goddard (2014), *Polish Cinema in a Transnational Context*. Rochester: University of Rochester Press.

Ostrowska, Elzbieta, and Joanna Rydzewska (2007) 'Gendered Discourses of Nation(hood) and the West in Polish Cinema', *Studies in European Cinema* 4(3): pp. 187–198.

Žižek, Slavoj (2001), *The Fright of Real Tears: Krzysztof Kieślowski Between Theory and Post-Theory*. London: BFI.

The national cinema as limiting

Finally, we return to one of our initial key referents: Andrew Higson. Despite 'The Concept of National Cinema' being a seminal article in the theorisation of national cinemas, Higson later returned to the concept to problematise it and point towards the theorisation of a transnational cinema. In the last chapter, we encountered Higson's argument about how foreign cinema can be considered as an invader, in ways that seek to protect national cinemas from outside influence. In 'The Limiting Imagination of National Cinema' he contends that the imagined community of nation may be more fragmented and diverse than previously imagined. Indeed, he suggests 'that the concept of the "transnational" may be a subtler means of describing cultural and economic formations that are rarely contained by national boundaries' (2006, p. 16). He returns to Benedict Anderson and his image of the national narrative as a means of constructing a unified image of nation and nationalism; the nation is always produced in a tension between 'us' and 'them', or 'home' and 'away' as Higson puts it. This image of nation pictures a unified nation that creates a single image of its culture, people and history. In addition, this discourse also presumes that borders are stable boundaries, fixed and impermeable, 'effective in containing political and economic developments, cultural practices and identity'. Instead, 'borders are always leaky and there is a considerable degree of movement across them' (2006, p. 19). Higson identifies a few ways in which national cinemas are subject to cross-border movement:

- Production: filmmakers and capital move easily across borders. Many films are co-productions, and produced with multinational cast and crews. Higson's example is *The English Patient* (Anthony Minghella, 1996), a film adapted from a novel about 'the contingency of identity' written by a Sri Lankan-born resident of Canada (Michael Ondaatje), produced by an American (Saul Zeantz), directed by a Brit (Minghella), with a multinational cast (British Ralph Fiennes, French Juliette Binoche and German Jürgen Prochnow amongst others) and crew (including John Seale, an Australian cinematographer, with music by Gabriel Yared, who is Lebanese) with American capital.
- Distribution: films regularly circulate beyond their borders, sometimes regionally and internationally.
- Reception: films are often received differently by audiences in different cultural circumstances. While this can often be a result of films being re-edited, dubbed, subtitled or even censored, audiences will still often read films in multiple ways. Films might be viewed as unwelcome, signs of cultural imperialism, or might be part of a move to broaden the cultural range of films seen by local audiences. Films might also be localised through local reception practices. (2006, p. 19)

One aspect not explored by Higson, who is more concerned with questions about production, distribution and state policy towards a national cinema, is the permeability of borders for filmmakers whose work explores identity in the context of diaspora or exile, a key subject for many scholars of transnational cinemas. At the level of form and/or content, films exploring hybrid or conflicted, often minority, identities or ethnicities form a crucial component for thinking about transnational cinema. As Higson argues, the imagination of national cinema is limiting, as is the focus on identity that can limit the range of diversity in multicultural societies. Many of the films we'll explore in later chapters will engage with this discourse.

Higson's article is careful not to completely undermine the agency of the national, as the term 'transnational' implies. As a prominent state entity, the nation remains in place as a legal entity that oversees media policy. Therefore, it:

> remains important to conduct debates at that level and in those terms. It would be foolish in this context to attempt to do away altogether with the concept of national cinema ... [which] is hardly able to do justice either to the internal diversity of contemporary cultural formations or to the overlaps and interpenetrations between different formations. (2006, p. 20)

As we considered at the beginning of this chapter, the images we hold of national cinemas can often be blind to the range of films produced by a nation's cinema culture, a construction at the behest of distributor practices, choices made by film festivals or broadcasters or sometimes by education, where some kinds of films (often those at the margins of a country's film culture) are favoured over others. Taking into account the arguments of John Hill (1992) and Paul Willemen (2006), Higson criticises their 'enclosed' notion of the nation within stable borders; for Willemen, the only viable national cinema is a marginal, counter-hegemonic one that opposes the multinational popular cinema. Nationalism and national cinemas are therefore particular kinds of address, rather than stable sets of meanings and practices or a unified myth. Higson takes objection to the underlying acceptance of the nation as a stably bordered entity that limits the identification with transnational practices. For him, national cinemas have always been 'impure'. As he asks:

> Are the limits of the national the most productive way of framing arguments about cultural diversity and cultural specificity? It is certainly valid to argue for a film culture that accommodates diverse identities, images and traditions, and it is undoubtedly important to promote films that deal with the culturally specific. But it doesn't seem useful to me to think through cultural diversity and cultural specificity in solely national terms: to argue for a national cinema is not necessarily the best way to achieve either cultural diversity or cultural specificity. In any case, the contingent communities that cinema imagines are much more likely to be either local or transnational than national. (2006, p. 23)

Higson here helps us consider how the range of diversity within a cultural formation might be better considered in relation to the more local narratives of multiculturalism – here we might more productively imagine minority or ethnic communities outside the main national narrative – or how production, distribution and questions of identity are considered as part of more transnational communities, including questions of diaspora, resistance to or questioning of dominant national myths. This would also include the ways in which national cinemas are always subject to connections with other cinemas or nations in a variety of ways not necessarily covered in terms of thinking about national cinemas as a site of struggle or resistance from a hegemonic popular cinema. While hegemonic interests still hold sway in many cases, the concept of national cinema limits thinking in ways that can consider the diverse interests and concerns of industries and individuals as they interact with global formations. As we've seen, this doesn't necessarily mean getting rid of the notion of the national as a paradigm of criticism. Indeed, the national retains its agency in thinking about how cinema and identity are formed, and the concept of the transnational helps us to understand the current state and formation of the nation as borders become more permeable and processes of multinational and global capital function to spread culture, capital and individuals around the world. In the next chapter, we'll begin to consider some of the historical and conceptual issues that have impacted on our thinking both about national cinemas and about alternative cinemas that reflect on issues of struggle, colonialism and postcolonialism.

Discussion questions:

- How useful do you think concepts of 'the nation' are in an era of globalisation?
- Is Hollywood a national cinema? Why, or why not?
- If national cultures are defined though comparing centres and margins, where do you think the centres of film culture might lie today?
- How might conceptions of transnational cinemas help us understand the cross-border and transcultural dimensions of national cinemas? How about nations-within-nations, such as Scotland?

Third and Postcolonial Cinemas

In the first chapter, we saw how Ella Shohat and Robert Stam argued that the ways in which we view the media have been derived from a Eurocentric mindset in which Europe is seen as the centre of the world, and that all meaning derives from how other cinemas either differ from or imitate a dominant Eurocentric cinema (including neo-European countries such as the United States and Australia). They proposed shifting from a monocentric point of view to one of a polycentric multiculturalism, to see the world as 'having many dynamic cultural locations, many possible vantage points' (1994, p. 48). Throughout this chapter, we'll look at Third World and postcolonial cinemas, including what has been termed 'Third Cinema'. Third World countries are those who aren't aligned either with the industrialised capitalist world of the US or Europe (also including industrialised US-allied countries such as Japan, South Korea and Israel, along with former British colonies like Australia and New Zealand); these encompass around three-quarters of the world across Latin America, Africa and Asia. The Second World covers the former socialist Eastern Bloc countries, the former Soviet Union and countries in Eastern Europe, such as Poland, whose cinema we encountered in the last chapter. A Fourth World has also been defined, by George Manuel and Michael Posluns in their book *The Fourth World: An Indian Reality* (1974), to refer to indigenous populations within, or dispersed across, nation-states, including Native-Americans in North and Latin Americas, Maoris in New Zealand and Australian Aborigines whose cultures have been colonised or dominated. We touched upon cultures such as these previously, where national cinema models were seen as inadequate to encompass the diversity of cultures within a nation-state.

In looking beyond the First and Second Worlds, we'll see how cinemas that have been shaped through their encounters with or struggles against colonialism are necessarily transnational, given the cultural influence of the dominant power in the colonised country. This accounts for one way in which cultural influence extends beyond national boundaries, through the exercise of imperial power. While in some ways this constitutes an approach towards national cinema, it also extends beyond, to think about neo-colonial cinemas where the imperial influence is exerted not through military might, but through capital, as is the case with US intrusions into Latin America. Consequently, this chapter will extend our look at approaches to national cinemas in the context of Third Cinema. With Fernando Solanas and Octavio Getino's manifesto 'Towards a Third Cinema' as a starting point (1985), the chapter introduces world cinema's engagement with issues of colonialism, poverty, domination and the struggles for recognition in cinemas in the Third World. It's important to highlight at the outset, however, that the study of transnational cinemas might be considered as detrimental to the recognition of Third World cinemas, positing Hollywood as a global centre, or overshadowing or absorbing postcolonial emphases, as we'll come to see when we look at Naficy's notion of an accented cinema. Alternatively, it might help us go beyond a simple binary of First and Third World to show the more complex interactions in an era marked by increased mobility of individuals and culture.

Third Cinema

In 'The National Revisited,' Paul Willemen argued that any 'cinema which seeks to engage with the questions of national specificity from a critical, non- or counter-hegemonic position is a minority and a poor cinema, dependent on the existence of a larger multinational or nationalised industrial sector' (2006, p. 35). It is therefore immediately a counter-cinema, one that seeks to resist or question prevailing ideological norms of a dominant cinema. The term poor cinema is not used to suggest that those films are in some way cheaply made or low budget (although by most measures counter-cinemas will be relatively low budget), but in reference to the poor theatre of Jerzy Grotowski, which has affinities with other socialist and revolutionary Marxist approaches to theatre such as those of Bertolt Brecht in Germany in the 1920s and 1930s or Brazilian Augusto Boal's 'Theatre of the Oppressed' under military dictatorship between the 1960s and 1980s.

Fernando Solanas and Octavio Getino were two young (33 and 34 years old respectively) filmmakers who, alongside the production of their film *The Hour of the Furnaces* (*La Hora de los Hornos*, 1968, in collaboration with the Cuban filmmaker Santiago Álvarez Román, Figure 3.1), wrote a manifesto for an avant-garde anti-colonial cinema. Solanas was an upper-middle-class Argentinian from Buenos Aires whose previous artistic works had brought him into contact with other militant anti-establishment practitioners. Getino was of Spanish birth but had been resident in Buenos Aires since he was 16; while he directed few films, he worked regularly as a writer and critic. Solanas

Figure 3.1 *The Hour of the Furnaces* (Fernando Solanas, Octavio Getino and Santiago Álvarez Román, 1968) critiques ideology's neo-colonial transmission through mass communication (Grupo Cine Liberación)

and Getino were members of the *Grupo Cine Liberación* (The Liberation Film Group), a politically militant group that followed the populist Leftist philosophy of Peronism, named for the Justicialist Party president Juan Perón. Perón was the president of Argentina from 1946 until his overthrow by a military dictatorship in 1955. Alongside his wife Eva (Evita), Perón espoused a revisionist view of neo-colonial Argentina. Previous visions of the country had been Eurocentric, civilisation viewed as something intrinsically European and cultured, unlike the perceived barbarity of the local population. Peronism saw this differently, that the *pueblo* (people) were exploited by the forces of colonial capitalism (the land was owned by a core upper class) and that action was required to overthrow this colonialist authority. Solanas and Getino, along with other intellectuals, artists and filmmakers, shared this vision and the need for the masses to free themselves from oppression. Two of their films, *Perón: The Justicialist Revolution* (*Perón: la revolución justicialista*, 1971), and *Perón: Doctrinary Update for the Taking of Power* (*Perón: actualización doctrinaria para la toma del poder*, 1971), interviewed the ousted president in exile in Spain, exploring his political plans and how the Peronists might retake power. As the titles suggest, the films advocated the revolutionary overthrow of the current military regime in Argentina, and in so doing positioned Perón's beliefs close to those of other militant revolutionary struggles of the time, such as that of Che Guevara (*The Hour of the Furnaces* is dedicated to Guevara 'and to all those who have fallen in the struggle for Latin American liberation'). The two sides were difficult to reconcile, however, and when Perón returned to power in 1973 he distanced himself from the Marxist revolutionaries in a divisive way.

Solanas and Getino's contribution to the understanding and theorisation of Third Cinema during this time is immense, with the publication of the *Grupo Cine Liberación's* manifesto, 'Towards a Third Cinema', first published in 1969. Making its first appearance in the Cuban journal *Tricontinental*, the manifesto concluded that 'the birth of a *third cinema* means, at least for us, *the most important revolutionary artistic event of our times*' (1985, p. 64). They argued that mainstream culture in a neo-colonial country like Argentina could only ever be an expression of the colonising, imperialist culture. There can only ever be the culture of the rulers and that of the nation, the people, the oppressed. Solanas and Getino saw in art a tendency to depoliticise aesthetics and turn the viewer towards the universality of beauty that emphasised the absence of politics in the work, a beauty that could only be understood through a colonialist and Eurocentric point of view that imposed all values as universal. In cinema, this universalising tendency is seen in the Hollywood film, which Solanas and Getino dub the '*first cinema*'. The ideological norms of the first cinema were found in the technical competence and common language of the American film:

> The 35mm camera, 24 frames a second, arc lights, and a commercial place of exhibition for audiences were conceived not to gratuitously transmit any ideology, but to satisfy, in the first place, the cultural and surplus value needs *of a specific ideology, of a specific world-view: that of US financial capital* ... but it also leads to the *absorption of forms of the bourgeois world-view* which are the continuation of 19th Century art, of bourgeois art: man is accepted only as a passive and consuming object. (p. 51)

This final point about the conditioning of the spectator, and their pacification – assuming the viewer as unable to question or critique the material on-screen as a natural consequence of their ideological positioning through processes of identification – is an important one. In many respects, Solanas and Getino's comments about bourgeois art and the nineteenth-century context are very similar to those of Brecht, whose Marxist-inspired aesthetics sought to reject the naturalism of Aristotle's poetics. Brecht sought an agitational response, to distance the viewer and shake them into consciousness through techniques of distanciation (*verfremdungseffekt*) that historicise the action and make the viewer aware of the social conditions portrayed on stage (or on-screen, as many of these ideas were later adopted or adapted by filmmakers). The first cinema, however, is in the service of specific ideologies of American cultural and financial imperialism, particularly in countries in Latin America such as Argentina, Brazil, Cuba and Venezuela (where *The Hour of the Furnaces* was banned).

A fully-realised Third Cinema rejects the establishment's system, although it might exploit funds made from overseas distribution of their films in art cinemas in European countries (its surplus value). '*Third cinema* is ... the cinema that *recognizes in* [the anti-imperialist struggle of the people of the Third World] *the most gigantic cultural, scientific, and artistic manifestation of our time* ..., the *decolonization of culture*' (p. 47). It is a guerrilla cinema, democratic and proletarian, without recourse to the cosmeticised beauty of the films of the first cinema, and therefore without the need for a standardised industry hierarchy of production, both artistic and technical, alongside its rejection of the narrative and stylistic norms of the Hollywood film (narrative coherence, continuity editing, identification, heroes and villains). Its subject material is the worker's reality, and its force of expression is violent; as they explain, the 'camera is the inexhaustible *expropriator of image-weapons*; the project, *a gun that can shoot 24 frames per second*' (p. 58). Likewise, the exhibition of Third Cinema is intended to circumvent the establishment's traditional spaces and means of engagement with cinema, aimed at producing a revolutionary participant consciousness in the viewer rather than first cinema's easy and comfortable passive identification. In screenings to militant groups, workers, middle-class intellectuals, university students and activists, the filmmakers would seek to 'disinhibit' the spectators and turn them into actors by providing a free space for discussion, education following the film's lead as 'a detonator or pretext' (p. 62) and the transformation of engagement into revolutionary action.

The Third Cinema manifesto was strongly influenced by the postcolonial criticism of Frantz Fanon, particularly his book, *The Wretched of the Earth* (first published in 1961). Rather than aligning with the separation of the world into First, Second or Third Worlds, Solanas and Getino's first and second cinemas and their Third Cinema echo Fanon's argument about the ways in which the artist can either assimilate or reject the colonial culture in their work. As Fanon argued: 'first, the colonized intellectual proves he has assimilated the colonizer's culture. His works correspond point by point with those of his metropolitan counterparts', and his or her expression evidences the influence of the culture of the occupying power: the artist assumes the guise of pretend European. 'In a second stage, the colonized writer has his convictions shaken and decides to cast his mind back': the artist retains the assimilation of the occupying power, but there is a return to memories 'just-before-the-battle' although those are still interpreted through a colonial gaze (becoming the 'progressive wing' of the dominant culture). 'Finally, a third stage, a combat stage where the colonized writer, after having tried to lose himself among the people, with the people, will rouse the people ... Combat literature, revolutionary literature, national literature emerges' (2004, pp. 158–159). In these three stages, we can see reflected the influence of Fanon on the manifesto for Third Cinema, its turn towards an agitational aesthetics that rejected the grammar and practice of neo-colonial influence, towards a 'combat cinema' in which a national cinema expression might emerge. In some respects, elements of the manifesto by Solanas and Getino are shared with those expressed by Cesare Zavattini in the previous chapter, and reflected in some of the tenets of neorealism (Third Cinema did adopt some of the techniques of neorealism, albeit in a very different context). These principles were also shared with other Latin American filmmakers.

An aesthetic of hunger

In January 1965, before Solanas and Getino's manifesto was published, the Brazilian filmmaker Glauber Rocha had given a speech at a retrospective of Latin American cinema in Genoa. Later published in Brazil and in French in the Leftist journal *Positif*, with the title 'An Esthetic of Hunger', Rocha's polemic, influenced, like that of his Argentinian contemporaries, by Fanon's *The Wretched of the Earth*, was a manifesto for the Brazilian cinema movement known as *Cinema Novo* (new cinema). At the time, Rocha was just 25 years old. Like Solanas and Getino, Rocha's films straddled fiction and documentary. His most famous work, *Black God, White Devil* (*Deus e o Diabo na Terra do Sol*, literally *God and the Devil in the Land of Sun*, 1964) focuses on the plight of a worker on a ranch in the *sertão* (the largest section of Brazil that is mostly arid land) who is swindled out of money by the ranch owner. Powerless in the face of the law, Manuel (Geraldo Del Rey) brutally murders the man and flees with his wife Rosa (Yoná Magalhães) for Mount Monte Santo. There they meet a preacher, Sebastião (Lidio Silva), and begin to follow him on a tour as he preaches, espousing against the ruling classes. The authorities begin to take notice of Sebastião and hire a bounty hunter, Antonio das Mortes (Maurício do Valle, who reprised the role in Rocha's follow-up, *Antonio das Mortes* (*O Dragão da Maldade contra o Santo Guerreiro*, literally *The Dragon of Evil against the Saint Warrior*, 1969), to track him down. Sebastião's ritualistic demands become more extreme, including carrying a large rock up a hill and sacrificing a baby. Rosa kills him to protect her husband. Left as the only survivors of a religious massacre, Manuel and Rosa then begin to follow another charismatic anti-establishment figure, the bandit Corisco (Othon Bastos), who is also being pursued by the bounty hunter. In the end, Rocha leaves his main character running, even abandoning Rosa, in a long take tracking alongside Manuel, then the sea. The film eschews comfortable formal devices associated with Hollywood cinema, such as shot-reverse-shot editing and smooth camera work. The camera, particularly at moments of violence, moves vertiginously, often looking at characters with whom we're offered no point of identification. Editing uses principles of montage, often to highlight pain. The film also presents individuals framed in space, in tableaux or in formations that express shifting relationships. In the sequences with Corisco, the film resembles an absurdist Western. Music plays a key role also, and the film is narrated by a folk ballad that directly addresses the viewer. In the end, the film offers no solution for Manuel, between the authoritarian rulers and the lawless injustice of the *sertão*, and therefore no solution for those he represents. Its final shots emphasise this absence with a lack of closure.

Rocha's manifesto formalised some of the commentary in *Black God, White Devil*. Echoing Fanon, he saw violence as the only viable expression of the hungry. Rocha argues that *Cinema Novo* 'shows that the normal behaviours of the starving is violence; and the violence of the starving is not primitive' (1995, p. 70). This is a revolutionary aesthetic: it shows 'the initial moment when the colonizer becomes aware of the colonized. Only when confronted with violence does the colonizer understand, through horror, the strength of the culture he exploits' (p. 70). In *Black God, White Devil*, this strategy is not simply one that uses tropes of on-screen violence as a representation of the colonised's need to turn towards revolutionary violence; it is also a formal strategy (Figure 3.2). While the film uses a degree of realism, in its long takes and documentary-style handheld camera work, it also exhibits disjunctive editing, jump cuts and moments of formal distanciation that seek to shock the viewer. Watching the film is not a comfortable experience (particularly the scene in which Sebastião ritualistically kills the baby), and is not intended to be. As the 'Esthetic of Hunger' critiques, the view of the coloniser is one that 'cultivates the taste of … misery, not as a tragic *symptom*' (p. 69). The European viewer is concerned not with the politics of the suffering of the neo-colonised in Brazil, but merely a 'formal exoticism that vulgarizes social problems' that goes hand in hand with 'a nostalgia for primitivism' (p. 69). The violence of *Cinema Novo* makes such a viewpoint impossible to marry with an 'old colonizing humanism' (p. 70), a Eurocentric paternalism that sees the 'uncivilised' as objects for condescension, as though the colonised subjects were children in need of care or 'civilising'. The recourse to violence for the hungry is separate from the demands of an industrial cinema,

Figure 3.2 *Black God, White Devil's* (Glauber Rocha, 1964) tableau-style *mise en scène*, depicting the preacher Sebastião's religious extremism (Copacabana Filmes/ Luiz Augusto Mendes Produções Cinematográficas)

just as Solanas and Getino were later to see a Third Cinema as a guerrilla cinema that rejected the formal cosmetics of Hollywood and a first cinema that served the neo-colonial purposes of capitalism. *Cinema Novo*, Rocha explains, also sought to reject this in favour of a specifically Brazilian and Latin American specificity: 'We understand the hunger that the European and majority of Brazilians have not understood. For the European it is a strange tropical surrealism. For the Brazilian it is a national shame.' (p. 70) As Randal Johnson and Robert Stam noted in the introduction to the article in their collection *Brazilian Cinema*, Rocha's manifesto made a seminal plea to blend together a social and political theme with a style and production methodology specific to Brazil at the time. In many respects this plea foreshadowed the contribution of Solanas and Getino, albeit in a different national context (which must still be acknowledged despite the common significance of their shared critiques of neo-colonialism in Latin American), in its focus not just on telling stories appropriate to the suffering of people living under neo-colonial oppression, but in adopting formal and production strategies that turned away from Hollywood-style polish and comfortable identification to articulate the struggle against colonial oppression and poverty. Although Rocha lived out most of his career in exile following the ascension of a US-validated military government in the 1960s and his flight from the country in the early 1970s, his work has held a strong influence on subsequent Brazilian filmmakers.

Case study: *City of God* (*Cidade de Deus*, Fernando Meirelles and Kátia Lund, 2002)

In many respects, the choice of *City of God* as a representative of the *Cinema Novo* tradition or of the influence of Rocha and of Third Cinema concepts is problematic. Made three decades after the end of the second wave of the *Cinema Novo* movement, Meirelles and Lund's film is a product of a different globalised era, although it still focuses on something we might call, using Rocha's terms, 'a national shame'. The film is about the drug culture of the *favelas* (slums or shantytowns) around Rio de Janeiro, specifically the eponymous *Cidade de Deus*, one of the most notoriously violent *favelas*. Following the end of military rule in Brazil at the end of the 1970s, and the transition to democratic governance, the country saw an escalation in the drug trade and related violence in the *favelas*. Around two-thirds of *favela* populations are black (in relation to around half of the overall population) and young black men in Rio are more than twice as likely to be victims of homicide than their white counterparts. Many of these deaths have been at the hands of the local police, who have asserted their control with brutal violence and little accountability. Since 2009, *Cidade de Deus* has been occupied by the police in an effort to tackle the drug trade.

Based on the semi-autobiographical novel by Paulo Lins, the film follows Buscapé (literally Firecracker, but translated as Rocket, played by Alexandre Rodrigues), a young man growing up in *Cidade de Deus* who aspires to a career in photography – he succeeds initially by photographing the *favela*'s gangsters. The story is split over three time periods. The first, in the 1960s, pictures the *favela* as semi-rural, and follows Buscapé's brother Marreco's (Goose's) 'tender trio' of small-time crooks: him, Cabeleira (Shaggy), and Alicate (Clipper), as they carry out petty crimes, the proceeds of which they share with local residents. A young local boy, Dadinho (Li'l Dice), follows them on a heist of a local motel, where he guns down a couple in one of the rooms. The violence of the crime brings the police to the *favela*, with consequences for the gang: Alicate dies running from the police, Cabeleira turns his back on crime, while Marreco is killed by Dadinho. The film then switches its focus to the 1970s, and colours become brighter, despite the drug trade's escalation. Dadinho, now known as Zé Pequeno (Li'l Zé) runs a gang alongside his right-hand man Bené. Li'l Zé's only remaining competition is Cenoura (Carrot), whose ascension to power we see in a single scene ('The Story of the Apartment'); a single camera angle shows us how Cenoura came to inherit, through violence and the neglect of other gangsters to pay off the police, with dissolves compressing time under Buscapé's voiceover. When one of Cenoura's hitmen kill a retiring Bené at his leaving party, Zé turns to violent retribution, and the *favela* descends into gang warfare as it reaches the 1980s. Buscapé's pictures inflate Zé's infamy, but offer a way out for the photographer. When the police capture Zé and Cenoura, they arrest the latter 'for the press' but take Zé's money and release him. Buscapé photographs the corruption, and subsequently Zé's body after he has been murdered by the very young children from a gang known as 'The Runts'. The film ends with those same kids plotting their future supremacy in the drug trade.

City of God tackles themes of poverty, institutional corruption and race that can place it within a historical lineage of *Cinema Novo*. However, what problematises *City of God* is its transnational circulation and reception, something that saw it considered as both a national product – a descendent of Third Cinema practices – and as evidence of a global hybridity. Rocha's point that mainstream cinema exhibits a 'formal exoticism that vulgarizes social problems' is an accusation that can be levelled at *City of God*. The film's thrilling mix of MTV-style aggressive editing, confrontational documentary-style filming, stylised cinematography and non-linear storytelling could be accused of turning a social problem into a film of 'formal exoticism' (Figure 3.3). But, as Rosalind Galt has argued in her book, *Pretty: Film and the Decorative Image*, such an argument might problematise the

Figure 3.3 Violence is inscribed in *City of God* (Fernando Meirelles and Kátia Lund, 2002) from the outset, with this opening montage of close-ups depicting the sharpening of a knife (O2 Filmes/VideoFllms/Globo Filmes/ Lumiere/Wild Bunch)

relationship between aesthetics and sociopolitical commentary. Galt notes that many critics referenced Rocha in their criticism of *City of God's* stylisation. She remarks that several critics pointed out that Meirelles and Lund had replaced an aesthetics of hunger with a 'cosmetics of hunger' since the film was more an image of postmodern depthlessness than a sign of social protest. She notes:

> contemporary filmmaking will almost always fall short [of the preeminent Marxist countercinema model of aesthetics and politics] because the color palette, camera movement, and editing strategies of more recent world cinema rarely continue untouched the strategies of Latin American Third Cinema. (Galt, 2011, p. 18)

Pretty films can still engage with social commentary, as they engage with their own aesthetics, a point also made by Lúcia Nagib when she remarked that 'the film has the revelatory quality of a "hidden reality" that previously characterised neo-realist films, which depicted the ravages of war, or the films of the Brazilian Cinema Novo movement, which depicted the misery of the Brazilian backlands'. However, that attempt is no 'mere attempt at copying reality' (2004, p. 244). And, returning to Galt, we need to remember that an 'aesthetics of poverty is still an aesthetics, and Rocha's films draw fully on the expressive qualities of cinematic space' (Galt, 2011, p. 18). The stylisation of the film therefore need not position it as an example of 'formal exoticism' but a film that engages with the social reality of poverty, in the *Cinema Novo* tradition, albeit in an updated form.

What problematised the film's engagement with its social themes was its international reception. As Miranda Shaw (2005) has noted, there was a recurrent trend in English-language criticism in the US and UK to see the film in generic terms, as a gangster film, through repeated reference to American films, including *Goodfellas* (Martin Scorsese, 1990), *Pulp Fiction* (Quentin Tarantino, 1995) or *Reservoir Dogs* (Tarantino, 1991). She also highlights how the film was repeatedly received as 'The Brazilian *Goodfellas*' (Figure 3.3), 'a kind of Boyz in the Brazilian hood', or 'Gangs of Rio de Janeiro' (p. 58). Shaw argues that this is to see the film not through the lens of a nationally specific social problem, but through the ill-fitting norms of a genre that has specifically American themes and icons. Like other critics, Shaw sees *Cinema Novo* as a more fitting way of critiquing the film's images of violence, such as the montage used in the opening shots of the sharpening of a knife, where violence is not just an on-screen trope, but a stylistic device, a powerful and political one. In her sampling of Brazilian reviews of the film, she observed repeated references to Rocha and to the legacy of *Cinema Novo*.

Transnational reception and distribution can often problematise films in this fashion (Miramax distributed the film with 'the Brazilian *Goodfellas*' on posters), but this can also be the case with films that hybridise or adopt features associated with western, or specifically Hollywood, cinema. Else Vieira (2007) has noted that Meirelles' films engage 'in dialogue with US cultural forms', notably the gangster and Western genres, in ways that disturb them, exposing cracks in their racism and exultant attitude towards capitalism and manifest destiny. In some ways, this echoes a comment made by Robert Stam in 'Beyond Third Cinema: The Aesthetics of Hybridity' in which he argued that:

> Brazilian Cinema proliferates in the signs and tokens of hybridity, draw- ing on the relational processes of Brazil's diverse communities. Rather than merely reflect a pre-existing hybridity, Brazilian cinema actively hybridizes in that it stages and performs hybridity, counterpointing cultural forces through surprising, even disconcerting juxtapositions. At its best, it orchestrates not a bland pluralism but rather a strong counterpoint between seemingly incommensurable yet nevertheless thoroughly co-implicated cultures. (2003a, p. 39)

In many respects, for a global audience, the hybridity of *City of God* has been constructed through marketing and the need to see the film through a more local frame of reference, given the invisibility of the *favelas* and their occupants internationally and locally. The dialogue discussed by Vieira, though, can be understood as a form of the hybridity explored by Stam (the era he examines is largely a *Cinema Novo* one), a 'counterpoint' or 'juxtaposition' of co-implicated cultures, as the film parodies the values of the Western in relation to its discourse on race. As the title of Stam's article implies, this might be a means of seeing the film as going 'beyond Third Cinema' but still in the wake of its legacy. The stylisation of the film need not be seen simply as 'cosmetic' but as a contemporary hybrid political aesthetics, even if it might be viewed by some critics as incompatible with the Marxist-inflected aesthetics of the 1960s and 1970s.

> Meirelles was certainly critical of this viewpoint. As he argued:

> if you ask some journalistic film critics, they will tell you that it is just a film made to sell popcorn. It's amazing how dialectics ruins people's minds. They are unable to conceive of entertainment, emotion, and reflection in the same package. They always think in an exclusive and antagonistic way: it's either art or entertainment. It's sad. (quoted in Johnson, 2005, pp. 13–14)

With his pop at Marxism ('dialectics ruins people's minds'), he argues a similar point to that of Rosalind Galt, that many critics find it difficult to see a pretty film as political. The question of entertainment is also important, since Meirelles, an experienced producer in television prior to his career as film director, produced the film without the support of the local film industry (it had the support of noted director Walter Salles's VideoFilmes). Like many neorealist or Third Cinema films, it relied on a largely non-professional crew. Apart from Matheus Nachtergaele, who played Cenoura, none of the cast had professional experience, and most came from the *favelas* (a point of the film's realism). The cast was drawn from the local neighbourhoods, including a theatre group, *Nós do Morro* (Us from the Hillsides), and lead to the development of non-profit film company Cinema Nosso, that began life as the film acting workshop, *Nós do Cinema* (We are Cinema), formed around the production of *City of God*. The film also spawned a sequel *City of Men* (*Cidade dos Homens*, Paulo Morelli, 2008) and a television series of the same name (2002-2005) that featured some of the same actors from the original film. This has been a social project associated with the film, where art works as means of social transformation. The legacy of the film has been explored in the documentary *City of God – 10 Years Later* (Luciano Vidigal and Cavi Borges, 2013), and the social project is still ongoing. As Cavi Borges told *The Hollywood Reporter*: 'if we want a fair and democratic country we need to invest more in education and culture' (Zulian, 2013).

Recommended viewing:

Third Cinema:
The Adventures of Juan Quin Quin (*Las aventuras de Juan Quin Quin*, Julio García Espinosa, 1967)
Lucía (Humberto Solás, 1968)
Memories of Underdevelopment (*Memorias del Subdesarrollo*, Tomás Gutiérrez Alea, 1968)
Blood of the Condor (*Yawar Mallku*, Jorge Sanjinés, 1969)
The Battle of Chile (Patricio Guzman): *The Insurrection of the Bourgeoisie* (1975), *The Coup d'état* (1976), *Popular Power* (1979)

Brazil, *Cinema Novo* and after:
Barren Lives (*Vidas Secas*, Nelson Pereira dos Santos, 1963)
Entranced Earth (*Terra em Transe*, Glauber Rocha, 1967)
Antonio das Mortes (*O Dragão da Maldade contra o Santo Guerreiro*, Glauber Rocha, 1969)
Bye Bye Brasil (Carlos Diegues, 1980)
Twenty Years Later (*Cabra Marcado para Morrer*, Edward Coutinho, 1984)
Central Station (*Central do Brasil*, Walter Salles, 1998)
Elite Squad (*Tropa de elite*, José Padilha, 2007)

Recommended further reading:

Aspects of Third Cinema:

Armes, Roy (1987), *Third World Film Making and the West*. Berkeley and London: University of California Press.

Chanan, Michael (1997), 'The Changing Geography of Third Cinema', Screen 38(4): pp. 372–388.

—— (2003). *The Cuban Image: Cinema and Cultural Politics in* Cuba. Minneapolis: University of Minnesota Press.

Eshun, Kodwo, and Ros Gray, eds (2011), Special Issue: The Militant Image: A Ciné-Geography, *Third Text* 25(1).

Guneratne, Anthony R., and Wimal Dissanayake, eds (2003), *Rethinking Third Cinema*. New York and London: Routledge.

Mestman, Mariano (2003), '*La Hora de los Hornos*' in eds Alberto Elena and Marina Díaz-López, *The Cinema of Latin America*. London: Wallflower Press, pp. 119–129.

Stam, Robert (2000), 'Third World Film and Theory' in *Film Theory: An Introduction*. Oxford: Blackwell, pp. 92–102.

Wayne, Mike (2001), *Political Film: The Dialectics of Third Cinema*. London and Sterling: Pluto.

Cinema Novo and Brazilian Cinema:

Dennison, Stephanie, and Lisa Shaw (2004), *Popular Cinema in Brazil, 1930–2001*. Manchester: Manchester University Press.

Freire-Medeiros, Bianca (2011) '"I Went to the City of God": Gringos, Guns and the Touristic Favela', *Journal of Latin American Cultural Studies: Travesia* 20(1): pp. 21–34.

Nagib, Lúcia, ed. (2003), *The New Brazilian Cinema*. London: IB Tauris.

—— (2007), *Brazil on Screen: Cinema Novo, New Cinema and Utopia*. London and New York: IB Tauris.

Pinazza, Natália, and Louis Bayman, eds (2013), *Directory of World Cinema: Brazil*. Bristol and Chicago: Intellect.

Proppe, Hans, and Susan Tarr (1976), 'Pitfalls of Cultural Nationalism in Cinema Novo', *Jump Cut: A Review of Contemporary Media* 10: pp. 45–48. Available online: www.ejumpcut.org/archive/onlinessays/JC10-11folder/CinemaNovo.html. Accessed 19 September 2017.

Stam, Robert (1997), *Tropical Multiculturalism: A Comparative History of Race in Brazilian Cinema*. Durham and London: Duke University Press.

Stam, Robert, and Randal Johnson (1979), 'Beyond Cinema Novo', *Jump Cut: A Review of Contemporary Media* 21, pp. 13–18. Available online: www.ejump-cut.org/archive/onlinessays/JC21folder/BrazilStamJohnson.html. Accessed 19 September 2017.

Shades of Third Cinema's conceptualisation can be seen in many global film-makers; in Africa, perhaps the most notable example is Ousmane Sembène, from Senegal, whose films critique colonialist subjectivities, including *Xala*

(1975), based on his own novel, which denounces post-colonial governmental rule through the metaphor of erectile dysfunction (the title is a Wolof word that translates closer to 'impotence' than its English subtitled translation as 'a curse'). Its protagonist, El Hadji, is a polygamist who has internalised colonialism and Eurocentrism, his affliction the revenge of an oppressed underclass exploited by the emerging ruling class. Sembène's earlier film *Black Girl* (*Le Noire de...*, 1966) explored colonial relationships and privileges through the story of a Senegalese maid employed by a wealthy French couple. The servant, Diouana, is contrasted with her employers, who aren't named (as subjects under colonialism tended to be shown, as undifferentiated and nameless) and fail to understand their employee as a human being on an equal standing (Figure 3.4). The film shows the continued privilege of colonial Europeans in the post-colonial era, but also the residual self-Europeanising of subjects after the end of colonial rule, retaining the Frenchness (in fashion particularly) and the symbol of France as a kind of promised land, prosperous and elegant. Sembène's films are often held as a model for African *auteur* filmmaking, with roots in the realist traditions of many world cinemas, but also in his postcolonial examination of identity and racism following the end of French rule.

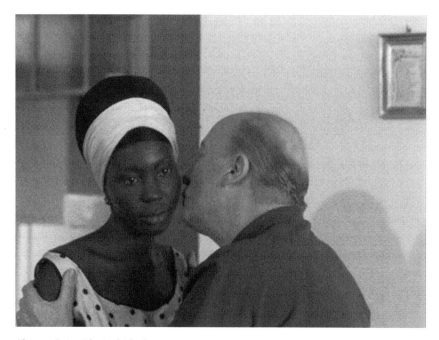

Figure 3.4 *Black Girl* (Ousmane Sembène, 1966): Diouana is objectified by a white European dinner guest who has never kissed a black woman before (Filmi Domirev/Les Actualités Françaises)

Third Cinema theories have also resonanted with filmmakers in Asia. In India, Bengali filmmakers such as Satyajit Ray and Ritwik Ghatak, or the Hindi art film director Saeed Mirza have been explored as representatives of Third Cinema traditions. Their films, including Ghatak's *The Cloud-Capped Star* (*Meghey Dhaka Tara*, 1960), *The Gandhar Sublime* (*Kormal Gandhar*, 1961) and *The Golden Line* (*Subarnarekha*, 1962), and Mirza's *Why Should Albert Pinto Be Angry?* (*Albert Pinto Ko Gussa Kyoon Aata Hai*, 1980) and *Summons for Mohan Joshi* (*Mohan Joshi Hazir Ho!*, 1984), belonged to a wider movement referred to as Parallel Cinema (considered as an Indian new wave), as it developed in parallel with the growth of popular cinemas in India. It's important to acknowledge that while it's often Hollywood that is resisted by many oppo-sitional global cinemas, in India the norms of a mainstream (or first) cinema are more local than global. Ray's films are very much in the global tradition of neorealist films, while Ghatak, whose career began in theatre, and Mirza have more diverse influences, including Brecht, local cultural forms such as Sanskrit, and filmmakers like Robert Bresson, that also locate them within a global art cinema tradition. They also formed a resistant cinema in India that explored social, political and economic conditions (for Ghatak, particularly those following the end of British rule and the partition in 1947 that split the Bengal province). We can see similar themes in the films of the Chinese fifth and sixth generation filmmakers, such as *Red Sorghum* (*Hóng Gāoliáng*, Zhang Yimou, 1987), *Temptress Moon* (*Fēng yuè*, Chen Kaige, 1996) and *Beijing Bicycle* (*Shí Qī Suì de Dānchē*, Wang Xiaoshuai, 2001), whose films have been implicated in debates about Third Cinema. Fifth generation filmmakers like Zhang and Chen were popular features on the festival circuits with their films that explored historical ruptures in China and sociopolitical issues relating to poverty and state control – many of which were banned by the Chinese authorities (this was also around the time of the pro-democracy Tian'anmen Square protests in 1989). While they have gone on to make major blockbust-ers in more mainstream modes, such as martial arts spectacles like *Hero* (*Ying xiong*, Zhang Yimou, 2002) and *The Promise* (*Wú Jí*, Chen Kaige, 2005), sixth generation filmmakers like Wang have continued to explore these sociopo-litical themes, and *Beijing Bicycle* demonstrates the continuing influence of neorealism, as a partial remake of *Bicycle Thieves*, about a young man whose bicycle is stolen after he gets a job as a courier. Unlike the earlier Italian film, Wang's film is more about the relationship between two teenage boys, one whose bicycle is stolen, and another who buys it from the thief. The consid-eration of Third Cinema continues, as its influences and motivations can be seen across continents (this would also include diasporic or marginal cine-mas, such as in Britain where black filmmaker John Akomfrah's *Handsworth Songs* (1986) has been discussed as an example of Third Cinema), but we shouldn't see the movement as homogeneous or unified, and need to consider how cinemas resist different forms of hegemony locally, cinematically, politically and historically.

Postcolonialism

The post-colonial era precipitated an intense scrutiny of issues of discourse and power relations in literature, theatre, film, theory and criticism. These concerns remain of paramount importance in analyses of transnational cinemas, which continue to engage with the ways in which power imbalances are negotiated or constructed through cinema's crossing of borders or engaging with stories about people crossing borders. As we'll see in later chapters, some of the spread of individuals is a consequence of the displacement experienced by colonialism, especially in the relationship between Britain and India, and postcolonialism (without a hyphen to distinguish between the post-colonial era and postcolonial culture) has been considered a key part of transnational film studies, although it's important not to consider it a sub-discipline of transnational film, but an important related field of cultural studies (particularly in the sense used in British academia). In Chapter 1, we encountered Shohat and Stam's seminal text on Eurocentrism and their call for a need for pluralism to defy the 'mania for hierarchies' that positioned marginalised groups of people as Other to European or neo-European 'civilisation'. The means through which that imbalance is produced has been a key subject for postcolonial artists and scholars.

One such scholar is Frantz Fanon. Born on the island of Martinique (at the time a French colony), he served in the Free French army in the Second World War, and worked as a psychiatrist in Algeria during the 1950s, later joining the Algerian forces against French rule. In a much-cited passage of his *Black Skin, White Masks* (originally published in 1952), Fanon discusses the ways in which black children living under colonisation identify with the protagonists of adventure stories that produce a 'collective catharsis'. That catharsis takes the form of an outlet whereby the accumulated effects of aggression can be purged, through games, psychotherapy or in children's stories. Hence, stories featuring Tarzan, Mickey Mouse or junior explorers take on the same function as a means of releasing this accumulated force. These comic books always feature the image of blackness in relation to figures of 'the Wolf, the Devil, the Evil Spirit, the Bad Man, the Savage ... always symbolized by Negroes or Indians'. Consequently, Fanon argues, 'there is always identification with the victor, [and] the little Negro, quite as easily as the little white boy, becomes an explorer, an adventurer, a missionary "who faces the danger of being eaten by wicked Negroes"' (2008, p. 113). The colonial child therefore identifies with the colonising subjectivity, 'the explorer, the bringer of civilization, the white man who carries truth to savages – an all-white truth', and the youngster 'adopts a white man's attitude' (p. 114). The construction of a colonial subjectivity, in which the colonised identifies with the coloniser, means that subjects internalise the inferiority of the colonised: for Fanon, it is 'The Other [in the guise of the white man] alone [that] can give him worth' (p. 119). Stories such as those featuring Tarzan, in which the white European masters the 'native skills' better than the 'native' to promote their superiority, are colonial fantasies. It's a myth that has been seen more recently in *Avatar* (James Cameron, 2009), in which the white protagonist not only infiltrates the native group but comes to organise and lead them better than they could themselves. Although the film also engages in critique of neo-colonial interests, at its core is a similar fantasy that posits the superiority of the white male over colonial Others (a white saviour narrative). In later life, Fanon contends, this internalisation of racism is a source of trauma – as the title of his book attests, the black colonised subject wears a white mask.

One of the important considerations in postcolonial theory is the heterogeneity of experience. We've already seen how approaches to world cinema have tended to see the world through the lens of binaries, dominant modes of cinema expressed in terms of Hollywood, and others seen through their opposition to or difference from those norms, as Other cinemas. This extends to the production of an Other through processes of identification. As Robert Stam and Louise Spence argue in 'Colonialism, Racism and Representation: An Introduction', published in *Screen* in 1983:

> Europe constructed its self-image on the backs of its equally constructed Other – the 'savage', the 'cannibal' – much as phallocentrism sees its self-flattering image in the mirror of woman defined as lack. And just as the camera might therefore be said to inscribe certain features of bourgeois humanism, so the cinematic and televisual apparatuses, taken in their most inclusive sense, might be said to inscribe certain features of European colonialism. The magic carpet provided by these apparatuses flies us around the globe and makes us, by virtue of our subject position, its audiovisual masters. It produces us as subjects, transforming us into armchair conquistadores, affirming our sense of power while making the inhabitants of the Third World objects of spectacle for the First World's voyeuristic gaze. (Stam and Spence, 1983, p. 4)

As 'audiovisual masters', we're placed in a position of superiority over the objects on-screen. Just as concepts of the male gaze of phallocentric cinema have problematised the ways in which women's bodies are conceived as objects of speculation, so with the images of the Third World. This raises an important question of who speaks in postcolonial discourse. In the examples offered by Fanon and Stam and Spence, the speaking subjects are often the colonisers (or neo-colonisers), not the colonised. Just as Tarzan or Jake Sully (in *Avatar*) come to master the Other's domain, the filmmakers speak on behalf of the Other. Gayatri Chakravorty Spivak raised this question in her influential essay 'Can the Subaltern Speak?'. An Indian scholar from Kolkata in West Bengal, Spivak drew on the Italian Marxist theorist Antonio Gramsci's notion of an underclass subaltern beneath a dominant or elite class. Spivak significantly challenges the ideas of the collectiveness of a subaltern, especially in relation to women as subaltern, where 'the possibility of collectivity itself is persistently foreclosed through the manipulation of female agency' (1988, p. 283). One of her most persistent arguments is with First World intellectuals, including Gramsci, but also Michel Foucault and Jacques Derrida, their project to speak *of* the voice of the Other, and the issue of a collective group of a subaltern class: she insists 'that the colonized *subject* is irretrievably heterogeneous' (p. 284). The question in its title – 'can the subaltern speak?' – is consistently posed through the article. The subaltern subject is marked by its difference from a set of norms or ideals, and therefore for that group, 'whose identity is its difference, there is no unrepresentable subaltern subject that can know and speak itself' while 'the slippage from rendering visible the mechanism [by which the unseen are made visible] to rendering vocal the individual ... is consistently troublesome' (p. 285). Spivak's argument was motivated by the suicide of a 'sixteen or seventeen'-year-old woman named Bhuvaneswari Bhaduri in 1926. Bhaduri had been involved in revolutionary circles in the armed struggle for Indian independence. When she found herself unable to carry out an order to assassinate a political target, she hanged herself, but, as Spivak explores, she did so at the time of her period, to ensure that her suicide couldn't be read as a consequence of illicit sex or pregnancy. In the writing of the incident, however, the hegemonic account of the male leaders of the movement is the loudest voice. As such, Spivak contends, the subaltern (in which poor, black women are triply articulated as difference) are unable to speak, not necessarily because they don't have voices of their own, but because the 'subaltern as female cannot be heard or read' (p. 308):

> Between patriarchy and imperialism, subject-constitution and object-formation, the figure of the woman disappears, not into a pristine nothingness, but into a violent shuttling which is the displaced figuration of the 'third-world woman' caught between tradition and modernization. (p. 306)

This final point connects significantly with the issue raised previously by Stam and Spence. The objectification of the colonial subject is a way of speaking on their behalf, ensuring that they are seen but not heard. Spivak's point – a particularly contentious one that has led to accusations of accepting the patriarchal account rather than its critique – of poor black women being a triple articulation of difference and therefore interpolated into the subject position of 'third-world woman' and spoken on behalf of, where their articulation is not heard or is misunderstood, is resonant in this case. It demonstrates the need not just for postcolonial figures to write their own narratives, but for those receiving them to read those articulations not simply for their difference or through hegemonic frames of reference (where difference from norms is the consequence) but to consider how those articulations are formed.

Edward Said's seminal book *Orientalism* has similarly explored the ways in which colonialism articulates a vision of colonised areas, specifically of the Middle and Far East. For Said, 'The Orient' embodies everything that the 'The Occident' doesn't: it is separate and distant from Europe, despite Franco-British and American colonisation of the areas. This understanding of the Middle and Far East relied on binaries of 'us' and 'them'. As Said explains: 'Orientalism was ultimately a political vision of reality whose structure promoted the difference between the familiar (Europe, the West, "us") and the strange (the Orient, the East, "them")' (2003, p. 43). Orientalism is a product of Eurocentrism. In regard to its approach to the Orient, Said points out, 'Europe was shut in on itself.' The Orient was therefore constructed as a region wholly Other: 'it was not merely a place in which one traded, [it] was culturally, intellectually, spiritually *outside* Europe and European civilization' (2003, p. 71). This final reference to civilisation reminds us that Europe defined itself, as we've already seen, as the centre of civilisation and that therefore that which is *outside* Europe is uncivilised and in need of civilising, that which Fanon mentioned led to a form of internalised racism in the colonial subject. Similarly, Orientalism 'depends for its strategy on [a] flexible *positional* superiority, which puts the westerner in a whole series of possible relationships with the Orient without ever losing him the relative upper hand' (p. 7). Again, like Fanon, Said defines colonial discourses through power relationships between the coloniser and colonised, which put the latter at a continual disadvantage, in language and discourse and through violence.

Attitudes such as these, seeing Asian countries as exotic, unusual, have persisted. The Asia Extreme cinema phenomenon that was popular around the turn of the twenty-first century often relied on the exoticism of Orientalist attitudes to see the Far East as brutal, weird and excitingly different from the norms of western cinema (see Shin, 2008 and Rawle, 2009). Such a point of view Others the Far East through the same perspective explored by Said, to see it as strange. Perspectives on films such as those from Japan, China and South Korean have persisted – around the time of the release of the remake of Park Chan-wook's *Oldboy* (*Oldeuboi*, 2003) in 2013 (directed by Spike Lee), *The Guardian* ran an article titled 'Why Hollywood Doesn't Get South Korean Cinema' that rehashed the discourse of the Asia Extreme movement when it remarked that the remakes 'often end up drained of the weirdness that made them so bracing' (Rose, 2013). The reasons behind the 'weirdness' ('inventive murder weapons, deranged storylines, genre-bending, varied menus, epic ambitions') position that cinema as strange and exotic, from its use of hammers and fish hooks in scenes of violence to animal cruelty (the eating of a live octopus in *Oldboy*), or the blurring of genre boundaries ('kimchi Westerns', such as *The Good, The Bad, The Weird* (*Choŭnnom, Nappŭnnom, Isanghannom*, Kim Jee-woon, 2008)). The image of South Korea presented is one of extremes, especially in the context of the article as a source of praise for a cinema seen as co-opted by Hollywood in Lee's remake of a recent world cinema classic. Said's focus on western attitudes towards the representation of the Middle and Far East are therefore not relics of the colonial era, but reflected in ongoing attitudes towards Others, and Othered cinemas, from outside Europe. While we might see these attitudes as positive, since they promote the works of cinemas from outside the Hollywood tradition, they can tend to warp our image of those cinemas, since distributors and festival programmers can sometimes be highly selective in the films they choose to show, and therefore those attitudes, however positively intentioned, can continue to foster standpoints that persist in reinforcing Orientalist positions in regard to films as representative of other cultures.

Colonial memories in transnational cinema

Discourses of colonialism and postcolonialism are recurring features of transnational cinema; transnational films are often by diasporic or exilic filmmakers, or about subjects that remind us of the transnational individuals or groups that have moved, or been moved, around the globe. One film that we might consider is Michael Haneke's *Hidden* (*Caché*, 2005). The film deals with the return of the colonial subject in the figure of the long-forgotten and repressed guilt of France's colonial past. The film's main characters are a bourgeois family: Georges (Daniel Auteuil) and Anne (Juliette Binoche) are both successful cultural figures, the host of TV show about literature and a publisher respectively. They begin to receive videotapes in the mail that show the exterior of their house (Figure 3.5). The film begins with one of these tapes, a long static shot of the outside of their house, ultimately revealed to be a videotape rather than an objective shot. Eventually, the tapes lead Georges to the home of Majid (Maurice Bénichou), a middle-aged Algerian man. Majid had lived with Georges's family after his own parents had been killed in 1961 during a massacre that occurred in Paris during the

Algerian war. Georges accuses Majid of sending the tapes, something the other man denies. During their encounter, Majid suddenly and shockingly slits his own throat – something he had wanted Georges to be present to witness. As we discover later, Georges had pressured Majid into cutting the head off a chicken and then told his parents of what he had done, something that led to Majid being sent to an orphanage instead of being adopted by Georges's parents (Figure 3.6). The film ends as ambiguously as it began; the

Figures 3.5 and 3.6 Haneke's repetitive use of long static shots in *Hidden* (Michael Haneke, 2005) implicates the viewer in voyeurism, including complicity with the 'forgotten' history of Majid's past (Les Films du Losange/Wega Film/ Bavaria Film/BIM Distribuzione)

central mystery of the film goes unresolved (who had sent the tapes?), and it ends with another long, static shot, this time of Georges and Anne's son's school after a discussion between him and Majid's son (who also denied sending the tapes).

Hidden positions the spectator in points of view that makes them voyeurs (the long, static shots of the central characters' home), or complicit (the viewpoint of Majid's suicide is uncomfortably detached, as though we are present observers). This is subsequently mapped onto French history, especially in relation to the child Georges, and whether he shares the guilt of the past as a child or as a helpless bystander. Georges, however, isn't innocent – he perpetrated a cruel wrongdoing against Majid, and later attempted to cover up the event in adulthood. His mother is even more complicit: she can't even remember the child she nearly adopted. The shades of French history are undeniable in the film, however. The 1961 massacre is referenced explicitly: on 17 October that year, French police attacked a demonstration against the imposition of a curfew on Algerians in Paris. An estimated 200 people were killed, and their bodies thrown into the Seine. Like the events of the past in *Hidden*, the incident was covered up, and it was only in 1998 that the prefect of police, Maurice Papon, was brought to trial and convicted (albeit for other crimes), which led to the French state having to acknowledge the massacre and confront the past. As Catherine Wheatley points out in her BFI Classics book on *Hidden*:

> It is easy enough to spot the allegorical significance of Georges's child-hood actions here: Majid, the intruder on his territory, is perceived as a threat, a usurper. He is defamed as dirty and dangerous and is eventually dispatched with ... Majid doesn't stand a chance against the combined forces of a malicious equal, a hand-washing authority figure and a powerful body of enforcers. (2011, pp. 58–59)

Majid's positioning as the colonial Other is especially significant in the film. Georges and Anne live a comfortable life in the city; their large, gated home is emphasised in the film's opening shot, and we're reminded of their lifestyle, sophisticated and comfortable, throughout the film. Majid and his son live in very different circumstances, in the *banlieue* (suburbs) of Paris, at the margins of the city. Like many ethnic residents of France, largely from Maghrebi North Africa (across Morocco, Tunisia, Algeria and Libya), Majid and his son live in modest, rent-controlled, poorer areas. This offers a stark contrast with the upper-middle-class life of Georges (the son of a family who owned a large country home). The marginality of Majid reminds us of the Othering of colonial subjects. Paul Gilroy has commented on the complexity of the representation of the colonial native in the film, particularly regarding the self-inflicted violence through which Majid commits suicide. As Gilroy argues, the film is at great lengths to present the complex psychology of Georges, through dreams and recollections, whereas this is denied to Mahid:

> When the Majids of this world are allowed to develop into deeper, rounded characters endowed with all the psychological gravity and complexity that is taken for granted in ciphers like Georges, we will know that substantive progress has been made towards breaking the white, bourgeois monopoly on dramatizing the stresses of lived experience in this modernity. (2007, p. 234)

So, while we might acknowledge the way in which *Hidden* explores the weight of colonial guilt and the problems of dealing with that past, we still have to acknowledge that Majid might not appear as a fully rounded character in the same way as the European subject, wherein Georges's subjectivity is much more developed, and Majid more representative. We also have to remember that while it is a film that deals with the ramifications of the colonial past, it is a film made by a European (Austrian) director who is also a white male. Most troubling for Gilroy, though, is how Majid commits suicide, 'that the colonial native can be made to disappear in an instant through the auto-combustive agency of their own violence' (p. 234). For Gilroy, this is a 'comforting idea', even if it is a step forward from previous representations. The death of Majid is not an event that is *about* Majid for Gilroy, but an event that reveals something about Georges's past, and as such it plays a narrative role, not one that develops the psychology of Majid or the colonial subject. The comforting nature of the self-immolation is problematised, as Gilroy explains: 'Getting the Arabs to do away with themselves is a timely fantasy in the context of today's pervasive Islamophobia.' (p. 234) In this context, the film makes a challenging intervention in the debate regarding multiculturalism and colonialism. Its politics implicate the make-up of contemporary France (in debates regarding centre/margin oppositions about the location of colonial Others), the growth of multiculturalism and developing transnational awareness that explores the ways in which the memory of colonialism is conceived in former colonial metropoles. Unlike some of the films we've encountered in this chapter, such as those by Sembène, this is a film produced not by a former colonial subject, or a postcolonial one, but by a European, something that might be implicated in the arguments of Gilroy that sound a measure of reservation about the film's examination of the colonial past.

Case study: *The Battle of Algiers* (Gillo Pontecorvo, 1966)

Pontecorvo's *Battle of Algiers* is a canonical example of postcolonial cinema. The film is a dramatisation of events that took place in Algiers during the period of guerrilla warfare by the *Front de Libération Nationale* (FLN) between November 1954 and December 1957. The film was largely based on the memoir written by Saadi Yacef, a leader of the FLN during the conflict. It was after his imprisonment in September 1957 that he began to write the book on which the film would later be based. Following the country's independence in March 1962, and after an amnesty offered by French president de Gaulle, saving him from a death sentence, he was released and founded a film company (see Harrison, 2007). He co-wrote an initial treatment for the film's story in 1964 with the French documentarian René Vautier, one of whose films, *One Nation, Algeria* (*Une nation, l'Algérie*, 1954), had been supported by Frantz Fanon. Backed by the Algerian government, Yacef had initially tried to approach the Italian director Luchino Visconti to direct the film, but was unsuccessful. Instead, he met with Pontecorvo, and, impressed by his leftist politics and background in the Italian Resistance in 1944 and 1945, engaged him to make the film. Pontecorvo and his screenwriting partner, Franco Solinas, had previously visited Algeria, shortly before the declaration of independence, to research another film that never came to fruition (largely because Paul Newman wasn't available and the film couldn't find an American distributor). Provided with press cuttings, documents and with access to those who had taken part in the Battle of Algiers, Solinas eventually produced a screenplay with which Yacef was satisfied and the film went into production in 1965, featuring Yacef in a prominent role, as Djafar, a charismatic leader of the FLN (Forgacs, 2007). With other non-professionals in the cast (French paratroopers were played by white tourists in Algiers), the film is strongly neorealist, shot on location in a documentary aesthetic, but most importantly it is one of the most significant examples of postcolonial cinema, something demonstrated by the renewed interest in the film at a number of points: in the run up to the Iraq war, when the film was screened at the Pentagon to aid in the planning for the aftermath of the invasion; and during its 50th anniversary in 2016, with numerous screenings and academic events reflecting on the film's sustained relevance.

The Battle of Algiers has a strongly episodic structure across the three years of the events depicted. It doesn't strongly feature a single protagonist, but focuses on a number of characters central to the conflict: Ali-la-Pointe, whose impending capture begins the film, which then flashes back to the story of his recruitment before returning to the scene of his capture; Ben M'Hidi, an FLN leader (both M'Hidi and Ali-la-Pointe were real people); and a trio of Algerian women who perpetrate a series of bombings. The

French are largely represented as military occupiers, the main antagonist being Colonel Mathieu (Jean Martin), an image of sophisticated western culture who advocates torture and the brutal repression of Algerian resistance, including the bombing of civilians. Robert Stam has noted the character of Mathieu is based largely on that of General Jacques Massu, the military leader who oversaw the strike depicted in the film and commanded a vicious campaign that led to the disappearance of 3,000 suspects.

Drawing on Fanon, Stam has explored the ways in which processes of identification work in the film to produce a form of 'revolutionary syncretism' (as a form of the 'combat literature' spoken of earlier in the chapter), and that 'the film sees the events through a Fanonian anti-colonialist prism' (2003b, p. 27). If we first go back a couple of decades to an earlier French film set in Algeria, we see the colonial image of the country. Julien Duvivier's *Pépé-le-Moko* (1937) gives a clear indication of the Othering of images under colonialism. Set in the Casbah of Algiers, the film is about a French gangster (the eponymous Pépé played by star Jean Gabin) on the run from the police. The Casbah is presented as an exotic, dangerous place, filled with shady characters. The film's trailer acts as a signifier of attitudes towards colonial others. A brief montage of exotic characters is presented with a caption that reads '*peupleé d'une étonnante faune humaine*'. The subtitles on the trailer translate this as 'populated by a colorful crowd', but the term *faune* translates more correctly as fauna or as wildlife. Despite being accompanied by the word *humaine* (human), the trailer is comparing these colonial subjects with animals; the subtitle's use of the 'colorful' implies the Orientalist exoticism of the gaze at these characters, the montage also summarising a range of groups of black, Asian and Middle Eastern characters. We are reminded that '*la Casbah est le plus pittoresque du monde*' (the Casbah is the most picturesque place in the world), but also that '*Pépé-le-Moko est son idole!*' (Pépé-le-Moko is their idol!). We can see, therefore, the colonial perspective with the white Frenchman as the main point of identification for the audience, albeit as an anti-hero. As Michael Vann has noted, this is in 'keeping with the colonial order of things and its racist logic, the white male colonizer maintains all agency' (2002, p. 188). The dominant language of the film is also French, rather than indigenous languages. This presents the classic colonial fantasy of mastery and control, the colonised country full of Othered subjects as a colourful backdrop to the action.

The Battle of Algiers, as a form of Fanonian 'combat' cinema, stands in stark contrast with an earlier film such as *Pépé-le-Moko*. As Stam notes, the film avoids the exoticisation of its Algerian protagonists, and its linguistic focus is not solely French. 'Algerian characters, although bilingual, generally speak Arabic with English subtitles; they are granted linguistic dignity.' (2003b, p. 25) Likewise, agency is not granted only to the colonial master:

'Instead of being shadowy background figures, picturesquely backward at best and hostile and menacing at worst, they are foregrounded. Neither exotic enigmas nor imitation Frenchmen, they exist as people with agency.' (p. 25). This final point is especially important – characters in the film exist as fully formed subjects, not just 'colourful' fauna, nor do they stand as Eurocentric figures whose agency is defined simply because they are most like French people. The Algerian characters in the film speak their own language, adhere to their own customs and history. This isn't to say also that the film presents a simply binary narrative of good Algerians versus bad French colonisers. The French are presented as being guilty of atroci-ties; they torture FLN members and innocent Algerians, such as the old man who leads them to Ali-La-Pointe's hiding place; they bomb domestic dwellings as retaliation; Algerian demonstrators are seen being fired upon. The Algerian resistance are seen committing terrorist acts, and the audi-ence is placed in a position of identification with them. When Ali-La-Pointe first joins the FLN, he is tasked with shooting a French police officer in the street. The gun turns out not to be loaded as a test of his loyalty. Islamic women conceal weapons within their burkas. Public places are bombed, with innocent victims. The conflict is presented as more complex than a simply good/bad dichotomy. And, although the French are victorious in the Battle of Algiers (the film ends with a caption that reminds us that the war for independence went on beyond the events in the film until independence was won), the film does not ask us to identify with the colonial saviour, nor turn the natives into spectacles of patriarchal humanist gazes (nor are they heroes).

The processes of identification used in the film can be difficult for the viewer. In perhaps the film's most discussed and analysed sequence, the audience is placed in a position of uncomfortable knowledge follow-ing three women as they bomb a series of targets in French occupied areas of the city. First, we see their planning and preparation. The three women disrobe from their traditional Algerian dress, removing veils. The three are then shown having their hair cut, being styled and dressed as French colonial subjects. In many cases, we would understand this as self-objectification, adopting the position of 'to-be-looked-at-ness' and therefore as a removal of agency. Within this context, however, this is an exercise of their agency, adopting the disguise of European modernity to 'pass' in the colonial city (to do so, they must shed all signs of their Alge-rianness). The sequence relies strongly on their look in the mirror – a kind of Lacanian mirror-stage identification in which the women take on the subjectivity of the coloniser (the colonial 'ideal ego') to carry out their plans (Figure 3.7). Having assumed the colonial agency, the women are able to pass beyond the checkpoints in the city, out of the Casbah. One of the women takes her child with her to pass the army, while another

Figure 3.7 *The Battle of Algiers* (Gillo Pontecorvo, 1966): The women remove the signs of their oppression to allow them to pass as colonising subjects with the identifying mirror as a form of alienation (Igor Film/ Casbah Film)

Figure 3.8 *The Battle of Algiers* (Gillo Pontecorvo, 1966): One of the women is able to pass through checkpoints because she is actively objectified by the soldiers on duty (Igor Film/Casbah Film)

flirts with the soldiers (Figure 3.8). In the background are numerous Algerians, men and women, unable to pass, conspicuously too 'native' to be allowed to do so. In performing as neo-European citizens, the women are visible enough as colonial subjects to be Othered as women rather than as Algerians.

When the women reach their targets, after collecting their bombs, the film doesn't simply reverse the logic of the colonial object/subject distinction. The citizens in the bars being targeted are not presented simply as faceless objects to fulfil the narrative's objectives. Pontecorvo offers a series of shot-reverse-shot close-ups to show us both the reluctance of the women in carrying out their task (although all three do). We cut between close-ups of the women, either ordering a drink in a French-style bar or watching young people dancing and listening to music in a milk bar, and the faces of the individuals in the locations, including a child eating an ice cream. These aren't military targets, although they are complicit with the occupying forces. The sequence uses close-ups throughout, while point-of-audition sound is used to highlight the women as listening subjects. So strongly are the women sutured within the text as speaking subjects, that we must identify with them while we simultaneously have to understand the consequences of the actions that we have just witnessed, and our complicity in that. Stam argues that the construction of the sequence invites us to contemplate 'our often simplistic attitudes toward anticolonial violence' as 'historical contextualization and formal mechanisms have short-circuited' during the sequence (2003b, pp. 27–28). The humanised victims of the bombings – of which we see much of the confused and shocked aftermath – aren't simply a 'colourful' bunch but have to be acknowledged as being individuals, through which we're invited to reflect on such actions and our relationship with them.

Even past its 50th anniversary, the film retains a place in contemporary culture, particularly after 9/11, and a strong relevance – it was condemned in the 1960s as a terrorist instruction film – but is also an important example of postcolonial cinema, one that has been much examined and written about. This analysis merely scratches the surface, and further investigation is strongly encouraged. Colonial narratives in the film are critically deconstructed: the truth is no longer an 'all-white' narrative, nor does it allow the European to comfortably witness the action as an 'audiovisual master'. This is strongly complicated by the issues of identification in the film's construction. Characters in the film are granted agency, not as imitation Europeans or as background actors, and as such the consequences of that agency must be contemplated by the spectator in its anti-colonial context.

Recommended viewing:

Yeelen (Souleymane Cissé, 1987)
Camp de Thiaroye (Ousmane Sembène, 1988)
Surname Viet Given Name Nam (Trinh T. Minh-ha, 1989)
Bye Bye Africa (Mahamet Saleh-Haroun, 1998)

Beau Travail (Claire Denis, 1999)
Monsoon Wedding (Mira Nair, 2001)
Whale Rider (Niki Caro, 2002)
Tsotsi (Gavin Hood, 2005)

Recommended further reading:

Ashcroft, Bill, Gareth Griffiths and Helen Tiffin (2013), *Post-Colonial Studies: The Key Concepts*. London and New York: Routledge.

Bignardi, Irene (2000), 'The Making of *The Battle of Algiers*', *Cineaste* 25(2): pp. 14–22.

Celli, Carlo (2005), *Gillo Pontecorvo: From Resistance to Terrorism*. Lanham: Scarecrow.

Diawara, Manthia (1992), *African Cinema: Politics and Culture*. Bloomington: Indiana University Press.

Ford, Hamish (2012), 'From Otherness "Over There" to Virtual Presence: *Camp de Thiaroye – The Battle of Algiers – Hidden*', in eds Sandra Ponzanesi and Marguerite Waller, *Postcolonial Cinema Studies*. London and New York: Routledge, pp. 63–77.

Harrison, Nicholas, ed. (2007), Special Issue: Gillo Pontecorvo's Battle of Algiers, 40 Years On. *Interventions: International Journal of Postcolonial Studies* 9(3).

Haspel, Paul (2006), 'Algeria Revisited: Opposing Commanders as Warring Doubles in *The Battle of Algiers*', *Journal of Film and Video* 58(3): pp. 33–42.

Higbee, Will (2007), 'Locating the Postcolonial in Transnational Cinema: The Place of Algerian Émigré Directors in Contemporary French Film', *Modern & Contemporary France* 15(1): pp. 51–64.

Khanna, Ranjana (1998), '*The Battle of Algiers* and *the Nouba of the Women of Mont Chenoua*: From Third to Fourth Cinema', *Third Text* 12(43): pp. 13–32.

Koch, Gerhard (2014), '*The Battle of Algiers* Revisited', in eds Geoffrey Nash, Kathleen Kerr-Koch and Sarah Hackett, *Postcolonialism and Islam: Theory, Literature, Culture, Society and Film*. London and New York: Routledge, pp. 217–226.

Mellen, Joan (1973), *Filmguide to The Battle of Algiers*. Bloomington: Indiana University Press.

Moore, Lindsey (2008), 'Fanon's "Algeria Unveiled" and Pontecorvo's *The Battle of Algiers*', in *Arab, Muslim, Woman: Voice and Vision in Postcolonial Literature and Film*. London and New York: Routledge, pp. 36–41.

Reid, Donald (2005), 'Re-viewing *The Battle of Algiers* with Germaine Tillion', *History Workshop Journal* 60: pp. 93–115.

Riegler, Thomas (2009), 'Gillo Pontecorvo's "Dictatorship of the Truth" – a Legacy', *Studies in European Cinema* 6(1): pp. 47–62.

Wayne, Mike (2001), 'Third Cinema as Critical Practice: A Case Study of *The Battle of Algiers*', in *Political Film: The Dialectics of Third Cinema*. London and Sterling: Pluto, pp. 5–24.

Post-Third World cinema

Ella Shohat's article 'Post-Third-Worldist Culture: Gender, Nation, and the Cinema', originally published in 1996, pointed towards an adoption of a 'post-Third-Worldist' perspective. As she discusses in one of the article's notes, she proposes the term:

> to point to a move beyond the ideology of Third Worldism. Whereas the term 'postcolonial' implies a movement beyond anti-colonial nationalist ideology and movement beyond a specific point of colonial history, post-Third-Worldism conveys a movement 'beyond' a specific ideology – Third-Worldist nationalism. A post-Third-Worldist perspective assumes the fundamental validity of the anti-colonial movement, but also interrogates the fissures that rend the Third-World nation. (Shohat, 2003, p. 75 n. 2)

Shohat's argument focuses particularly on Third World feminist practices in film and video that had previously been seen to fall outside the boundaries of feminist film theory as well as the patriarchal discourses of nationalism. Feminist film theory, she argues, is a Eurocentric and western construct, a universalising and essentialising project that assumes a shared interest of all women regardless of their location, race or ethnicity. As Shohat posits, this often leaves Third-Worldist feminists stuck between stations, traversing 'excommunication as "traitors to the nation" and "betraying the race" by patriarchal nationalism, and the imperial rescue fantasies of clitoridectomized and veiled women proffered by Eurocentric feminism' (p. 52). Third-Worldist feminists do not suddenly become western feminists through their engagement with political, social and aesthetic movements devoted to empowering women. Post-Third-Worldist feminist practices are embedded within specific geographical identity politics that are located in the reference to ethnicity and race in regional and national contexts.

Many of the filmmakers we've encountered in this chapter, along with many of the key theorists, were men. Shohat draws attention to the phallocentric bases of Third-Worldist cinema, and that those men were largely unconcerned with a feminist critique of nationalism. She draws attention to the scene from *The Battle of Algiers* referenced in the case study, where the three women adopt the visage of the coloniser to pass army checkpoints. The film, she argues, avoids exploring the revolutionary movement's tensions surrounding gender, class and religion – colonised people are not as unified as the project might suggest. While the three women in the film exercise their agency through the adoption of the coloniser's 'look' in more than one sense – their appearance and the soldier's gazes – Shohat points out that they are still at the behest of male revolutionaries, and that it remains a patriarchal revolution. Indeed, she quotes Anne McClintock's observation that nationalisms are generally founded in terms of their gendered power and that women who were unable to organise prior to a revolution will remain without the power to organise following it. Women's empowerment therefore had to wait in line for its turn – the national struggle subsumed other struggles yet to take shape.

A great deal of Shohat's thinking in this area relates to the growth of post-modern culture, the 'end of history' (in Francis Fukuyama's term, although Shohat asks whose history that was) and the waning of a 'Third-Worldist euphoria' that has given way to more fragmented or heterogeneous concerns that Third-Worldist theory collapses or masks. This euphoria has:

> given way to the collapse of Communism, the indefinite postponement of the devoutly wished for 'tricontinental revolution,' the realization that the 'wretched of the earth' are not unanimously revolutionary (nor neces-sarily allies to one another), the appearance of an array of Third-World despots, and the recognition that international geopolitics and the global economic system have forced even the 'Second World' to be incorporated into transnational capitalism. (p. 55)

In many cases, this gives way to more heterogeneous explorations of identity politics in films by women filmmakers, and Shohat implicates some of the issues that we will begin to consider more in the next chapter, including exile and diaspora. She explores a number of films by Palestinians in exile, such as Elia Sulieman's *Homage by Assassination* (1992) and Mona Hatoum's *Measures of Distance* (1989), both of which, she argues, affirm 'the process of recreating identity in the liminal zone of exile' (p. 65) through a number of distancing aesthetic techniques such as video layering, voice-over and play with language. Hatoum's film examines the female body and nudity, and relationships between mother and daughter. Both films engage with the broader concerns of displacement, exile and the fluid, unfixed identities of those with diasporic subjectivities. Many of the films explored by Shohat's article tackle historical and racialised concerns regarding women's bodies, including Julie Dash's *Illusions* (1982), about a black singer whose voice dubs a white star, or Tracey Moffatt's experimental short *Nice Coloured Girls* (1987), which challenges historical discourses relating to Aboriginal sexual-ity in Australia in ethnographic traditions; they are post-Third-Worldist in the sense that they interrogate nationalist discourses through 'grids of class, gender, sexuality, and diasporic identities' (p. 74). Their film practice is neither solely feminist, nor nationalist, but much more heteroglossic in its approach to the multi-layered and complex identities for diasporic or post-independence women.

As we move onto the next chapter, and the ways in which transnational cinema explores some of these issues more specifically, Shohat demonstrates the way in which moving beyond purely Third-Worldist and nationalistic perspectives, without leaving them behind altogether, can help us understand a world in which existence is becoming subject to increasing levels of globalisation. Instead of merely trapping us in a 'deterritorialised' domain in which we become 'atomized consumers or self-entertaining monads', transnationalism offers the potential for more positive impacts, post-Third-World:

> In a transnational world typified by the global circulation of images and sounds, goods, and peoples, media spectatorship impacts complexly on national identity, communal belonging, and political affiliations ... Just as the media can exoticize and disfigure cultures, they have the potential power not only to offer countervailing representations but also to open up parallel spaces for anti-racist feminist transformation. (pp. 74–75)

Discussion questions:

- If postcolonialism becomes just another part of transnationalism, in what ways might that make post-colonial issues less prominent in studying Third World cinema?
- How important do you think it is to historicise postcolonial discourses in approaching transnational cinemas?
- What questions are faced by film studies in responding to films that travel across borders from former colonial or neo-colonial countries?
- What challenges do you think might be faced by a transnational feminist movement today?

CHAPTER 4

Globalisation, Border-crossing, Migration

In this chapter, we'll begin to explore concepts of transnational cinema more closely as a means of understanding how the flows of individuals, boundary-crossing and the instabilities of national institutions and imaginaries have been explored in cinema in the era of globalisation. Unpacking several approaches to transnational cross-border encounters, the chapter engages with methods that explore the experiences of border-crossing, migration and globalisation. During the first section, we'll return to Deborah Shaw's 'Deconstructing and Reconstructing "Transnational Cinema"' (2013) and consider her categorisation of transnational cinema, unpicking its thematic significance for stories of journeying or globalisation, and for issues of production and distribution that will become more significant in later chapters. We'll also examine Mette Hjort's (2010) conception of marked and unmarked transnationalisms, introducing her discourse on works that are transnational by nature, but that 'encourage thinking about transnationality' as a means of engaging with the experiences of displacement, migration, exile and diaspora. Most prominently, however, we'll look at issues of globalisation and themes relating to the movement of people across borders and national territories. This and the next chapter, therefore, consider what Ezra and Rowden term 'cinematic depictions of people caught in the cracks of globalization' (2006, p. 7).

In the opening chapter, we encountered several thinkers who defined transnational cinema in terms of the ways in which it engages with globalisation and flows of individuals, of capital and culture. During this chapter, we'll consider flows of individuals across borders, returning to Appadurai's notion of Ethnoscapes, groups of people whose movement across borders reflect the shifting boundaries of the world that are challenging the politics of and relationships between nations: 'tourists, immigrants, refugees, exiles, guestworkers and other moving groups and persons' (1990, p. 297). We'll explore these and their cinematic representation during this chapter and the next.

Shaw introduced us to a range of categories across a variety of approaches to transnational cinema. Here, we'll engage with a few of those: transnational modes of production, distribution and exhibition; the cinema of globalisa-tion; films with multiple locations (we'll consider exilic and diasporic filmmaking in the next chapter); also included along with this would be a term from Shaw's earlier editorial with De La Garza: migration, journeying and other forms of border-crossing. Border-crossing is imagined in a num-ber of ways cinematically, as Shaw discusses. Production, distribution and exhibition are necessarily transnational. In some cases, as she highlights, this tends to favour Hollywood's hegemonic power, as an institution that produces films in collaboration with many nations, and also across national borders (the old term for which used to be 'runaway productions'). During this chapter, though, we consider filmmakers, such as the Mexican director Alejandro González Iñárritu, who work across national borders within the institutional and aesthetic structures of Hollywood. Similarly, we'll consider filmmakers making films about the condition of border-crossing, in stories such as Courtney Hunt's *Frozen River* (2008), about a single working-class mother trying to make a living to support her children, who becomes embroiled in people trafficking across the US-Canadian border with a Native-American widow. Stories of migration and journeying such as these are central to the representation of being transnational, part of the Ethnoscape of globalisation.

The cinema of globalisation is characterised by Shaw as films that explic-itly address questions raised by globalisation, particularly 'the ways in which relations of power between nations and peoples are played out on screen' (2013, p. 54). Here she draws on a definition developed by Tom Zaniello in his book *The Cinema of Globalization: A Guide to Films About the New Economic Order* (2007). Zaniello's guide gathers together 213 films, across drama and documentary, selected for the ways in which they address key indicators of globalisation, particularly as they relate to issues of global labour histories, multinational corporations, and the daily lives of working-class people in the context of developing multinational globalisation, or as they relate to a series of indicators of globalisation (p. 17). These indicators cover: transna-tional organisations; global labour; global capital; digitalisation; changes in the workplace; outsourcing and offshoring; deregulation and privatisation; oil; scarce resources; intellectual property rights; China and other export processing zones; containerised shipping; and anti-globalisation (pp. 2–16). Films included under these headings by Zaniello include *Beijing Bicycle*, *The Constant Gardener* (Fernando Meirelles, 2005), *Dirty Pretty Things* (Stephen Frears, 2002), *Lilya 4-ever* (Lukas Moodysson, 2002), *Syriana* (Stephen Gaghan, 2005), *Zoolander* (Ben Stiller, 2001), and TV show *The Wire* (HBO, 2002–2008). To this list, Shaw adds a number of other films that deal with issues of global capital, labour and working-class life under globalisation, and particularly films set in or around conflict zones: *Blood Diamond* (Edward Zwick, 2006),

Children of Men (Alfonso Cuarón, 2006) and *Babel* (Iñárritu, 2006), one of our case studies. Questions of power, identity and the consequences of border-crossing, for individuals and organisations, as we'll see, form a core part of the thinking about cross-border issues in transnational cinema.

Marked/unmarked transnationalisms

In 'On the Plurality of Cinematic Transnationalisms' (2010), Mette Hjort articulates one of the key issues of many studies of transnational cinema, the indistinct use of the term and its lack of theoretical clarity. She argues that the term 'transnational' has been used 'as a largely self-evident qualifier requiring only minimal conceptual clarification' (p. 13) and as a means of discussing topics that would previously have been explored under the terms of the national cinema paradigm just a decade previously. In some ways, this mirrors some of the theorisation that we've encountered so far in this book. We've seen how the national cinema paradigm gave way to thinking about transnational cinema due to its limiting nature; the paradigm of the national became constraining, as cinema came more and more to be both a product of transnational organisation, production and distribution, and as a way of telling stories about individuals and groups across borders. Despite this tendency towards a more pluralistic and/or hybridised form of cinema, Hjort sees a tendency to use the term 'transnational' as 'shorthand for a series of assumptions about the networked and globalized realities that are those of a contemporary situation', whereby those assumptions end up 'playing a strangely homogenizing role' in the face of a lack of conceptual definitions of the term. While we've seen some theorisation of transnational cinema already in this book, by the likes of Shaw, Higson, Ďurovičová, Higbee and Lim, Iwabuchi and Ezra and Rowden, some of these have followed Hjort's argument (she also offers a list of texts that have avoided this pitfall, including Hess and Zimmerman's 'Transnational Documentaries: A Manifesto', Shohat and Stam's collection, *Multiculturalism, Postcoloniality, and Transnational Media*, and Naficy's *An Accented Cinema: Exilic and Diasporic Filmmaking*). In effect, though, Hjort's identification of a plurality of transnationalisms reminds us that not all transnational cinemas are the same, and that they don't promote the same agendas:

> Cinematic transnationalism comes in many different forms and promotes a wide range of values, some of which are economic, artistic, cultural, social, or political. Any given instance of cinematic transnationalism may involve the pursuit of more than one kind of value, the various kinds of value being themselves differentially weighed depending on the type of transnationalism in question. (p. 30)

Hjort gives us a taxonomy of transnationalisms that we can apply to a range of different cinematic texts. She argues that 'there are a number of different types of cinematic transnationalism that combine genuine hybridity, traceable to distinct national elements'. That transnationalism is defined by two aspects: 'a resistance to globalization as cultural homogenization; and a commitment to ensuring that certain economic realities associated with filmmaking do not eclipse the pursuit of aesthetic, artistic, social, and political values' (p. 15). These values may also stem significantly from national contexts.

For Hjort, transnationalism is not an absolute category. A range of different kinds of production can be determined as transnational, weakly or strongly across a scale. Strongly transnational productions would exhibit indicators of transnationalism over a number of levels of production, distribution, reception and in the work itself. Hjort's example is Mehdi Charef's 2001 film *Daughter of Keltoum* (*La Fille de Keltoum*), a work of *cinéma beur*, that exhibits transnationalism across a number of levels: it is a French-Belgian-Tunisian co-production; its distribution was supported by the Global Film Initiative (a group whose mission is to 'promote cross-cultural understanding through film'); the director is a French resident born in Algeria; French and Arabic are the film's dominant languages; and its theme explores identity as formed through multiple national cultures (it is about a young woman returning to her homeland, Algeria, from her adopted home of Switzerland, to kill the woman who abandoned her at birth). A film such as Gurinder Chadha's *Bend It Like Beckham* (2002) might be positioned lower down the scale of transnationalisms: its production was heavily supported by the UK Film Council (just under half of its overall budget), although it was a British-German-American co-production; its distribution was largely handled by British company Redbus (now part of the Canadian mini-major Lionsgate) and internationally by 20th Century Fox; the writer-director is of Punjabi descent, born in Kenya and raised in Britain; the film is mainly in English and Punjabi, with some Hindi and German; the film engages with multicultural identity in Britain thematically (more of which in the next chapter). On a broad scale, the film remains strongly transnational, whereas a film such as *The Bourne Ultimatum* (Paul Greengrass, 2007), despite its global locations, British director and transnational distribution, is more weakly transnational, since it retains a core interest in hegemonic American values.

Hjort places intention at the heart of this process, where there are 'marked' 'properties that encourage thinking about transnationality' and 'unmarked' transnational cinema projects that don't locate a notion of transnational endeavour politically at the forefront of production and reception (p. 14). We see marked transnationalisms in films where issues relating to transnationalism are heavily implicated in the formal and thematic basis of the film, as intended by the film's principal creative team, comprising directors, actors, writers, producers, cinematographers and editors. A film's editing, camerawork or narrative structure may foreground concepts relating to transnationalism (as such, we will largely be looking at marked works of transnationalism throughout this chapter). Unmarked transnational films may not draw attention to these issues through their style or stories. Hence, Hjort is keen to note that films that have marked qualities of transnationalism may not be produced through transnational production routes, and could be products of a purely national cinema framework, and therefore would not be strongly transnational, but might be marked that way. Conversely, strongly transnational films might be unmarked as transnational in their texts, and that strong transnationalism might only be uncovered through research and investigation about the film's production and distribution. Hjort uses Andrea Arnold's *Red Road* (2006) as an example of a film that is strongly transnational, but not marked as such. The film's story – about a CCTV operator in Glasgow – doesn't engage with transnationalism in any way. However, as a British-Danish co-production, the film promoted particular forms of European collaboration, and hence was strongly transnational.

As previously mentioned, Hjort's goal was to define the ways in which cinematic transnationalisms are conceptualised in a number of ways. As such, she identifies nine different modes of transnationalism: epiphanic; affinitive; milieu-building; opportunistic; cosmopolitan; globalising; auteurist; modernising; and experimental. Each one articulates a different set of values in relation to transnationalism. They are not exclusive, however, and may be found combined in certain texts in different ways.

Epiphanic: the term relates to an epiphany, and Hjort defines this category as the ways in which shared qualities of national belonging are disclosed. The emphasis here is on how cinema articulates forms of deep-rooted national belonging that exhibit shared aspects with other national identities to produce a deep transnational belonging.

Affinitive: as the term suggests, this category stresses affinities across borders and national identities. This is often defined in terms of shared ethnicity, languages that are either similar or mutually intelligible, and a longstanding history of interaction that has produced commonalities and shared core values, practices and cultural institutions.

Milieu-building: a filmmaking milieu (environment) might be shared across boundaries as a way of resisting the globalising homogenisation of Hollywood. Hjort offers the example of a project called *Advance Party*, a collaborative undertaking between Scottish and Danish filmmakers to build a small-nation milieu as an alternative or complementary form of cultural policy. This *Dogma 95*-style project sought to bring positive elements of the Danish milieu across to Scotland as a means of influencing cultural policy to develop a commercially viable environment.

Opportunistic: this form of transnationalism is less positive than the first three, since it seeks not to leave any lasting legacy or network, but capitalises on economic realities as they arise at a particular moment (it merely takes advantage of whatever financing exists to get a project made, wherever that funding may come from – hence it may produce a strongly transnational but unmarked product).

Cosmopolitan: cosmopolitan filmmakers, often through their ethnicity, can exhibit multiple belonging through their films. Hjort mentions the work of Evans Chan, an ethnically Chinese filmmaker, born in mainland China, raised in Macao, but educated in Hong Kong and America, based in New York, whose films are targeted at Chinese audiences in Hong Kong, and beyond China. Works in this category explore various issues of migration, and the intersections of national, transnational and postcolonial issues. In preference to the term exilic, Hjort notes that cosmopolitan filmmakers are free to migrate and circulate globally.

Globalising: globalising transnationalisms acknowledge the shortfalls of national cinema funding streams, by producing films with strongly transnational audience appeal in terms of genre and stardom. To access distribution beyond their national context, they must include factors that leave behind many of the qualities associated with a committed and political national cinema in favour of Hollywood-style production values, cross-border stars, and a lack of themes typical of Third Cinema. Hjort's example is the major blockbuster *Hero* (*Ying xiong*, 2002), a *wuxia pian* ('chivalrous martial arts film'), directed by Zhang Yimou, a member of the Chinese fifth generation, whose later film *The Great Wall* (2017), starring Matt Damon, would also sit comfortably in this category.

Auteurist: as the name of this category makes explicit, this form of transnationalism is concerned with the investment made by *auteurs* in matters of transnational collaboration. Whereas cosmopolitan transnationalism described the works of *auteurs* who were at the margins and intersections of different forms of national belonging, auteurist transnationalisms may not be strongly marked in their regard for transnational issues, although they may set up projects that are unmarked but strongly identified as cross-border collaborations. Hjort gives the example of the *portmanteau* film that brings together several *auteurs* from different nations to produce variations on a theme.

Modernising: modernity is not a totalising concept, and it has been identified that there are multiple modernities across the globe. Routes of modernity sometimes criss-cross transnational developments. Modernising transnationalism is thus often seen in cultural policy, such as in Hong Kong and South Korea, in which the idea of state-of-the-art filmmaking practice is designated as a cultural expression that brings modernisation and transformation. Hong Kong, for instance, promoted a strong self-image of its global city state through its cinema as a transnational expression, the cutting edge seen as distanced from what is traditionally national culture, but outward looking and necessarily transnational.

Experimental: this final category in some cases resists that of the other eight; it often seeks not to build milieus or capitalise on deeply shared cultures, nor to engage with global cinemagoers. Its value is ascribed through artistic experimentation, through which filmmaking engages socially, politically and aesthetically with transnationalism. Strongly transnational production strategies combine with a marked transnationalism that encourages *thinking* about the transnational, often at an abstract level.

Hjort's categories here give us a series of ways of thinking about how films engage with the transnational on different levels, from cultural policy (affinitive, milieu-building, globalising, modernising) to production (auteurist, opportunistic, globalising) and within texts themselves (epiphanic, affinitive, cosmopolitan, globalising, modernising, experimental). Because many relate to social, political, economic, artistic and cultural values, they can intersect to different degrees and in different ways depending on how strong or weak, marked or unmarked aspects of the film are understood. Sometimes, these qualities will be self-evident in the text, while at others they may be uncovered through deep textual analysis, or through research about a film's production, distribution or reception contexts.

Case study: *Babel* (Alejandro González Iñárritu, 2006)

Babel is a strongly marked transnational text, one that, for many scholars, is a key work of transnational cinema. For Deborah Shaw, the film is 'one of the best examples of cultural exchange', featuring a multinational cast and crew from Mexico, Italy, France, North America and Morocco; it was filmed in the US, Japan, Morocco and Mexico and features dialogue in five different spoken languages (English, Spanish, Japanese, Arabic and Berber) alongside Japanese Sign Language (2013, p. 57). Shaw here draws upon Tom O'Regan's notion of cultural exchange (1999), the circulation of cultural texts and materials across different sociocultural areas and formations. As O'Regan notes, we need to remember that 'partners to cultural exchange in the cinema come to that exchange on an undeniably and permanently unequal basis with disparities of language, wealth, size, resources, infrastructures, and culture. Few film relations are based on free and open exchange' (p. 270). Therefore, it's important to keep in mind here that *Babel* is a Hollywood film, produced by the speciality (or niche/independent) wing of Paramount Pictures, Paramount Vantage (hence its blended approach to the Hollywood star system and tropes of world cinema, including often-subtitled dialogue). As such, there is little to note in terms of milieu-building transnationalism in which the film's partnerships might have left a legacy beyond the film itself.

Katarzyna Marciniak, Anikó Imre and Áine O'Healy echo this point in their introduction to *Transnational Feminism in Film and Media* (2007) when they argue:

> Highlighting transnational encounters between the so-called first and third worlds, *Babel* submits a critique of U.S. entitlement to unhindered mobility, and delivers its argument with an uncompromising force: no matter who crosses borders, the crossing is potentially risky and difficult. But not all crossings are equal: when privileged first worlders venture abroad, border crossing is a matter of 'cosmopolitan' choice; and their trauma can be alleviated by the international apparatus of embassies and rescue helicopters. When the third worlders cross borders in the film, however, there is no aid, only the risk of severe punishment. (p. 2)

Marciniak et al. place the film in the context of post-9/11 anxiety, the war on terror and US domestic policy towards 'undocumented' illegal immigrants and the ways in which they amplify cross-border tensions and fears. They argue that it 'depicts its cross-cultural dramas with striking sensitivity to gender, ethnoracial, economic, national, and (il)legal realities. It de-romanticizes "travel" and, to some extent, de-exoticizes "otherness"' (p. 6). This is not to say that the film makes Otherness disappear, but in many cases it demonstrates how Otherness is constructed by Eurocentric gazes, the privileges of white, western travellers, and the tensions manifest in George W. Bush's war on terror.

The film tells four interconnected stories across as many continents. They are told in a slightly time-shifted fashion – a conversation heard early in the film from one side is heard from the other towards the end. The final story ends five days after the drama begins. In Morocco, a goat herder (Mustapha Rachidi) buys a rifle to kill jackals that have been killing his sheep. He sends his two sons (Boubker Ait El Caid and Said Tarchani) out to the desert with it to watch over the flock. In childlike fashion, they play with the gun. Disappointed with its quality, they argue about how far it can shoot. They aim it at traffic on a nearby road. Firing at a bus, they see no sign of contact, until the bus screeches to a halt. On the bus are an American couple, Susan (Cate Blanchett) and Richard (Brad Pitt). They have come to Morocco to patch up their marriage. Both are tense, while she is fearful of the hygiene in a Third World country: she throws away ice they're given with cola because it might be unsafe. He is more concerned with why they are there. Later, on the bus ride, Susan is hit by the boy's bullet. A local guide helps them to his nearby village, where there is a doctor, and Richard can contact the American embassy for help. This sparks an international incident, and a terrorist panic. Meanwhile, in the US, Susan and Richard's children are being looked after by their Mexican nanny, Amelia (Adriana Barraza). She is due to be at her son's wedding across the border, but the delayed return of her employers complicates her plans. When she can't find anyone else to look after them, she decides to take them with her, driven by her nephew, Santiago (Gael García Bernal). The children enjoy the wedding, but when it's time to go home to San Diego, Santiago drives Amelia and the children across the border drunk. The guards are aggressive in their questioning; Santiago panics and speeds through the border. He leaves Amelia and the children in the desert on the American side. She hides them in shelter to go looking for help in the searing heat of the day; when she returns with the border patrol, the children are missing. In Tokyo, deaf schoolgirl Chieko (Rinko Kikuchi) is struggling to overcome the death of her mother and the distance of her father, Wataya (Kûji Yakusho). Her anger and confusion is palpable – when we first encounter her, she is protesting a referee's decision in a volleyball match and being sent off. She reaches out to others for connection, often sexually, exposing herself to a group of young men, and a policeman who visits her father to ask some questions. When she calls him to their apartment late at night, after a night out with friends, she confesses to him about her mother's suicide, that she threw herself from the apartment's balcony. When the detective meets her father, however, he points out that it's not that with which he's concerned, but the ownership of a gun – Wataya had previously been on a hunting trip to Morocco, and had given the gun to his guide, who had subsequently sold it on to the farmer, who had given it to his sons.

It is not just the gun that ties the stories together, but family is a common thread through each of the stories. As a means of structuring the film, this is an example of strongly affinitive transnationalism. In each of the four stories, we encounter different family relationships: the brotherly conflict between the two boys in Morocco, with the elder Ahmed scolding the younger Yussef for spying on a local street girl undressing (something he reveals to their father in an attempt to deflect from their guilt for shooting Susan); Amelia is obviously a caring mother (literally and as a surrogate), and the wedding scenes are warm and family-centred; Susan and Richard's relationship is damaged following the death of their third child; while the relationship between Chieko and her father, in the absence of her mother, is the focus in the Japanese segment of the film. This shared dynamic of familial relationships is strongly affinitive in the film, revealing similarities across cultures. This is also reinforced in some of the cutting in the film, which often uses match cuts from one story to another – right at the outset, the running of one of the boys in Morocco is visually matched with that of one of Richard and Susan's children in San Diego. Other cuts are more disjunctive, and there is a tendency to cut across sound, from quiet to loud or vice versa, and to contrast colour and light through montage. This is due to the film's other focus on the dissimilarities between the stories, and the focus on ethnic Otherness and the power imbalances across and comparatively between borders.

Throughout the film, it's clear that the American and European tourists occupy a privileged space in travelling across borders for leisure purposes. Susan's reluctance about the trip, and her fears about dirty water, constitute a Eurocentric gaze at the Othered North African country. This is echoed through the other tourists on their bus, who are afraid for their lives in the small rural village, hysteria fuelled by terrorist anxiety. One of them relates a story about other tourists who had their throats cut in a similar instance, and fears the same. Their gaze Others both the country and its occupants. Fears about terrorism also fuel the international and Moroccan response to the accident. The local police aggressively pursue the culprits under pressure from outside – when the father returns home one night, he remarks he's late because the road is closed due to an American tourist being shot by a terrorist. Yet, while the white American tourists are afforded embassy support, a helicopter to ferry them out, there is no such support for the family at the heart of the tragedy – the boys initially lie to the police about where they can find the owner of the gun, and when tracked down by the police, they attempt to run. Ahmed is killed, and Yussef shoots back at the police, wounding one of them. The international nature of the incident, in combination with post-9/11 anxieties, produces an imbalanced response, with the white Americans' privileged position restated. As Marciniak and Bruce Bennett remind us:

> *Babel* shows us an unequal world in which, for some, border-crossing is a matter of a travel to an 'exotic' location, while for others, it is an experience of abjection. While the American children, blond, blue-eyed, fragile, and innocent, are ultimately 'rescued,' there is no such outcome for the Moroccan children. (2016, p. 6)

We see something similar in Amelia's crossing of the border with the children (Figure 4.1). She has no trouble crossing into Mexico, but the return trip is much more problematic. Borders are not permeable for everyone

Figure 4.1 In *Babel* (Alejandro González Iñárritu, 2006), border-crossings have different consequences for those Othered by race, gender and disability (Paramount Vantage)

in every direction. For Richard and Susan, and the other tourists, border-crossing is a luxury, but for others (literally Othered), it is a difficult ordeal. Amelia and Santiago are treated with suspicion and aggression by the border guards. While it was possible for her to cross the border with the two white children, it is not so easy to return to the US. Along with questioning, they are met with torchlight in their faces. Santiago's response is to act like a criminal when treated like one. Amelia's undocumented status is more problematic, as she's deported, despite her obvious motherly care for the two children. This is a reminder that the experience of border-crossing, here exacerbated by US border policy, is not equal for everyone. Similarly, for Wataya, a middle-class Japanese salaryman, there is an ease about crossing borders and tourism denied others. So, while the film does have elements of affinitive transnationalism, it exposes some of the processes through which individuals and social groups are Othered, be that through domestic and foreign policy, Eurocentric gazes, ethnicity, assumptions regarding the Third World or through discrepancies between languages. As such, we must finally acknowledge the film's title, which very clearly references the biblical story of the Tower of Babel, in which all people lived in harmony, until God scattered them to different parts of the Earth and made their languages incomprehensible to each other. *Babel* reflects on these difficulties of language and understanding, and the imbalances between different social, ethnic and economic groups, often due to those misunderstandings of language (even between Wataya and his daughter, due to her deafness), but that there are transnational affinities between those groups. Having said that, though, the film does not trivialise those affinities in striving for some pat 'universalism' (which would be to impose a westernised perspective onto those Othered in the Third World) that deflects criticism from political responsibility for those fundamental differences encountered in cross-border transnationalisms. Hence, it is a strongly transnational work whose text is clearly marked as encouraging thinking about transnational relationships and imbalances.

Recommended viewing:

Before Night Falls (Julian Schnabel, 2000)

JSA: Joint Security Area (*Gongdong gyeongbi guyeok JSA*, Park Chan-wook, 2000)

Journey to Kafiristan (*Die Reise nach Kafiristan*, Donatello and Fosco Dubini, 2001)

Guardians of the Frontier (*Varuh meje*, Maja Weiss, 2002)

The Syrian Bride (Eran Riklis, 2004)

Gypo (Jan Dunn, 2005)

Unveiled (Fremde Haut and Angelina Maccarone, 2005)

Shelter Me (*Riparo*, Marco Puccioni, 2007)

Biutiful (Alejandro González Iñárritu, 2010)

I am Nasrine (Tina Gharavi, 2012)

Recommended further reading:

Del Mar Azcona, Maria (2015), '"We Are All Uxbal": Narrative Complexity in the Urban Borderlands of *Biutiful*', *Journal of Film & Video* 67(1): pp. 3–13.

Kerr, Paul (2010), '*Babel's* Network Narrative: Packaging a Globalized Art Cinema', *Transnational Cinemas* 1(1): pp. 37–51.

Manning, Caitlin, and Julie Shackford-Bradley (2010), 'Global Subjects in Motion: Strategies for Representing Globalization in Film', *Journal of Film and Video* 62(3): pp. 36–52.

Pellicer, Juan (2010), 'Bridging Worlds: Transtextuality, Montage, and the Poetics of *Babel*', *Mexican Studies/Estudios Mexicanos* 26(2): pp. 239–249.

Podalsky, Laura (2010), 'Migrant Feelings: Melodrama, Babel and Affective Communities', *Studies in Hispanic Cinemas* 7(1): pp. 47–58.

Rothlisberger, Leisa (2012), '*Babel's* National Frames in Global Hollywood', *Jump Cut: A Review of Contemporary Media* 54, Available online: http://ejumpcut.org/archive/jc54.2012/RothlisbergerBabel/index.html. Accessed 19 September 2017.

Shaw, Deborah (2011), '*Babel* and the Global Hollywood Gaze', *Situations: Project of the Radical Imagination* 4(1): pp. 11–31.

Tierney, Dolores (2009), 'Alejandro González Iñárritu: Director Without Borders', *New Cinemas: Journal of Contemporary Film* 7(2): pp. 101–117.

Border narratives

Like *Babel*, there are many films engaged with experiences of individuals or groups who cross borders, and their consequences. Some of those films explore the violence of border-crossing experience, such as Moodysson's *Lilya 4-ever* about a young woman from a post-Soviet republic who is trafficked to Sweden for prostitution, or *The Sisters* (*Sestre*, Vladimir Paskaljević, 2011), a Serbian film about two sisters who become victims of sex trafficking in Italy. From a slightly different perspective, we can also include *Taken* (Pierre Morel, 2008) under this heading, although, like *Babel*, it reminds us of the privileged position of white American tourists, albeit with a more individualistic approach than Iñárritu's in its saviour narrative, where Liam Neeson's paternal authority rather than direct state intervention defeats the ethnic criminals. Some horror films also engage in tropes of transnational border-crossing, including *An American Werewolf in London* (John Landis, 1981), and its sequel, *An American Werewolf in Paris* (Anthony Waller, 1997), and *Hostel* (Eli Roth, 2005), about three American backpackers in Slovakia. Horror films have long had a metaphorical and literal interest in borders and boundaries, often the boundaries of the body, but these are also translated into fears relating to the liminality of experience across borders and the abjection of tourist bodies. Often these fears are conservative or reactionary, as fears of Otherness or the unknown experiences of being outside familiar territory (such as forests, oceans and deserts, as in the Australian outback horror *Wolf Creek* (Greg McLean, 2005)), are projected onto 'foreignness' as characters cross or transgress national boundaries.

Narratives about border-crossings or border experience can be fairly diverse, but what we'll explore in this section are works that examine or discuss border-crossings as they relate to migrant journeys or those who become involved in migration in some form or another. Earlier in the chapter we heard briefly about Courtney Hunt's *Frozen River*, about how a single mother's struggle to provide for her children draws her into a people-smuggling operation. An independently produced American film by a female director, the film won the Grand Jury prize at the Sundance festival in 2008. Like *Babel*, it uses family to focus on affinities in cross-border cultures, and Klaus Dodds has referred to it as 'manifestly preoccupied with matters of biopolitics and border crossings, both geographical and social' (2013, p. 561). The film's central character, Ray Eddy (Melissa Leo), is an abandoned mother of two living in New York State, whose Mohawk husband, a compulsive gambler, has absconded with their savings. Her search for her husband takes her across borders, although not across national lines. The film makes it clear that there is a clear cultural and legal divide between the US and Mohawk nations; the Akwesasne St. Regis Reservation has its own police force, and the local force has no jurisdiction there. This encounter between the First and Fourth Worlds reinforces boundary lines within the US, although Ray's poverty seems a far cry from the luxury experienced by the First World middle-class travellers in *Babel*. To alleviate her poverty, she forms an uncomfortable partnership with Lila Littlewolf (Misty Upham), a similarly poverty-stricken Mohawk widow separated from her own son by her mother-in-law. They begin to smuggle undocumented immigrants over the US-Canadian border across the frozen St. Lawrence River because travelling through the reservation allows them to evade detection by the police. During one crossing, they transport a couple from Pakistan; struck by post-9/11 hysteria, Ray panics and throws a bag she suspects may contain a bomb out of the car. Instead, it contains their baby, which they recover alive. A subsequent encounter with a strip club owner, smuggling two Asian women across the border, goes wrong. They battle with the man, and, fleeing, are pursued by the police, resulting in their car breaking the ice, from which the four women escape. Shot in a gritty, realist style, emphasising the stark, grey environment, the film examines fundamental social inequalities, and the geopolitical space occupied by these women, within the US and across the border with Canada. Wilfred Raussert has argued that '*Frozen River* opens up a series of perspectives for conceiving borders as multidimensional in the context of human relationships, legal jurisdiction, and geopolitical power' (2011, p. 20). By focusing on two powerless individuals, Hunt's film stresses the ways in which border-crossings become means of mobility and agency. In some regards, this is symbolised by the first interaction between the two women, which is about Ray's missing husband's car – she turns up at Lila's trailer home with a gun, wrongly believing that her husband is there. This provides mobility for their ability to cross the border, itself a (literally) fluid boundary that is liquid by day, but solid by night. As Raussert notes, this agency allows for a new translocal, trans-ethnic community, Lila raising Ray's and her own children, symbolising a dissolution of psychological boundary lines. The additional border between translocal spaces – the US and the Mohawk nation – provides another space to navigate, one suffused with colonial memories, another signifier of imbalanced power in the film, for the poor white and Native-American women as well as the generally nameless migrants that Ray and Lila smuggle across the border to an uncertain future. As this demonstrates, border narratives need not have a solely global dimension, from one country to another, but can have strongly translocal dimensions, again stressing affinitive and epiphanic transnationalisms, in the ways that globalisation impacts individuals on a local basis, but also in ways in which those discourses intersect here with those relating to power, gender and ethnicity.

Due to the scope of this issue in transnational cinema, it isn't possible to be inclusive of all films that engage with border-crossing in a literal sense, but what we'll do here is look at how this is figured on a regional basis, demonstrating some of the discourses relevant to different kinds of border narratives that can lead to further investigation. In her book, *Immigration Cinema in the New Europe* (2015), Isolina Ballesteros argues that mobility is a central feature of what she calls the Border-Crossing Road Movie. Like the classical iteration of the road movie, Ballesteros contends that there is a central metaphor in the genre that posits the road as a signifier of freedom. In this version of the road movie, the road points west, away from poverty or the realities of persecution. Citing the American roots of the road movie, in the counter-cultural literature of Jack Kerouac, the journey is often one in search of liberation, although it ends in futility. It places a central importance on the journey itself, on the move, but also with passages of stasis that provide means for self-examination. A critical cinematic example might be *Easy Rider* (Dennis Hopper, 1969), in which the two central characters, with a motorcycle gas-tank full of cash from a drug deal set out to discover spiritual transcendence. Instead, they encounter an American south full of bigotry and suspicion, leading to their disillusionment and death on the road at the hands of locals. As it relates to border-crossing narratives:

> the journey is determined by the characters' desperate need to reach the ultimate goal, and their movement across open space is curtailed by visible and invisible borders and thus not necessarily liberating, as it usually carries with it fears of being captured or deported, suffocating inside a vehicle, dehydrating in the desert, or drowning at sea, among other hazards. Border-crossing films are often adaptations of the outlaw road movie, in which characters are on the road out of necessity rather than choice; they are fugitives escaping from oppression, persecution, or economic disadvantage whose liberation depends on the success of their flight, their survival, and their arrival at their destination. (Ballesteros, 2015, p. 179)

Ballesteros gives us several examples of such narratives about the journey to reach Europe and the difficulties of traversing impenetrable borders: *Letters from Alou* (*Las cartas de Alou*, Montxo Armendáriz, 1990); *In This World* (Michael Winterbottom, 2002); *14 Kilometers* (*14 kilómetros*, Gerardo Olivares, 2007); *Return to Hansala* (*Retorno a Hansala*, Chus Gutiérrez, 2008); and *Eden is West* (*Eden à l'Ouest*, Costa-Gavras, 2009). For Ballesteros, each of the films draws attention to the ways in which displacement is presented as the most logical consequence of poverty, war, destruction or oppression, and each is presented in a *cinéma vérité* style. Like Ballesteros, Thomas G. Deveney, in *Migration in Contemporary Hispanic Cinema* (2012), sees a growth of films that have responded to migration from Africa to Europe, and Latin to North America. He draws a direct line between *Letters from Alou* and *14 Kilometers* as part of a core set of films that investigate the impact of African immigration in Spain, which saw a significant wave of immigration (not just from North Africa) in the 1990s and 2000s. Deveney cites figures (p. 4) for Madrid that demonstrate a six-fold increase in immigrant populations, split between EU and non-EU citizens roughly 40 to 60 per cent. The two films that both Deveney and Ballesteros mention follow the experiences of young men who attempt to cross from Africa to Europe. In *Letters from Alou*, the title character arrives in Spain from Senegal by boat, in a frightening sequence at night, and finds himself undocumented and therefore unable to find secure or permanent work. The film uses journeying as an ongoing metaphor (indeed it ends with a series of journeys, by train, by plane and again by boat after Alou is deported). As Ballesteros notes, this second crossing by Alou after his deportation 'defines immigration's circular nature and exposes the futility of border controls in a country that keeps demanding a cheap labor force' (2015, p. 180). The narrative is structured by Alou's voice-over, in the form of letters back home, which demonstrates the importance of links with home, a core theme of many transnational films that posit a strong connection across borders, between those who traverse them and those who are left behind. Indeed, much immigration is based around this connection as migration is often a case of journey to family in other countries, or in advance of a family joining the successful journey once a new home has been established.

14 Kilometers demonstrates a different kind of journey. Taking its title from the distance between the final stretch of the journey between North Africa and the Spanish coast, it follows the attempts of two brothers to reach Europe in search of a better life. The younger of the two brothers, Buba, is a promising footballer, and he is encouraged to make the journey to Europe to try to make it as a professional. He is accompanied by his older brother Mukela as they attempt to travel from Niger across the Sahara. In so doing, they meet Violet, a young girl fleeing an arranged marriage to a much older man. After paying smugglers to transport them across the desert, they are abandoned. Olivares's background is as a documentary filmmaker, and this is demonstrated repeatedly throughout the film – as Ballesteros points out, this is a *cinéma vérité* style (complete with passers-by looking at the camera in uncontrolled crowd scenes) – the narrative drive of the film is weakened, while there is a predominance of handheld cameras. In some regards, this is reminiscent of some of the principles of Third Cinema and the lack of decorative *mise en scène*. However, the film also offsets the claustrophobia of many scenes with wide shots of the engulfing Sahara and the smallness of the characters (Olivares has also made many wildlife documentaries). The final crossing to Spain is shot with the familiar green look of night vision cameras

Figure 4.2   After their long journey across the desert, in *14 Kilometers* (Gerardo Olivares, 2007) Buba and Mukela join other migrants to make the journey across the titular 14-kilometre sea crossing at night (Explora Films/Wanda Visión S.A.)

(Figure 4.2) – again demonstrating a documentary aesthetic (although we're used to this from many war films and 'real war' footage on YouTube) – and harks back to the journey of Alou, and an image with which we're becoming very familiar from news footage, of migrants crammed into a small boat for a pitch-dark crossing; the *mise en scène* reminds us how uncertain and terrifying this journey is for those who undertake it. We don't see the landing, though, just the aftermath as the two boys are immediately discovered and chased by a policeman. What many of these border narratives demonstrate is a focus on characters who might be defined through their Otherness, or through the processes by which they are Othered: racism, legal border controls (or their futility), exploitation and violence. There are many more examples of films that focus on these issues, or that turn border-crossing journeys into metaphors for relationships between nations in a transregional or translocal sense, as we've seen above. For reasons of space, it's not possible to explore all of these in detail, and so you are encouraged to seek out your own examples, with the list at the end of this section as a starting point.

The migrant journey across the borders between North Africa and Europe is mirrored in films from different regions. Winterbottom's *In this World* is, like *14 Kilometers*, a docudrama, this time about two Afghan refugees attempting to reach one of their uncles in England from Pakistan, across Iran (twice), through the mountains to Turkey by foot. From there, they are transported to Italy by people smugglers in an unventilated container, in which many migrants, including one of the two protagonists, suffocate.

The surviving character, Jamal, eventually reaches France, and the Sangatte camp near Calais (which was closed in 2002, during the film's production, after rioting), from which he is able to hide on a lorry to make it to London, where he's refused asylum. This journey is echoed in another film, *Welcome* (Phillipe Lioret, 2009), about a Kurdish Iraqi refugee who has made it to Calais (this time to the camp known as 'The Jungle') and decides to swim the Channel to England, to join his girlfriend, but can't swim. The core of the film follows the relationship that builds between him and the French swimming coach who agrees to teach him for the journey.

Contemporary discourses around migrants and migration have often used dehumanising language, such as then-Prime Minister David Cameron's comment in 2015 that the refugees in Calais were a 'swarm' (which might remind us of insects), presenting refugees and migrants as sub-human or animalistic. This echoes some of the discourses around colonial Others (many refugees are leaving former European colonies); therefore many border, or cross-border, stories engage with these discourses, looking at some of the ways in which refuges are Othered, or related legal processes, such as policy around border controls, undocumented people, refugee camps and people smuggling. Such films are strongly marked as transnational – they take place in multiple countries and languages – and they encourage thinking about transnationalism, about how globalisation impacts individuals and social groups who are disenfranchised, persecuted or oppressed. Unlike those tourists in *Babel*, these are people without the advantages of cosmopolitanism, unable to travel as a luxury or for economic purposes, for whom attempts to cross borders are dangerous, obstructed and subject to public perception that can often see them as sub-human.

Another border area that echoes these concerns is the border between the US and Mexico. We've seen how the border between Canada and the US has been imagined, but there is a much broader group of films that investigate the US-Mexican border. There has been a long tradition of both Mexico and America making films about immigration and crime along the border areas, and the experiences of those who cross the border. These range from major Hollywood films, such as *Babel*, *No Country for Old Men* (Joel and Ethan Coen, 2007) and *The Three Burials of Melquiades Estrada* (Tommy Lee Jones, 2005), to the Charles Bronson-starring revenge film *Borderline* (Jerrold Freeman, 1980), *Touch of Evil* (Orson Welles, 1958), with Charlton Heston in Latino-face (a term used by Brian D. Behnken and Gregory D. Smithers in their book *Racism in American Popular Media* (2015), although brownface is a more commonly used term for white actors playing Latino characters), or *Border Run*, starring Sharon Stone (Gabriela Tagliavini, 2012). The setting is also relevant to popular television series such as *Breaking Bad* (2008–2013), *Weeds*

(2005–2012), and the animated show *Bordertown* (2016). As the subject matter of the former two shows testifies, the border can be presented as a place of lawlessness and criminality, and Mexican characters can be stereotyped as gangbangers or undocumented workers (often without names). These are not strongly marked transnational texts – they have a transnational dimension in the ways that they frame the border region, but there is little attempt to encourage thinking about categories of the transnational or ideological problems relating to the border.

This is not to say that Mexican films about the border and immigration have always been sensitive portrayals, although they may constitute counter-hegemonic approaches. David R. Maciel identified dozens of examples of films about immigration and crime around the US-Mexican border, in his short book *El Norte: The U.S.-Mexican Border in Contemporary Cinema*, published in 1990. They range from *The Deported Ones* (*Deportados*, Arturo Martinez, 1977) to *Santo and the Border of Terror* (*Santo en la Frontera del Terror*, Rafael Pérez Grovas, 1969), starring the popular wrestler El Santo. Maciel finds these films to be formulaic, sharing more or less the same elements:

(a) production is done purely for commercial and exploitative purposes, (b) there is an excessive use of violence and sex, (c) the plots and action usually take place with the United States, (d) the main emphasis is on violence and oppression directed at Mexican workers by Anglo-American individuals and institutions, and (e) generally, there is a total disregard for the 'push' factors within Mexico that are partially responsible for immigration. Never shown are the structural problems, political questions, and the socio-economic effects of the contemporary Mexican crisis upon society. (Maciel, 1990, pp. 42–45)

In some sense, Maciel here defines an exploitation cinema, a generic term for filmmaking that capitalises upon popular trends or ideas for short-term financial return. In defining this, however, he notes several films to have been very popular – hence there are affinities here with films such as *The Big Boss* (*Táng Shān Dà Xiōng*, Lo Wei, 1971) or *Way of the Dragon* (*Měng Lóng Guò Jiāng*, Bruce Lee, 1972), both starring Bruce Lee, about cross-border exploitation or oppression of workers. Similarly, neither of these two films make serious examinations of the issues confronting migrant workers and the reasons for emigration, they merely use their scenarios as a means to make populist statements on the oppression of migrant workers by exploitative owners, or the mafia in the case of *Way of the Dragon*, which even begins in an airport, a liminal space in-between national boundaries that marks its central character as an Othered body (Figure 4.3).

Figure 4.3 *The Way of the Dragon* (Bruce Lee, 1972): Bruce Lee's body is Othered by the gaze of the white woman as they wait in the airport's liminal space (Concord Productions/Golden Harvest)

Case study: *Sleep Dealer* (Alex Rivera, 2008)

Subsequent to Maciel's study, there have been many films that have examined the US-Mexican border from different perspectives, from independent American and Mexican cinemas. This would include *Lone Star* (John Sayles, 1996), *Under the Same Moon* (*La Misma Luna*, Patricia Riggen, 2007), *Backyard* (*El Traspatio*, Carlos Carrera, 2009), *Sin Nombre* (Cary Jôji Fukunaga, 2009), *Monsters* (Gareth Edwards, 2010) and *Cronos* (Guillermo Del Toro, 1992). Francisco R. Monar (2014) has argued that these form a genre that he refers to as *fronterizo*, 'a category of films in which issues related to *la frontera* form the overarching narrative or thematic structure'. Some, such as *Sin Nombre* and *Under the Same Moon*, follow those who are attempting to cross the border to reach family (a Honduran family in the former, and a 9-year-old boy in the latter), while others explore issues of neo-colonialism (*Cronos*, about the vampiric corporate relationship between the US and Mexico), or global capitalism and the *maquiladoras*, manufacturing plants owned by multinational corporations (*Backyard*, based on the real-life case involving the deaths of hundreds of women around the *maquiladoras* in Juárez).

The film we'll look at more closely in this section is a science fiction film that tackles issues around outsourced or migrant labour, difficulties in traversing boundaries, and American foreign policy towards Third World nations. Alex Rivera's *Sleep Dealer* (2008) is a prophetic dystopian vision of the near future in which the US has built a wall along the border with Mexico. Behind the wall are thousands of migrant workers – instead of crossing the border, they work in shops in which they're plugged into a *Matrix*-style cyber network through nodes in their arms and torsos

Figure 4.4 *Sleep Dealer's* (Alex Rivera, 2008) factories echo the maquiladoras of the real Tijuana, with multiple workers packed into cramped spaces (Likely Story/This Is That Productions)

(Figure 4.4). They are 'sleep dealers', so called because they are likely to collapse if they work long enough (a term taken by Rivera from John Berger's *A Seventh Man*, about migration in Europe, where sleep dealers would rent beds, by the hour, to migrants in search of work in Northern Europe who are too exhausted to carry on (Carroll, 2014, p. 223)). When our hero Memo (Luis Fernando Peña) takes on his first job in the sleep dealer shop, his foreman explains to him:

> This is the American dream. We give the United States what they've always wanted – all the work, without the workers. Jose is in a slaughter-house in Iowa. Maria is a nanny for a little girl in Washington. You three will be on a big job in San Diego. Plug in, your future starts today.

Here, the foreman explains one of the key issues in the film regarding migrant labour – the neoliberal, neo-colonial economy requires and demands cheap migrant labour, but they are not willing to deal with the workers themselves, to provide health care and social security. The film is partly a follow-up to an earlier short film by Rivera entitled *Why Cybraceros?* (1997), which cut together archival footage from government films promoting cross-border migration from Mexico to the US with that of violence against such border-crossers. The resulting solution is the creation of 'cybraceros', robots remotely controlled by Mexican workers in Mexico: 'all the labour without the worker', the film brags. The term cybraceros is also seen in *Sleep Dealer* on a sign in the factory. In both films, the term refers to an earlier American experiment, the bracero programme (that ran between 1942 and 1964), which encouraged controlled immigration by temporary guest workers, mainly to fill demand for workers in the agrarian sector (in *Why Cybraceros?* the robots are seen working in orange groves), a need intensified by America's entry into the Second World War. As Thomas Prasch quotes Rivera, the programme was fraught with tensions, bringing 'racial and economic suspicions' (Prasch, 2013, p. 44). The programme existed alongside ongoing undocumented migration, which led to a counter-response, a conservative crackdown in the 1950s known as 'Operation Wetback', that brought forced deportations. *Sleep Dealer* deals with many of these tensions, racial and economic, that have existed in the wake of these programmes and waves of immigration.

Prasch argues that one of the distinctive features of *Sleep Dealer* is its approach to genre, that 'relocates the film's center, taking us from traditional metropoles to the Third-World fringes of transnational labor mobilization' (p. 45). The film begins in the rural town of Santa Ana Del Rio, in Oaxaca province. Memo's father is a farmer whose efforts have been complicated by the damming of the local river by a company in San Diego, repurposing the water for commercial and metropolitan purposes. Water has become an expense commodity – Memo and his father, faced with machine guns and surveillance cameras, must buy water by the bag. Two small bags cost them $85. While his brother watches American television, Memo teaches himself hacking, and he builds a small radio with which he taps into the local satellite network to eavesdrop on others. In so doing, though, he inadvertently taps into a frequency used by the local water company's security forces. Due to widespread fears of 'aqua-terrorists', Memo and his family are targeted. Later, Memo is watching TV with his brother; they are watching a show called *Drones*, which shows live drone strikes against criminals and terrorists in Mexico. They suddenly realise that the terrorist target in this show is their family home; they escape, but their father is killed. It's after this that Memo moves to Tijuana (in reality, home to around 700 maquiladoras, making everything from Nike shoes to medical products), and meets Luz Martínez (Leonor Varela) en route there. She is a 'writer' who tries, with little success, to sell memories on TruNode (similar to an online video platform). It's only when she uploads her meeting with Memo (entitled 'A Migrant from Santa Ana Del Rio') that she meets some interest. The buyer asks her to learn more about the migrant and his background, and so she begins a relationship with him. We eventually learn that the interested buyer is Rudy Ramirez (Jacob Vargas), an inexperienced drone pilot who piloted the strike against Memo and his family. Rudy is also a node worker, and the son of a migrant family. He begins a quest to find Memo and quiet his conscience.

The film is shot in a combination of realist style and sci-fi techno-fetish-ism (literally in some cases, as the nodes are sexualised, alongside the film's focus on the fetishism for drones as a gamified form of war), something Rivera has referred to as 'third world cyberpunk' (Prasch, 2013, p. 45). As Prasch notes, the film's relocation away from major metropoles, such as Los Angeles, Hong Kong or Tokyo, to the border town reminds us of the impact and consequence of neo-colonial and transnational economic policies that exploit migrant workers while also casting them as Others. The scenes in which Memo, plugged into the factory, works on the construction site in San Diego demonstrate the highly alienating form of this labour. In one sense his labour is alienated, owned by the capitalist system, not by the individual worker. On another, it is more literally alienating. At one point he looks into the mirror and sees 'himself' reflected. But of course he doesn't see his body, he sees the robot, the cyber body that he controls (Figure 4.5).

Unlike those who can travel south, Memo and other Mexicans are not permitted the mobility to cross the border. Their only mobility is in the economic value of their labour, but not their value as human beings, only as service robots. Not that cross-border mobility is encouraged for those to cross the other way – the *Drones* show presents Mexico as a lawless land of dangerous aqua-terrorists unsafe for those travelling from the First World. When Rudy attempts to cross into Mexico, he is confronted with a giant sign that warns him that he crosses 'at his own risk'. At the border, he is met with a similar kind of machine gun surveillance camera that challenged Memo and his father at the water station (this presumably is another disembodied node worker). He is aggressively questioned about why he would want to go to Mexico, why he hasn't crossed in 12 years, and about his safety. The border is presented as a heavily militarised zone

Figure 4.5 *Sleep Dealer* (Alex Rivera, 2008): The alienating mirror reflection of Memo's robot body reminds us the alienation of his labour, his self Othered for its production value (Likely Story/This Is That Productions)

(citing Douglas Massey, Prasch (p. 49) also notes how this border in reality is the most heavily militarised border in the world between two neighbours at peace), unlike in *Babel*, where mobility into Mexico is relatively simple; it was returning that was fraught with tension. Samantha Kountz (as Maciel did earlier) points out how Hollywood representations of Mexico have tended to highlight these dangerous aspects of the US-Mexican border, in films like *Traffic* (Steven Soderbergh, 2000), 'a typical, damaging representation of Mexico as a land of poverty and a harbor for drug lords, where even its most reputable citizens turn out to be corrupt cops' (2015, p. 294). *Sleep Dealer*, through its reference to cross-border media (Memo's brother's obsession with American television) interrogates some of this stereotyping of the border region, as one filled with terrorists and criminals whose deaths are presented live on television for entertainment, in a crass *Cops*-style show. This engages with the ways in which the media characterises cross-border issues and the highly imbalanced transnational and transregional power relationships across such areas, as well as how transnational and neo-colonial economies exploit migrant workers, taking the value of their labour without providing them with recourse to legal rights (to make them 'documented'). *Sleep Dealer's* sci-fi response to such an imbalance highlights the economic, racial, political and identity issues complicated by transnational commerce and political policy that impact on those living in poverty and under persecution. The implications of these issues and of the violence often inherent in cross-border interactions and journeys are, as we've seen in this section of the chapter, common in films that deal with cross-border relationships or journeys. Whether we look at borders between Africa or the Middle East and Europe, between East and West Europe, in Latin America, between Latin and North America, and across tense political borders, such as those between North and South Korea, or Israel and Palestine, there are many issues that recur about racial, ethnic, economic or political considerations as well as the ways in which media representations stereotype, Other or demonise migrants or those who cross borders for many reasons.

Recommended viewing:

Born in East L.A. (Cheech Marin, 1987)
The Promise (*La Promesse*, Jean-Pierre and Luc Dardenne, 1996)
Bread and Roses (Ken Loach, 2000)
From the Other Side (*De l'autre côté*, Chantal Akerman, 2002)
Ghosts (Nick Broomfield, 2006)
Norteado (Rigoberto Perezcano, 2009)
Incendies (Denis Villeneuve, 2010)
Le Havre (Aki Kaurismäki, 2012)

Recommended further reading:

Anzaldúa, Gloria (2007), *Borderlands/La Frontera: The New Mestiza*, 3rd edition. San Francisco: Aunt Lute.

Brayton, Sean (2011), 'Razing Arizona: *Migrant Labour* and the 'Mexican Avenger' of *Machete*', *International Journal of Media & Cultural Politics* 7(3): pp. 275–292.

Deleyto, Celestino (2016), 'Looking from the Border: a Cosmopolitan Approach to Contemporary Cinema', *Transnational Cinemas* 8(2): pp. 95–112.

Dell'agnese, Ella (2005), 'The US–Mexico Border in American Movies: A Political Geography Perspective', *Geopolitics* 10(2): pp. 204–221.

Dickinson, Kay (2016), *Arab Cinema Travels: Transnational Syria, Palestine, Dubai and Beyond*. London: Palgrave Macmillan.

Kazecki, Jakub, Karen A. Ritzenhoff and Cynthia J. Miller, eds (2013), *Border Visions: Identity and Diaspora in Film*. Lanham: Scarecrow.

Mendes, Ana Cristina, and John Sundholm, eds (2015), Special Issue: Walls and Fortresses: Borderscapes and the Cinematic Imaginary, *Transnational Cinemas* 6(2).

Rosen, Philip (2006), 'Border Times and Geopolitical Frames', *Canadian Journal of Film Studies* 15(2): pp. 2–19.

Villazana, Libia (2013), 'Transnational Virtual Mobility as a Reification of Deployment of Power: Exploring Transnational Processes in the Film *Sleep Dealer*', *Transnational Cinemas* 4(2): pp. 217–230.

Wells, Sarah Ann (2014), 'The Scar and the Node: Border Science Fiction and the Mise-en-scène of Globalized Labor', *Global South* 8(1): pp. 69–90.

Discussion questions:

- Might we be able to see border-crossing films as a genre?
- How can we tell the difference between films *about* globalisation and films that are *products* of globalisation?
- In what ways could marked and unmarked transnational films help us think more about living in a globalised world?
- In what manner do you think films about migration could help challenge dominant media representations of migrants?
- How might thinking about literal borders help us to address questions about more conceptual borders, like race, sexuality or gender?

CHAPTER 5

Exilic and Diasporic Cinema

As an alternative to concepts of transnational cinema that struggle to locate a place for the postcolonial, Will Higbee has suggested a *trans*vergent cinema. Unlike a convergent cinema that is moving to a point of synthesis or consensus, the transvergent cinema 'aims to explore and foreground (celebrate even)' difference, where nationalist discourses would tend to 'paper over the cracks'. Hence, 'transvergence allows for a myriad of possibilities, an open-ended challenge to the fixed positionings typically offered by hegemonic structures of knowledge and power' (2007, p. 85). Previous binaries and hierarchies of centre/margins, self/other would no longer be applicable to such a construct open to potential chaos. He argues that the transvergent cinema becomes a potent means through which to explore postcolonial and diasporic cinemas as specifically transcultural in their relationship between global and local dimensions because they operate, not within a globalised framework but through a contextualised understanding of the hierarchised structures of power that ground filmmakers in specific national identities or cultures at a given time. This would be an 'engaged (politicized) site of resistance which foregrounds the experiences of the alienated, marginal other' (p. 87). The Algerian émigré filmmakers at the core of Higbee's argument are those that are neither purely national nor fully transnational, but 'negotiate a position that, at different times and in different contexts, alternates "between" French and Algerian cinema, while still maintaining a distinct position "within" the two film cultures and industries' (p. 88).

It is these filmmakers who move 'between positions of centre and margin' (p. 90) with whom we are concerned in this chapter, filmmakers who occupy often interstitial places in film cultures, but whose identities and politics are formed through identification with another culture, either through choice, by birth or by force. In this look at exilic and diasporic cinemas, we'll look closely at some key thinkers in transnational cinemas; this includes Laura U. Marks' concept of intercultural cinema and Hamid Naficy's notion of 'accented' cinemas, which challenge how we think about movements or filmmakers that mediate the relationship between local and global. This mediation is explored in ways that engage with the issues of history, power and identity that previously defined Third Cinema or the postcolonial.

Diaspora

One of the key dimensions of films and filmmakers that address border-crossing is diaspora, a term we've heard several times already in this book. The word diaspora, from the Greek, *diaspeirein* (meaning disperse), and comprising *dia* (across) and *speirein* (scatter) refers to groups of people who have been dispersed or spread from their original homeland. As Hamid Naficy describes it:

> Diaspora, like exile, often begins with trauma, rupture, and coercion, and it involves the scattering of populations to places outside their homeland. Sometimes, however, the scattering is caused by a desire for increased trade, for work, or for colonial and imperial pursuits. (2001, p. 14)

For many individuals, that scattering is caused by traumas relating to war, such as the migration of Syrians to Lebanon and Europe in 2016, fleeing the conflict involving Bashar al-Assad's state forces, a collection of oppositional forces across ideological divides, and the Jihadist Daesche (also ISIS or Islamic State), along with armed forces from the west and Kurdish forces. In June 2015, the United Nations High Commissioner for Refugees had reported that nearly 12 million people were displaced due to the conflict within and outside Syria (around five million outside the country). Many of those reaching Europe will settle in pre-existing diasporic communities, such as those in Germany, many of whom are of Kurdish descent. There is also a substantial Syrian diasporic community in Brazil. Other diasporic communities arose due to imperial concerns, such as Indians who left India to work in other parts of the British Empire (Naficy refers to these as 'labour/service diasporas'); for instance, many Punjabi workers were exported from Imperial India to Kenya to work as railway labourers, some of whom later settled in Britain (we'll return to this later in the chapter).

Higbee and Lim saw questions of diaspora and postcolonialism as central within transnational cinema, where films examine the 'consequences of ... uprootings and re-groundings ... frequently considered in the collective context of diaspora' (2010, p. 11). Productions such as these are continually examining and renegotiating the interrelatedness of global and local dimensions of diasporic communities (this might be through representation, as well as in questions of identity for diasporic filmmakers themselves), and relationships between home and host cultures. We'll return to issues such as these when we consider more fully the critical transnationalism of Hamid Naficy's approach to exilic and diasporic cinemas.

Since the 1980s, Britain has seen the growth of a wave of South Asian-British cinema produced by first generation South Asian-British writers and directors that have explored issues relating to diasporic identity in contemporary Britain. Key figures include Hanif Kureishi, writer of *My Beautiful Laundrette* (Stephen Frears, 1985) and *My Son the Fanatic* (Udayan Prasad, 1997); Meera Syal, an actor and writer, whose films include *Anita & Me* (Metin Hüseyin, 2002); playwright and screenwriter Ayub Khan-Din, author of *East is East* (Damien O'Donnell, 1999) and *West is West* (Andy De Emmony, 2010); and Harwant Bains, writer of *Wild West* (David Attwood, 1993). Perhaps the best-known figure in this group, certainly the one to achieve the most mainstream success, is the writer-director Gurinder Chadha. Chadha's films include: *Bhaji on the Beach* (1993), about a group of Indian women, including residents of a women's shelter, on a day out at the seaside in Blackpool; *Bend it Like Beckham* (2002), which follows the attempts of a teenage girl to break free of tradition to become a footballer; *Bride and Prejudice* (2004), a mash-up of Jane Austen in a Bollywood-style masala; and *Viceroy's House* (2017), about India's transition to independence. Born to Punjabi parents in Kenya, Chadha moved to Southall in West London when she was two years old. Near Heathrow airport, Southall is home to a large Sikh Punjabi community, and this has been the background for some of Chadha's work, including *Bend it Like Beckham* and her documentary work, such as *I'm British But...* (1989).

As Higbee and Lim argue, transnational filmmakers such as Chadha need not be 'ghettoize[d] ... in interstitial and marginal spaces' but can help us understand how their filmmaking practice negotiates 'with the national on all levels – from cultural policy to financial sources, from the multiculturalism of difference to how it reconfigures the nation's image of itself' (Higbee & Lim, 2010, p. 18). Critical of the ongoing focus on marginal cinematic practice, they explain how the 'deliberate focus on experimental and interstitial film-making ..., while reflecting the fact that ethnic minority and diasporic filmmaking continue to be marginalized within the West, cannot account for the recent mainstreaming of diasporic or postcolonial film-makers' (p. 13). Chadha is one of their examples. In many cases, this ongoing marginalisation can place a heavy burden on filmmakers as representative of underrepresented groups. As Meera Syal put it:

> Everything we do becomes representative ... If *West Is West*, *Anita and Me* and *Bend it Like Beckham* all came out in the same year, then you would be judged more fairly. But usually it's one Asian film a year, if that. (Manzoor, 2011)

While diasporic communities are often marginalised, Chadha's films represent a prominent example of how films can reflect and question issues of diasporic identity.

Bend it Like Beckham follows the attempts of the teenage daughter of a Punjabi Sikh family in Southall to be allowed to play football. Jasminder Bhamra (Parminder Nagra), known by the more westernised Jess to her friends, is infatuated with the game. In the film's opening scene, she dreams of playing for Manchester United, scoring a winning goal from a David Beckham cross, after which TV pundits Gary Lineker, Alan Hansen and John Barnes, from the long-running British television programme *Match of the Day*, discuss her performance as a potential England saviour. The dream is disrupted by the presence of her mother (Shaheen Khan), who demands she come home because she shouldn't be 'showing her bare legs to 70,000 people'. Much of the conflict in the film is expressed cross-generationally, a younger generation expressing a more hybridised identity, against a staid and conservative older generation (older women are presented as being the most resistant to change). The film doesn't simply explore this in terms of cultural identity, it's also expressed in terms of gender. Jess's friend Juliette, known as Jules (Keira Knightley), experiences similar conflict; her mother (Juliet Stevenson) believes she's too masculine, and later becomes convinced that Jess and Jules's relationship is a gay one, a misconception shared by some of Jess's family's friends. In many regards, this cross-generational theme is shared with other films in British-Asian cinema, particularly *East is East*, which uses similar tropes of gender, sexuality, religion and naming to explore diasporic identity and the shifting poles of home and host cultures in multicultural society.

Food and dress play key roles in both films (Figure 5.1). In *Bend it Like Beckham*, Mrs Bhamra is concerned that her daughters, especially Jess, will be unable to make good wives if traditional duties are neglected. 'What kind of family,' she asks, 'would want a daughter-in-law who can kick a football around all day but can't make round chapatis?' It's notable too that Jess has a scar on her leg from an accident while trying to make baked beans on toast (an English staple) as a child. As Guido Rings explains, films such as these demonstrate cross-cultural and transnational hybridity, in which 'cultural boundaries are transgressed, and it is usually second-generation migrants who select more or less consciously what aspects of each cultural background are acceptable and preferable for them' (2011, p. 117). Other scholars have similarly commented on the ways in which the film draws together different cultural spaces and rituals to demonstrate the experiences of being between two cultures, or within a blending of the two. Discussing Chadha's cross-cutting of the film's finale, in which Jess must choose between her sister's wedding and an important match, Irene Gedalof argues that:

Chadha offers a ... nuanced relationship between the two spaces. Both are sites of sexism, homophobia, and unequal gender dynamics, but

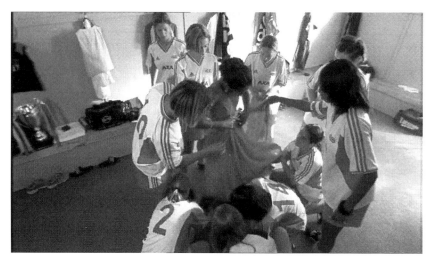

Figure 5.1 *Bend it Like Beckham* (Gurinder Chadha, 2002): Jess's teammates participate in dressing her to return to her sister's wedding, emphasising the blending of home traditions with host cultures (Bend It Films)

both are also sites of the embodied pleasures of the different rituals of dance and sport and of investment in and the pleasures of connectedness. It is the ways in which they are 'differently similar' that make it both necessary and possible for a girl like Jess to navigate both spaces. (2011, p. 138)

For Gedalof, this is a way in which older binaries of west and the rest might be destabilised, as a means of understanding changes not just in Britain, but across Europe (her comparison is with another film that concerns migrant experience, Paweł Pawlikowski's *Last Resort* (2000), about a Russian woman and her son awaiting an asylum application to be considered after they arrive in Britain). For Rings, though, this is more problematic. At the film's fantasy resolution, Jess and Jules leave for America, defined in the film as a paradise for women's football, and therefore for equality. This defines the 'lead culture' as distinctly Anglo-American for Rings, Jess as less hybrid, more English in her cultural status. The film's references to colonialism through her father's humiliation at the hands of English cricketers who shunned him 'like a dog' when he arrived from Nairobi (this passage from Punjab to Kenya and then to England mirrors that of Chadha's own family) are negotiated through his own rejection of that racism and his appeal to her to go and fight for what she wants. This throws the film back into the split between the west and the rest for Rings (unlike for Gedalof, who sees it as more complicated, through a lens of transnational cinema), in that Jess must choose between a monocultural Indian heritage or an Anglo-American one:

> you are either fully trapped in traditional Indian customs and cannot even prepare beans on toast without seriously injuring yourself, or you are fully geared up for an Anglo-American way of life marked by the capitalist cult of football heroes and do not want to cook Punjabi food, dress up traditionally, or pray to Guru Nanak, because it simply does not fit. (Rings, 2011, p. 121)

Rings sees the home and exterior spaces of the film as binary opposites, not the more equivalent spaces that Gedalof identifies, where the negotiation of 'differently similar' spaces are both alienating for Jess in different ways, and therefore make it possible for her to negotiate the two. Rings sees a more colonialist, self-Othering message:

> The solution proposed is for the Oriental Other to finally adapt to modern times, for his or her own sake and for everybody's well-being, which implies that the happy ending depends on the assimilation of Anglo-American cultural traits by all the main characters. (p. 122)

However we see this resolution in terms of the ways in which characters negotiate their hybrid diasporic identities culturally, we do see an example of how mainstream cinema has engaged with the politics of multiculturalism and transnationality (albeit in a way that is more playful than strongly politically engaged). We don't simply see such issues being discussed at the margins of art cinema, as Higbee and Lim demonstrated. *Bend it Like Beckham* is a key example that considers the second generation push and pull between hybridised identities, between the originary homeland and host culture. Diasporas often have a strong connection with homeland, which can be on a nostalgic or mythic level, that can produce a tension between the two cultures, particularly for those who are born in the new culture, as is the case for Jasminder/Jess or the children of the family in *East is East*.

Accented cinemas

Hamid Naficy's book *An Accented Cinema: Exilic and Diasporic Filmmaking* (2001) is one of the seminal works of theorisation about transnational cinemas. Naficy's book dovetails significantly with many of the themes that we've covered so far, about national, postcolonial, and transnational cinemas. As he contends, 'accented cinema not only constitutes a transnational cinema and identity but also is a constitutive part of the national cinemas and national identity' (2001, p. 95). He cites several film and video workshops in Britain by black British and Asian-British collectives that he argues made a distinctive contribution to broadening the scope of what was considered a British national cinema at the time. An accented cinema expands the parameters of what is defined as a national cinema, although, since it engages with aspects of border-crossing and is a particular mode of production, it is necessarily transnational as well. But, as we've seen a number of times already in the book, the very concept of the transnational does not do away with or replace thinking about national cinemas, but intersects strongly with the national on a number of levels. As Higbee and Lim also argue, this area of transnational cinema significantly acts as a critique of the national from the margins to the centre:

> Indeed, many of these transnational productions emerge from within a specifically diasporic configuration that, implicitly or explicitly, articulates the relationship between the host and home cultures, and is aware, at the same time, of the interconnectedness between the local and the global within diasporic communities. Such a cinema can be defined as transnational in the sense that it brings into question how fixed ideas of a national film culture are constantly being transformed by the presence of protagonists (and indeed film-makers) who have a presence within the nation, even if they exist on its margins, but find their origins quite clearly beyond it. (Higbee & Lim, 2010, p. 11)

This interconnectedness is also shared with Higbee's focus on transvergent cinemas that began the chapter. The category that encompasses accented cinema is 'a mammoth, emergent, transnational film movement and film style' (Naficy, 2001, p. 19) where it 'may be difficult to appreciate [its] geographic dispersion and the massive size' (p. 17) and, as such, 'unlike most film movements and styles of the past, [it] is not monolithic, cohesive, centralized, or hierarchized. Rather it is simultaneously global and local, and it exists in chaotic pockets in symbiosis with the dominant and other alternative cinemas' (p. 19). This final point of Naficy's is perhaps the strongest indicator of what constitutes an accented cinema: it is an alternative mode of cinematic production and expression, one produced by figures who are linked critically to national cultures and are either beyond those national boundaries or within others, in exile and/or diaspora. The figures that Naficy discusses range across many countries and regions: Latin America, Lithuania, Iran, Turkey, Palestine, Russia, and diasporic filmmakers with roots in many countries, in that, for instance, the hyphenated term 'Asian-American' might encompass roots as diverse as the Philippines, Vietnam, Cambodia, Korea, Japan, Thailand, China, Laos, Taiwan, Indonesia, Malaysia, India, Bangladesh and Pakistan.

Accented filmmakers are interstitial figures. They exist in spaces between different national or social formations, as well as within the interstices of cinematic practice. Most accented filmmakers are either independent and/ or experimental filmmakers, and many, Naficy notes, are from Third World or post-colonial countries, having, for one reason or another, relocated to northern metropoles. The filmmakers are 'products of [a] dual postcolonial displacement and postmodern or late modern scattering ... They have earned the right to speak and have dared to capture their means of representation' (p. 11). Again, this restates the scale of the accented cinema, across many different countries, identities and modes of production, with a range of differences from and connections with numerous dominant and alternative filmmaking cultures.

Dominant cinema, Naficy posits, is universal and without accent (realistic, for entertainment and free from explicit ideological commentary). The accent is not so much the accented voices in the film, although this is a consideration for Naficy, but an articulation of the displacement of the filmmakers and their production modes. To speak with an accented *cinematic* voice is to speak through alternative modes of address and production: a film produced in an artisanal, collective or independent mode might by accented, but that doesn't make it an exilic or diasporic film. The accent can also be a signifier of assimilation or legitimisation rather than defiance, and as such accented cinema 'is one of the dialects of our language of cinema' (p. 26). Exilic and diasporic cinema is produced in the connection between the filmmaker's and audience's deterritorialised location *and* through alternative modes of production. The accented style is both accent and dialect, permeating the 'deep structure' of a film: narrative, visual style, characters, subject matter, theme and plot (p. 23). Authorship and autobiography are key parts of the accent, as signs of the filmmaker's interstitial positioning, their deterritorialisation between host and home culture. They are not just texts, the postmodern position on authorship, as exclaimed by Roland Barthes (1978) or Michel Foucault (1979); for Naficy, they are real 'empirical' people. Their experiences and autobiographies have a significant impact on what they are attempting to express: to 'signify and signify upon exile and diaspora by expressing, allegorizing, commenting upon, and critiquing home and host societies and cultures' (p. 4).

Accented films are part of the legacy of Third Cinema, but accented films can be found anywhere, made anywhere or about any subject. Also, where Third Cinema was chiefly a Marxist cinema concerned with critiquing the First World and its neo-colonial intrusions and their impact on the proletarian masses, accented cinema takes its subject matter from specific individuals, ethnicities, nationalities and identities and the experience of being or becoming deterritorialised in exile or diaspora. Naficy mentions how

Fernando Solanas, one of the co-authors of the Third Cinema manifesto in the 1960s became an accented filmmaker in the 1970s and 1980s, making films in exile in Paris, including *Tangos, the Exile of Gardel* (*El exilio de Gardel: Tangos*, 1985), about exiled Argentinians producing tangos (a signifier of their connection to a home culture). This is an example of the ways in which, on the level of plot, 'Accented films ... usually posit the homeland as a grand and deeply rooted referent' (p. 27).

These formerly Third World filmmakers have become 'shifters,' exhibiting 'multiple perspectives, and conflicted or performed identities'. This is partly down to a 'border consciousness' that is liminal and where multiple, contradictory or divergent factors and identities converge or intersect, such as race, class or gender, or where 'membership of ... antagonistic, historical and national identities' might overlap. As we've already seen, borders can be uncertain or violent spaces, dangerous for those forced (or attempting) to cross them. Border consciousness or subjectivity is necessarily 'cross-cultural and intercultural', and border films (again, as we've seen) are characterised by:

> multifocality [awareness of multiple cultural emphases or ways of thinking], multilinguality [rendered in more than one spoken language], asynchronicity [temporally discontinuous, such as the use of flashbacks through epistolarity, such as letters or spoken words sent home], critical distance [a self-conscious narrational style, something we haven't always seen in some of the examples of border narratives], fragmented or multiple subjectivities [characters who are split between hybrid or performed identities], transborder amphibolic characters [ambiguous characters in flux who live contextually in the moment]. pp. 31–32

Given the scale of his project, we don't have time to summarise all of Naficy's examples and the many films he discusses. Instead, this section will briefly outline the key elements of the accented style, and we'll see how they can be applied through our case studies: *The Edge of Heaven* (*Auf der anderen Seite*, 2007), directed by Turkish-German diasporic filmmaker Fatih Akin, who has become a highly celebrated example of someone whose films engage with the politics of diasporic identity; and later when we explore the work of the Armenian-Canadian filmmaker Atom Egoyan, someone whose work has straddled both the independent cinema mainstream and works that explore intercultural connectivity, memory and hyphenated identity.

Naficy summarises the accented style under a number of headings. These are: visual style; narrative structure; characters/actors; subject matter/ theme/plot; structures of feeling; filmmaker's location; mode of production. We'll explore these category by category, bearing in mind that not all accented films will demonstrate all of these properties; they may demonstrate few or many, depending on the film (accented cinema is not homogeneous nor a unified style).

Visual style encompasses the overall look and narrative pacing of the film. Plots are usually driven more by word and emotion than by action, and are often rough, even amateurish, and lacking in closure. In many regards, this is seen in much of the realist *cinéma vérité* of many accented films. Films often use real locations, tight enclosed interiors (often with strong ethnic coding), frequently juxtaposed with exteriors emphasising the immenseness of the homeland. Many accented films are set in transitional, liminal spaces, such as airports, train or bus stations. The style therefore often oscillates between closed and open framing, the closed frame signifying entrapment and enclosure, and the open frame its opposite: potential, or exhilaration.

Narrative structure: Naficy contends that films in the accented mode are often concerned with forms of epistolarity (a work in the form of written letters). For cinema these encompass several types, not solely the more literary device of letter writing. They include film-letters (including letters written by characters within the narrative, such as in *Letters from Alou*), letter-films (which take the form of an address to those outside the diegesis, without necessarily including any letters) and telephonic epistles, including phone voice messages (electronic epistolarity). Such epistles are multivocal, featuring a range of different addresses: direct (first person characters), indirect (the third person narrating of story), and free-indirect discourse (a mixture of the other two). The free-indirect form, as multivocal, provides the best way of signifying the hybrid border consciousness of exile or diaspora.

Accented films are often asynchronous. Epistles can be delivered or spoken across time, space and cultural boundaries. They pose the lost or left-behind homeland as a cultural object, seen through a form of looking. As such, these films will often confuse the line between fiction and non-fiction through self-reflexivity. The texts also demonstrate aspects of incompleteness or incoherence, or feature structuring absences (things which should be there, but aren't, and are felt as such), and there is a special role in the films for sound, the voice, often asynchronous. Epistolarity can also be in the form of on-screen text, calligraphy or titling, in more than one language (as can also be spoken). As many of the films are from post-colonial nations, there is still a role for Third Cinema aesthetics, a critically engaged and political form of self-conscious filmmaking.

Under this heading, Naficy also finds a place for what he terms *daughter-texts*. In this set of films, there is a special emphasis on mother-daughter relationships. Ann Hui's Hong Kong-Taiwanese film *Song of the Exile* (*Kè tú qiū hèn*, 1990) is a key example here. The film concerns the autobiographical events following the reunion between a UK-based media student from Hong Kong travelling home for the wedding of her sister, and her mother, who yearns for a return to her native Beppu, in Japan. When the daughter accompanies her, she comes to understand her mother's exile, alienated by language and culture. The film examines issues of exile and diaspora through the mother-daughter relationship. Hatoum's *Measures of Distance* (1989), which we encountered in an earlier chapter, is another of Naficy's examples, in which mother-daughter orality is emphasised through letters from Hatoum's mother that produce 'an overall female consciousness and female solidarity, challenging the hegemony of patriarchal culture and mode of narration' as the mother's voice and writing is superimposed over shots of the daughter's body, crossing oceans and borders (p. 130).

Characters/actors: Like many of the films we've considered throughout the book so far, Naficy notes that many of the films he discusses demonstrate a preference for non-actors, with many of the cast playing themselves, including the filmmakers, either on-screen or in the soundtrack. Characters in accented films often speak a dominant language with an accent and are multilingual – they speak the language of the host culture, sometimes broken, and that of their home culture (at times, these can be the same language if it is a post-colonial country from which they originate). As we've also noted above, these characters can often be shifters, across borders and amphibolic, and likely to be those who slip between identities, one that is authentic, and one that is performed. Hence, there is a focus on characters who are hybridised, doubled or split between different identities, straddling more than one culture. They therefore often take on the role of outsiders or loners.

Subject matter/theme/plot: There are a number of common themes in accented films. Many films take on the form of a journey: they are often journeys that are seeking home, searching for home, or recounting the events that led to the original exile or departure from home. Conversely, they can be homecomings, returns or desires for such, where that return might eventually be impossible. Finally, journeys in search of home might simply be an open form of wandering, an ongoing homelessness. This investigation of home extends to the films' consideration of history, and ways in which accented cinema explores, narrates or explains national and personal pasts. Because of the use of self-reflexivity, there can be confusion about what is real and what is not.

Several themes fit with some of the categories that defined characterisation. There is a continual and ongoing focus on the deterritorialisation of the individual or group, a lack of belonging, through displacement or exile. Likewise, there is a continuing search for wholeness, for the split or hybrid identity to be healed or made whole. Identities that are performed are also recurring themes. Family is a recurring feature (as we've noted in daughter-texts above), under continual strain.

Structures of feeling: These represent a series of personal and social experiences of exile signified by accented films. They include a range of qualities that capture the experience of being interstitial. This includes a revelry in ambivalence, a heightened emotionality, nostalgia and sensuality, encapsulating synaesthesia (connections between sensations that trigger other senses, such as hearing prompting a taste sensation). This synaesthesia in the accented style covers all the signs of exile, loss, difference, a yearning for belonging, that are marked by sensorial triggers. There is a prevailing mood of melancholia, anomie, fear, as characters look backwards, yearning for a state before separation.

In many regards, accented structures of feeling are poised between binaries, located between cultures and nations, in different formations relating to memory and presentness. As such, characters and feelings are: liminal (between social structures and psychological positions); interstitial (on the border between languages, nations, cultures, as well as aesthetic forms); hybrid (the selective and ambivalent adoption of practices from other cultures held in conflict); multifocal (the awareness of multiple cultures and ways of thinking simultaneously and at all times); tactile (an awareness that is continually distracted rather than contemplative); and simultaneous (aware of multiple dimensions of time and space, here and there, then and now). This is regarded as a nomadic sensibility, in which time is personal and cyclical, past and present are co-present in simultaneous time, and the nomad is always deterritorialised, displaced. In many regards, this is combined with a fundamental loneliness, that of characters and of the filmmakers themselves – it can be a lonely, singular mode of production.

Filmmaker's location: In many regards, the same structures of feeling also define the filmmaker. They are interstitial figures, liminal in themselves. Accented films are such because the filmmaker is inscribed within them, and they are autobiographical to some degree. Authorship is overdetermined. Naficy's key accented *auteurs* include the nomadic Belgian director Chantal Akerman, Atom Egoyan, Turkish filmmaker Tevfik Baser (who made his most notable work in Germany), Fernando Solanas, Palestinian

Elia Suleiman, American-based Vietnamese director and postcolonial theorist Trinh T. Minh-ha, and Iranian Amir Naderi, and they have all produced work that presents authorship as a key determinant. We'll see how this works in more detail in our case study of Egoyan (who features in 'close-up' in Naficy's book seven times from various perspectives).

Mode of production: The *auteur* is at the heart of much of the accented mode of production. They are at the core of the production, from inception to exhibition, and take on multiple roles, not just as director, but often as writer, producer, performer, editor, even cinematographer; they are multiple and integrated, and usually interstitial. Not all are so individualistic, however – some are collectively produced by ethnically accented film collectives. Naficy points to a number of Asian-American groups, such as Visual Communications, Asian CineVision and the National Asian-American Telecommunications Association, that were proactive in challenging Asian-American stereotyping throughout the 1970s, 1980s and 1990s. He also refers to postcolonial groups in Britain that produced similar work to deconstruct Afro-Caribbean and Asian-British identities, in particular several groups comprising first generation children of migrants from the West Indies – Black Audio Collective, Ceddo Film and Video Workshop and Sankofa Film and Video Collective – and those of Indian and Pakistani parentage, such as the Retake Film and Video Workshop. Other 'collectives' were looser affiliations, but were united in similar goals of producing work that examined exilic and diasporic identity, in Iran and in *cinéma beur*. Naficy gives particular focus to festivals that provide a collectivising function by presenting home-produced films alongside those produced by filmmakers in exile, or those that solely programme films made in exile, such as those in Gothenburg in the 1990s that presented over 50 films by exilic Iranian filmmakers. Such festivals create an oppositional relationship between home-produced films and those that are exilic (which are often banned in their 'home' country). They can 'construct a national cinema identity and an auteur identity, but also distort both' (p. 87), and should the standing government change, this can shift alongside that. Hence, the transnational circulation and curation of film festivals can produce a collective identity for filmmakers in exile, but can just as easily limit its profile to those films unpopular with an unpopular government (but what happens to those films once a government becomes more liberalised?).

This important point of distribution is collectively shared across accented cinemas – they are artisanally produced outside a mass-production or dominant system, and their distribution can often be handled by niche distributors or through self-distribution (Rivera's *Sleep Dealer*, by a diasporic filmmaker, was a festival hit at Sundance, but its distribution was marginal, largely to Latinx audiences, as the film was mostly subtitled, and it had minimal distribution internationally, never released in the UK). Some films are handled by collectives with educational remits such as Women Make Movies or The Global Film Initiatives. Spectators are also transnational, across different national, cultural, ethnic communities, and the films address those audiences in complex ways due to the accented style's use of multiple modes of address.

In some regards, we might see this as defining a generic mode of production, albeit one that is alternative, independent and interstitial. The categories outlined here from Naficy's book help us understand some of the collective modes and forms in the accented style that define how exilic, diasporic and often post-colonial or post-Third World filmmakers address their place between, across or over borders, either through force, choice or by birth. As Arne Saeys argues, though, the categories are reductive (by Naficy's own admission), and Naficy tends to place 'filmmakers in a liminal nowhere, rather being part of the host country cinema, part of the home country cinema, or part of the international cinema', they are 'forever "homeless"'. Saeys contends that the whole category of accented cinema 'reinforces the Othering of migrant filmmakers … into a new discursive ghetto'. It is a model 'constructed as a stylistic category based on a generalized past of the filmmakers [that] fails to account for the personal and professional evolution of filmmakers over time', and it obfuscates how more mainstream political contexts (non-accented ones) have developed against which the accented films are then characterised (Saeys, 2013, p. 32). Therefore, as Saeys's criticism here demonstrates, it's important to contextualise the locatedness of migrant filmmakers to understand where they fit, not simply to be now and always liminal, regardless of when and where they produce work. Criticisms such as this should remain with us as we apply critical models such as that of Naficy.

Case study: *The Edge of Heaven* (*Auf der anderen Seite*, **Fatih Akin, 2007)**

Akin's *The Edge of Heaven* is a strong example of diasporic cinema. Akin is a German-born writer-director of Turkish descent (an example of one of many filmmakers considered interstitial who work in the countries of their birth). Akin's breakthrough film, *Head-On* (*Gegen die Wand*, literally *Against the Wall*, 2004), about a marriage of convenience between two suicidal Turkish-Germans (the title referring to one character's head-on car crash into a wall), became a significant hit when it won the Golden Bear at the Berlin Film Festival in 2004, a triumph claimed by both the Turkish and German media. Overnight, Akin was thrust into the limelight as a representative of a kind of identity politics and transnational *auteur*. As Daniela Berghahn notes in her book on *Head-On*, Akin, 'against his will ... became not only a "model migrant", whose artistic achievements testified that successful integration into German society was indeed attainable for Turkish immigrants, but also a spokesperson on fervently debated political issues'. She notes how Akin accepted this mantle on several occasions, interceding in environmental and political campaigns through his 'hyphenated identity' that promoted him as a detached political commentator on issues relating to Turkey, particularly its proposed membership of the EU (something referenced in *The Edge of Heaven*) (Berghahn, 2015, pp. 35–36). This makes Akin's later film an excellent example through which to consider some of the aspects of the film that make it demonstrable of Naficy's accented style.

Akin's accented style displays many of the elements of Naficy's mode: a connection to homeland, aspects of epistolarity, scenes of travel (at airports, on the road and petrol stations), an overlapping narrative structure and multilinguality, amongst others. (Its title translates more literally from German as *On the Other Side*, while the film's Turkish title, *Yaşamın Kıyısında*, is more literally *Bringing Out the Dead*, something that echoes the film's mirrored shots of coffins being either loaded on to or off planes as part of a posthumous homecoming (Figure 5.2).) The film begins with

Figure 5.2 *The Edge of Heaven* (Fatih Akin, 2007): Literally bringing out the dead, echoing the film's Turkish title, as homecomings are depicted by repeated shots of coffins being transported to home countries (Anka Film)

Nejat Aksu (Baki Davrak), a professor of German at a German university in Bremen, on the road, where he visits a petrol station (only later do we learn this is the end of the film). The film cuts quickly back to Bremen during a Mayday labour march. There, we meet Ali Aksu (Tunçel Kurtiz), an elderly Turkish immigrant. One day he visits a prostitute, Yeter Öztürk (Nursel Köse), choosing her because she is Turkish. He visits her again, and asks her to come and live with him, to have sex only with him in return for a monthly salary. Only after she's menaced by two Turkish men about her occupation does she agree to Ali's request. She moves in and becomes friendly both with Ali and Nejat, who we learn is Ali's son, and when Ali suffers a heart attack, her friendship with Nejat grows; she tells him about her grown-up daughter who she hasn't heard from in some time, who believes that Yeter works in a shoe shop. After Ali returns home from the hospital, he drunkenly accuses Yeter of having an affair with Nejat. She threatens to leave him, and he hits her, accidentally killing her. When Ali is imprisoned, Nejat travels to Istanbul in search of her daughter. He puts up posters around the town, and visits a German bookstore – when the owner mentions he's looking to sell up and move home, Nejat offers to buy it. We then cut back to another Mayday march in Istanbul, this one more violent than that in Bremen. An undercover policeman in the march is exposed and attacked. He drops his gun, which is picked up by a woman, who we discover is Yeter's daughter, Ayten (Nurgül Yeşilçay). She flees to Germany under an assumed identity, and, after being thrown out of the faction protecting her, meets Lotte (Patrycia Ziolkowska) while searching Bremen shoe shops in search of her mother. They begin a romantic relationship, and Ayten stays with Lotte and her suspecting mother (Hanna Schygulla). One night they are stopped by the police and Ayten runs, leading to her deportation back to Turkey. Lotte follows her, in a vain attempt to help free her. Lotte eventually meets Nejat – although she doesn't connect the flyer on the bookstore noticeboard with Ayten – and stays in his spare room. When she is eventually allowed to visit the prison, Lotte is asked by Ayten to retrieve the gun she hid. She does so, but is mugged by a group of young boys. When she catches up with them, one of them shoots and kills her. In the film's final section, Ali is released from prison and deported, back to Trabzon on the Black Sea coast. Lotte's mother arrives in Istanbul – she stays in the room Lotte rented from Nejat and takes on her daughter's mission to free her girlfriend. Nejat drives to Trabzon to visit his father, leaving Lotte's mother to look after his shop with Ayten. In the film's final, prolonged shot, under the end credits, Nejat sits on the beach waiting for his father to come home from fishing.

Considering the accented style, we find many aspects of Akin's film conform with Naficy's observations. First, the mode of production is particularly transnational. As a writer-director, Akin was involved from the film's inception to its completion. Second, as a film produced within the

European art cinema tradition, its release was by more marginal distribution. However, it would be difficult to see such a major production as artisanal in the low-budget tradition that Naficy discusses. It is a transnational production, though, as a German-Turkish co-production with a multinational cast and crew, with cast from Germany (including performers who have long histories in German cinema, such as Schygulla, who played the eponymous heroine of Fassbinder's *The Marriage of Maria Braun* (1979)), Poland (Ziolowska), and Turkey (Kurtiz has strong ties to important Turkish directors Yilmaz Güney and Erden Kiral), while crew originated from Germany, Turkey and Britain. The degree to which we might see Akin as an interstitial figure is debateable, however. He describes himself as German, with interests that are both or sometimes German or Turkish (Berghahn, 2015). His works engage politically with actions or characters who cross borders, are migrants, in exile or diaspora, but this is not the sole issue in his cinema. While interstitial themes are addressed, the degree to which this is autobiographical is debatable, and that direction of analysis may be limiting if we're just trying to 'find' the author's message in relation to their biography.

The Edge of Heaven, however, does demonstrate many aspects of the visual style, narrative structure, characters, themes and structures of feeling that help us understand how cinema can be accented. In terms of visual style, the narrative is not so much amateurish – it is a decidedly polished piece of work – but displays a highly complex form that interweaves several stories, as many transnational stories do. As Claudia Breger (2014) has argued, the film foregrounds 'the act of narration', not necessarily as a form of critical distance, but 'as much as it invites [audiences'] (affective as well as cognitive) curiosity in and for the process of storytelling, creating a space for engaged, overall affirmative, but simultaneously cautious – and at moments tongue-in-cheek – deliberation' (p. 73). She contends that the film initially introduces, but then seeks to move beyond, the prevailing media discourse of hate and fear in Europe, around Islam and Turkish masculinity vis-à-vis the oppression of women (the two men who intimidate Yeter). As though invoking the memory (from a national cinema) of Fassbinder's *Ali: Fear Eats the Soul* (*Angst essen Seele auf*, 1974), about a Moroccan migrant's relationship with an older woman (the title's incorrect German grammar refers to the title character's accented speech), Ali's first introduction to Yeter to 'please call me Ali' presents us with a stereotype, ironically. We encounter the cramped interior of Yeter's basement bedroom, something shared with many of the interior spaces of the film (which Naficy argued is a characteristic of the accented style). This is juxtaposed throughout the film with expansive exterior shots, especially the film's final shot – Nejat's return to his father's hometown (Figure 5.3) – and many of the landscape shots that depict journeys. There are also many scenes of travel or liminal

Figure 5.3 *The Edge of Heaven* (Fatih Akin, 2007): The film's final, ambiguous shot, as Nejat awaits his father's return, the expansive exterior demonstrating Naficy's accented style (Anka Film)

spaces – the most affecting would be the repetitive shots of coffins (Yeter's, then Lotte's) being loaded from or on to planes respectively. The shots mirror one another, thematically connecting the two characters (the first two segments of the film are 'Yeter's Death' and 'Lotte's Death').

With the accented style, the film shares numerous visual and thematic tropes and structures of feeling. The film is multilingual, in Turkish, German and English, and features brief elements of epistolarity, when Lotte's mother arrives in Istanbul and reads her daughter's diary, through a mixture of first and third person narration (although these moments are brief). Our characters display many of the characteristics of shifters, split or hybrid identities. Nejat is conflicted in his role as professor of German, as an outsider – the man from whom he buys the book store mocks him for this from a kind of shared space straddling the two cultures. Ayten displays many characteristics of slippage between identities; even with her strength of political conviction (she aggressively complains to Lotte's mother about the colonial countries at the heart of the EU and refuses to wear clothes with American company logos) she has little trouble adopting signs of globalised popular culture, as she does on a night out with Lotte (dancing to the 'Bukovina Dub' adopted by *Borat: Cultural Learnings of America for Make Benefit Glorious Nation of Kazakhstan* (Larry Charles, 2006)). The gay relationship between Lotte and Ayten, between the naïve blonde German and 'worldly' Turk, is never presented as a core element of their shared transformation, simply a part of their identities. The realisation of their sexuality is not a journey of discovery – nor a source of inter-generational conflict for Lotte and her mother – but a border that is crossed without question by the film and its characters. There is no sense that this is them living 'contextually' as shifters.

Musically, a soundtrack by Shantel, a Romanian-German producer and DJ, known for his reworkings of Balkan music, creates, as Berna Gueneli has argued, a heterogeneous soundscape for the film in which 'sounds of Akin's imagined Europe mirror on an acoustic level the contemporary sociopolitical shifts and changes of a geopolitically defined Europe' (2014, p. 338). The mixture of music here is more complex than an either/or of home and host cultures, but a shifting across different European borders and boundaries. Characters are engaged in journeys – there are a series of homecomings (alive and dead) and journeys in search of family (an element that is always under strain in the film), as well as a great source of loss (for Yeter, then Ayten, Lotte's mother, and finally Nejat in search of connections). Finally, amongst numerous other structures of feelings (loss, loneliness, nostalgia, a search for wholeness) the film's structure is circular and non-linear, with overlapping time frames, stressing simultaneity and a return to the past (in relation to a more literal return to the past as Nejat returns home to reconcile with his father), and the ambivalence of that meeting – that we are denied seeing – at the end of the film. In this regard, the film shares many aspects of the accented style in its engagement with issues of diaspora and exile that engage with the crossing of borders in the film. If we had more space, we might find more (although it's important to keep in mind Naficy's own point that not all accented films would demonstrate all of its aspects).

With that in mind, it's important to point out that there are criticisms of highlighting such a narrow analysis of the film. Tim Bergfelder has sounded a note of caution in pigeonholing Akin solely as a migrant or diasporic filmmaker, echoing other criticism to see filmmakers simplistically through their authorship via their ethnicity is reductive and essentialist as it continues to define such filmmakers as Other, despite the aim of the critical tendency to do exactly the opposite. As Bergfelder argues, 'studies ... continue to compartmentalize "migrant" and "diasporic" film-makers, now with the new framework of "transnationalism" where minorities and their particularities (sexuality, ethnicity, gender) remain structurally "Other"' (2012, p. 73). Importantly, he points to other Akin films that have received little by way of critical or academic focus, such as his earlier films *In July* (*Im Juli*, 2000) or *Solino* (2002) that don't focus on migrant or Turkish-German themes. Daniela Berghahn also promoted an image of Akin as a diasporic/migrant filmmaker – albeit a reluctant representative one – although she notes, just as Bergfelder does, that filmmakers such as Akin, whose works are hybridised, polyglot and multilingual, are heavily influenced by and influential for a global art cinema. They should not be ghettoised as always Other, but make telling contributions to the language and structure of international and national cinemas. Bergfelder's alternative positioning of *The Edge of Heaven* as a film that ironically analyses cosmopolitanism, through the film's many doublings, mirrorings and contradictions, importantly attempts to see the film 'separated from simplistic conflations of auteurist biographies and narrative concerns, and ... placed in longer ... discursive as well as cinematic historical continuities' (p. 79). This is worth keeping in mind as, although we have set Akin's work in the context of an accented style, the approach is not without its limitations (as with most critical approaches) and scholars have approached the film from different critical perspectives in response to the overdetermining focus on migrant and diasporic filmmakers as solely concerned with those issues. As Bergfelder reminds us, Akin is not a deterritorialised filmmaker, but a highly located one, and this is a film that does engage with the national as a way of then engaging with transnational issues.

Recommended viewing:

Accented cinemas in Germany and France:
Farewell to a False Paradise (*Abschied vom falschen Paradies*, Tevfik Baser, 1989)
Hexagone (Malik Chibane, 1994)
Bye-Bye (Karim Dridi, 1995)
Brothers and Sisters (*Geschwister – Kardesler*, Thomas Arslan, 1997)
Dealer (Thomas Arslan, 1999)
Lola and Billy the Kid (*Lola + Bilidikid*, Kutlug Ataman, 1999)
A Fine Day (*Der schöne Tag*, Thomas Arslan, 2001)
Chouchou (Merzak Allouache, 2003)
The Great Journey (*Le grand voyage*, Ismaël Ferroukhi, 2004)
Kebab Connection (Anno Saul, 2004)
Crossing the Bridge: The Sound of Istanbul (Fatih Akin, 2005)
Beur sur la ville (Djamel Bensalah, 2011)

Recommended further reading:

Bergfelder, Tim (2005), 'National, Transnational or Supranational Cinema? Rethinking European Film Studies', *Media, Culture and Society* 27(3): pp. 315–331.

Berghahn, Daniela (2006), 'No Place like Home? Or Impossible Homecomings in the Films of Fatih Akin', *New Cinemas: Journal Of Contemporary Film* 4(3): pp. 141–157.

Berghahn, Daniela, and Claudia Sternberg, eds (2014), *European Cinema in Motion: Migrant and Diasporic Film in Contemporary Europe*. London: Palgrave Macmillan.

Burns, Rob (2006), 'Turkish-German Cinema: From Cultural Resistance to Transnational Cinema?', in ed. David Clarke, *German Cinema Since Unification*. London and New York: Continuum, pp. 127–150.

Erdoğan, Nezih (2009), 'Star Director as Symptom: Reflections on the Reception of Fatih Akın in the Turkish Media', *New Cinemas: Journal Of Contemporary Film* 7(1): pp. 27–38.

Gramling, David (2010), 'On the Other Side of Monolingualism: Fatih Akin's Linguistic Turn(s)', *The German Quarterly* 83(3): pp. 353–372.

Grassilli, Mariagiulia (2008), 'Migrant Cinema: Transnational and Guerrilla Practices of Film Production and Representation', *Journal of Ethnic & Migration Studies* 34(8): pp. 1,237–1,255.

Higbee, Will (2013), *Post-beur Cinema: North African Emigre and Maghrebi-French Filmmaking in France Since 2000*. Edinburgh: Edinburgh University Press.

Khrebtan-Hörhager Julia (2015), 'De-constructing Monoculturalism on the German Screen: A Critical Cultural Reading of *On the Other Side*', *Crossings: Journal of Migration & Culture* 6(2): pp. 193–209.

Loshitzky, Yosefa (2010), *Screening Strangers: Migration and Diaspora in Contemporary European Cinema*. Bloomington: Indiana University Press.

Naficy, Hamid (1999), *Home, Exile, Homeland: Film, Media and the Politics of Place*. London and New York: Routledge.

Petek, Polona (2007), 'Enabling Collisions: Re-thinking Multiculturalism Through Fatih Akin's *Gegen die Wand/Head On*', *Studies In European Cinema* 4(3): pp. 177–186.

Tarr, Carrie (2005), *Reframing Difference: Beur and Banlieue Filmmaking in France*. Manchester: Manchester University Press.

—— (2007), 'Maghrebi-French (Beur) Filmmaking in Context', *Cineaste* 33(1): pp. 2–7.

Intercultural cinema

Laura U. Marks's 2000 book *The Skin of the Film: Intercultural Cinema, Embodiment, and the Senses* explores an alternative way of thinking about filmmakers who move across borders. Marks prefers the term 'intercultural' to understand how film mediates between two different cultural formations. In her introduction, she responds to an earlier article by Naficy, 'Phobic Spaces and Liminal Panics: Independent Transnational Film Genre' (2003), first published in *East-West Film Journal* in 1994, in which Naficy explores some of the issues that he later expanded upon in *An Accented Cinema*. Here, he posits 'transnational filmmakers as interstitial authors and configuration of claustrophobic spaces as one of the chief iconographies that characterizes this genre', with a focus on the contributions that 'transnationals, exiles, emigres, refugees, and expatriates' made to art in the west (Naficy, 2003, p. 203). Marks makes no claim to explore a similar genre (she does claim intercultural cinema to be a genre, unlike Naifcy's note that the 'accented style is not a fully recognized and sanctioned film genre' (2001, p. 39)) or configuration of filmmakers, but instead to look at filmmakers who strongly identify with multiple cultures but are working in the countries in which they were born. With Naficy, Marks shares a concern with the ways in which films act 'as sites for intertextual, cross-cultural, and translational struggles over meanings and identities' (Naficy, 2003, p. 205; Marks, 2000, p. 7).

There are some key overlaps between Marks's intercultural cinema and Naficy's accented one. While Marks's focus takes figures who are more marginal rather than solely interstitial, there is a shared emphasis on hybridity, politicisation of aesthetics and a mode of production that is generally artisanal, low-budget, often supported by public subsidies, and distributed by exhibitors outside the mainstream to audiences assumed to be more politically engaged and receptive than the mass audience. In its simplest terms (Marks refers to 'intercultural' as a 'mild term' without 'a great deal of conceptual weight'), intercultural cinema defines 'a context that cannot be confined to a single culture. It also suggests movement between one culture and another, thus implying diachrony and the possibility of transformation' (p. 6). Marks uses the philosophies of Gilles Deleuze, in *Cinema 1: The Movement-Image* (2001), *Cinema 2: The Time-Image* (2000) and (with Félix Guattari) *Anti-Oedipus: Capitalism and Schizophrenia* (1983) and *A Thousand Plateaus* (1987), to interrogate the discourses of intercultural cinema that must speak through already established cultural traditions. Because it is largely diasporic, intercultural cinema draws strongly on memories of home and histories of both home and host nations, for 'what official history overlooks' (Marks, 2000, p. 28).

Intercultural cinema, Marks argues, 'is constituted around a particular crisis: the directly political discrepancy between official history and "private" memory' (p. 60). Such a crisis is especially relevant for filmmakers who 'slip between the cracks' where official discourses and archives erase aspects of collective identity politics, like gender, ethnicity, nationalities or other associations that enable social groups to engage in ongoing political debates. For many, this can constitute an erasure, an absence or silencing, especially where official records or archives are grasped by colonisers and a culture is lost or denied to those conquered (pp. 55–56). Marks's Deleuzian-informed cinema is participatory. It seeks not to obfuscate or obscure, but often to interrogate registers of memory through experimentation. The past is always subjective, an intermingling of perception and memory. Through images that fail to extend into action – as pure optical and sound images, in Deleuze's terminology – the viewer has only recourse to personal memory to make sense of the image. Deleuze, following Henri Bergson, refers to this as attentive recognition. The actual image the audience sees before them is incomplete, inexplicable, and therefore fails to 'explain' itself fully. The viewer must then make use of their attentive recognition to bring to mind images from memory that help to explain or fully realise what is before them. The crystal-image is the moment where the actual and virtual meet most fully, mirroring each other to reveal their common falsehoods: censorings, absences, their lack of reality or inextension into interpretable action, as though trapped in a maze of remembrances. These 'powers of the false only undermine the hegemonic character of official images, clichés, and other totalizing regimes of knowledge. They do not privilege some other experience as truth' (p. 66). Intercultural filmmakers who negotiate and navigate between multiple regimes of knowledge extend into this crisis between what is presented as an official 'truthful' history and private memory that draws both into conflict; they both fictions. As Egoyan discovers as the photographer in his 'native' Armenia in *Calendar* (1993), the search for an authentic origin can produce empty clichés of an originary homeland that fail to speak as anything other than commodities. Marks highlights that this process doesn't simply return to the homeland to find the truth of home or of an originating culture, but to see the whole process of culture as a fiction. By functioning metafictionally, and exposing the processes through which culture and history are consti-tuted (or constitutive of absences, clichés and universalising absolutes) these films are 'making history reveal what it was not able to say' (p. 29).

As the title of Marks's book demonstrates, the revelation of attentive recog-nition is an embodied, sensory process. Recollections are tangible not simply as images, but as music, objects, through senses, touch, smell or taste. Memory is not just a visual register, although the use of the term recollection-image can imply as much in cinematic terms, but is multisensory, as we know from our everyday lives, and recollections can be sparked by many different sen-sory experiences. Marks explores this through many different examples in her book. Objects can take on the material qualities of fossils or fetishes. Trans-national objects can be as simple as a tin of pineapple in *Ananas* (Amos Gitai, 1983), flowers in *Love, Women and Flowers* (Marta Rodriguez and Jorge Silva, 1988) or the potato in *Papapapá* (Alex Rivera, 1996). Each of these examples highlights the 'knowledge gap' of 'capitalist abstraction' in which the object is stripped of its past to become a transnational commodity. The objects are transformed through their journeys, stripped of the agency of those who pro-duced, harvested or laboured to produce them. Marks argues that they cannot simply be considered as signs like others within a semiotic system, but that they take on a different value, as memory objects. Their transnational form gives them a volatile quality; they are invested with political value within which is contained the power to convey strongly personal private histories, particularly those of diasporic (and gendered) cultures, whereby those groups may only be granted the ability to speak through such remembered histo-ries motivated by fetishised or fossilised objects. Such intercultural conflict, between the official and unofficial histories of transnational movement, is evoked through the incompleteness of the image, its unintelligibility and through a sensorium that invites participation on the part of the viewer's attentive recognition. It is therefore through that active recognition on the part of the viewer that intercultural cinema's exploration of multiple cultural regimes is enacted. We'll explore more about how this functions in relation to our case study in the next section.

Case study: Atom Egoyan

Egoyan's films in the 1990s were critically lauded as the forefront of Canadian cinema, and, with the exception of David Cronenberg, he is perhaps the most celebrated of Canadian filmmakers. A run of films across the 1980s and 1990s produced a distinctive oeuvre that was celebrated for its auteurist integrity. The films played at and won awards at international festivals, including Montreal, Moscow and Cannes. The series of feature films that includes *Next of Kin* (1984), *Family Viewing* (1987), *Speaking Parts* (1989), *The Adjuster* (1991), *Calendar*, *Exotica* (1994) and *The Sweet Hereafter* (1997) made Egoyan a prominent figure in the alternative art cinema of the 1990s, alongside many American independent figures like Hal Hartley, David Lynch and Todd Haynes, his films distributed by major companies like Miramax. But, for critics such as Naficy and Marks, Egoyan's works are strongly evocative of accented and intercultural styles. A diasporic figure, Egoyan was born in Egypt to parents of Armenian descent who emigrated to British Columbia in 1962 where they established a successful furniture store, as they had run prior to leaving Egypt. Naficy argues that Egoyan's 'films embody many attributes of the accented style': 'including the inscription of closed and claustrophobic spaces':

> ethnically coded mise-en-scène, characters, music, and iconography; multilinguality and accented speech by ethnic characters and actors; epistolarity by means of letters, video, and the telephone; tactile uses of video and technological mediation of all reality; slippery, guarded and obsessive characters who camouflage or perform their identities and secret desires; ethnic characters who either are silent or are present but only on video; inscription of journeys of identity and of return journey to the homeland; the instability and persistence of memory that can be recorded, recorded over, remembered nostalgically, erased, and played back repeatedly; and fragmented structures of feeling and narratives.
> (Naficy, 2001, p. 37)

His experimental works 'confirm the importance of authorship as a marker of difference' (p. 38) while criss-crossing the hybridised aspects of exilic and diasporic cinema. Emma Wilson has responded to Naficy's claim that Egoyan's cinema is 'one of increased ethnicization' (Naficy, 2001, p. 35) by stressing 'that Egoyan's films are frequently about Armenia, memory, and ethnic identity but that these issues are interwoven with his other concerns, particularly fantasy, displacement, and loss'. The ancestral Armenian homeland has been a lost object for many exiled Armenians since 1915, following the genocide committed by the Ottoman Empire (its successor, Turkey, has always disavowed responsibility for the genocide). 'In exploring a geographical or historical relation to Armenia, as in *Calendar* or *Ararat* [2002], Egoyan draws attention to the problems of remembering in another generation: postmemory, a memory of trauma passed down within a family and the community' (Wilson, 2009, pp. 2–3).

As we've already seen, *Calendar* is considered a key film in this respect by Marks. For her, it is a key work of intercultural cinema and the processes of memory that question registers of the past. The film, she argues, 'confronts a tourist's commodified images of his ancestral Armenia with incoherent memory-images of that country, from which a profoundly repressed grief erupts' (2000, p. 31). In the film, the photographer (played by Egoyan) visits Armenia to take a series of photographs of churches for a calendar, presumably for diasporic communities back home (Figure 5.4).

Figure 5.4 *Calendar* (Atom Egoyan, 1993): The photographer captures the postcard images of Armenia that are incoherent, commodified memory-images incapable of fully capturing the past (The Armenian National Cinematheque/Ego Film Arts/ZDF Television)

He is accompanied by his wife (Egoyan's long-time collaborator and wife, Arsinée Khanjian) who becomes attracted to their driver, a local named Ashot (Ashot Adamyan), employed as their guide. She becomes attracted to him, all while the photographer shoots from behind his camera – she also has a video camera, but we're unsure if the imagery we see in the video, often rewound or fast forwarded, is from her perspective. As we watch these videos from the past, the photographer tries, unsuccessfully, to write to her, to articulate his feelings, and he has dinner with a series of women, each of whom resemble her. They all end the same way, with those women on the phone in the background of the shot, speaking in their native language unsubtitled or untranslated, such as Macedonian or Turkish (all languages of host countries of the Armenian diaspora). Meanwhile, his wife calls and leaves answer phone messages in an attempt to repair their marriage (12 of them, as though to mirror the 12 images of the calendar).

The return to Armenia is an act of attempting to reclaim the past, in glossy images, following the independence of the nation after the fall of the Soviet Union. For Marks, this attempt is constituted as a failure, as, she explains, the images he tries to capture are incomplete. They are fetishes of absence that offer little more than clichés, flattened commodities. 'Though the photographer attempted to manage memories by manufacturing virtual images, the inadequate visual and sound images of the video and answering machine force him to fill their gaps, with the painful memory of losing the woman he loved.' (p. 49) The official histories of the calendar are given the same weight as the private memories, both just as fictional as each other; while one is explicitly manufactured (the calendar), the other is only processed through the attentive recognition of the viewer, piecing together two virtual images, one visual, the other an important epistle, the wife's final voice message:

> In the pivotal scene in the film, the grainy, bluish Super-8 footage he shot of a flock of sheep running alongside the car [Figure 5.5] is paired with another virtual image, his wife's voice on the answering machine. 'As you were taping, he placed his hand on mine. I remember because I gripped his hand so hard, watching you grip your camera as if you knew all the time. Did you know? Were you there? Are you there?' (Marks, 2000, p. 48)

Naficy sees this final sequence as an important example of the epistolarity of diasporic narratives, not because they succeed in recuperating different registers of knowledge and memory, but because they fail: 'The failure of the epistolarity mechanisms to repair the husband and wife's personal relations signals their failure to reconcile the three modalities of Armenian national identity.' (2001, p. 139) For Naficy, this is Egoyan's most significantly ethnic and exilic film, and the one, therefore, with the most pronounced accented form.

Figure 5.5 *Calendar* (Atom Egoyan, 1993) The super-8 footage of a flock of sheep articulates the private memories of the film's characters in more complex ways than the perfect clichés of the calendar (The Armenian National Cinematheque/Ego Film Arts/ZDF Television)

As we heard earlier, Naficy returns to consider Egoyan's films seven times during the close-up sections of his book. He considers: his accented style generally; the transnational funding mechanisms of his work, from various public and private sources; the failed epistolarity of *Calendar*; the many fake homes and homelands of *The Adjuster*; *Next of Kin's* transitory narrative in which a suitcase becomes a signifier of the mobility of identities; and in his conclusion Naficy draws an analogy between the performativity of ethnic identities in Egoyan's films and Judith Butler's (1990) argument that posits gendered identity as contingent upon certain practices of performance. As Naficy argues,

> one could say that ethnic, diasporic, or exilic identities are performances that rely on certain practices of repetition that over time produce the effect of ethnic, diasporic or exilic identity. But this repetition is inexhaustible, since it will never completely capture 'identity' or 'home.' (Naficy, 2001, p. 285)

For Naficy, therefore, Egoyan's work forms a summary of many aspects of the accented style. For Marks, Egoyan is a key representative of the intercultural style. Both however, explore a concern for the haptic (touch) in his work. They both note a concern with different forms of video and film technology, and different processes of reprinting that produce a tactile effect. Naficy refers to this as a nostalgia for the image, which is the absence of a lost object, a signifier of the past lost in time. The image, therefore, takes on a 'haptic aura' for Naficy and for Marks a 'haptic character' that conceives how the viewer relates to the image. Marks sidesteps Deleuze's narrow focus on the haptic as a repeated concern with filming hands (as 'unnecessary'), although there is also a concern for Egoyan with the haptic and with hands, particularly at the end of *The Adjuster*. As the title character's model-home burns, he holds his hand up to it, which produces a tactile remembrance. We flashback to an earlier fire; he arrives to speak to the displaced family, which turns out to be the women who we have accepted as his wife and her sister throughout the rest of the film. It becomes a chronotope of a depthless or lost home that burns at the end of the film (Figure 5.6). The film cuts back and forth with the later shot – he continues to stare at his hand (in both time frames), a haptic, embodied connection to the memory, although one that again restates for us the fictionality of the 'home' as it burns (although it was only ever a façade, a fetish that stood in for something absent). It is a metonym for an absent home in Egoyan's diasporic, intercultural cinema.

Figure 5.6 *The Adjuster* (Atom Egoyan, 1991): The haptic connection between *The Adjuster's* lead character and the memory of past fires reminds us of how fictional the 'reality' of the film has been (Alliance Entertainment/ Ego Film Arts/Ontario Film Development Corporation/Téléfilm Canada)

Recommended further reading:

Abramson, Bram Dov (2001), 'The Specter of Diaspora: Transnational Citizenship and International Cinema', *Journal of Communication Inquiry* 25(2): pp. 94–113.
Baronian, Marie-Aude (2014), 'Archive, Memory, and Loss: Constructing Images in the Armenian Diaspora, in eds Chiara De Cesari and Ann Rigney, *Transnational*

Memory: Circulation, Articulation, Scales. Berlin and Boston: Walter de Gruyter, pp. 79–97.

Egoyan, Atom (2004), 'In Other Words: Poetic Licence and the Incarnation of History', *University of Toronto Quarterly* 73(3): pp. 886–905.

Ghosh, Bashnupriya, and Bhaskar Sarkar (1995), 'The Cinema of Displacement: Towards a Politically Motivated Poetics', *Film Criticism* 20(1–2): pp. 102–113.

Gilroy, Paul (1990), 'It Ain't Where You're From, It's Where You're At: The Dialectics of Diaspora Identification', *Third Text* 5(13): pp. 3–16.

Marks, Laura (1994), 'A Deleuzian Politics of Hybrid Cinema', *Screen* 35(3): pp. 244–264.

Mazierska, Ewa (2011), *European Cinema and Intertextuality: History, Memory and Politics*. London and New York: Palgrave Macmillan.

Meerzon, Yana (2012), 'Framing the Ancestry: Performing Postmemory in Atom Egoyan's Post-Exilic Cinema', in *Performing Exile, Performing Self: Drama, Theatre, Film*. London and New York: Palgrave Macmillan, pp. 254–292.

Naficy, Hamid (1997), 'The Accented Style of the Independent Transnational Cinema: A Conversation with Atom Egoyan', in ed. George E. Marcus, *Cultural Producers In Perilous States: Editing Events, Documenting Change*. Chicago and London: University of Chicago Press, pp. 179–231.

Pisters, Patricia, and Wim Staat, eds (2014), *Shooting the Family: Transnational Media and Intercultural Values*. Amsterdam: Amsterdam University Press.

Siraganian, Lisa (1997), '"Is This My Mother's Grave?": Genocide and Diaspora in Atom Egoyan's Family Viewing', *Diaspora: A Journal of Transnational Studies* 6(2): pp. 127–154.

Tschonfen, Monique, and Jennifer Burwell, eds (2007), *Image and Territory: Essays on Atom Egoyan*. Waterloo, Ontario: Wilfrid Laurier University Press.

Discussion questions:

- Why do you think cinema has become such an important medium for narrating migrant, diasporic and exilic experience?
- How do you think diasporic and exilic films imagine national belonging?
- Do you agree with critics of theories of accented cinema that it can promote a vision of diasporic filmmakers as always liminal and stuck between home and host nations?
- In what ways might diasporic and exilic filmmakers be helping to make national cinemas more multicultural?

CHAPTER 6

Transnational Film Production

With globalisation comes the increased mobility of people, capital and media texts. As we've seen Appadurai (1990) argue, ethnoscapes, technoscapes, finanscapes and mediascapes constitute a process of 'global cultural flow' with which all aspects of film production interact, at levels of finance, production, reception and textual meaning. Since its development as an industry in the early twentieth century, cinema has always been a global medium – its products circulate around the world, and film crews have worked across national boundaries. Hollywood has used this as a means to retain its hegemonic position, to attract talent from other countries (or offer haven for émigrés), to co-opt popular cultural material, genres or individual films, or to make films in exotic locations (so-called 'runaway productions' made outside the US). In most countries, Hollywood films, often dubbed, sometimes subtitled, outperform local cinema at the box office, attracting the biggest audiences with expensive advertising campaigns and wide releases. This has been considered a form of cultural imperialism, although, as we've seen, that position has been considered to be more complex as products and individuals move across cultural boundaries and are integrated into or work to negotiate different national contexts.

Throughout this chapter, we'll consider issues relating to film production as they relate to 'global cultural flow'. This will include explorations of flows of individuals, including stars and directors, both of whom negotiate different national contexts and ideological positions. For stars, this will often include their adoption by audiences and the ways in which those stars symbolise aspects of identity politics on local and global levels. In addition, we'll look at flows of capital in transnational film production and the ways in which supranational collaboration facilitates production across borders and how transnational co-productions can often be granted the same rights as national films in terms of funding, distribution and exhibition. We'll also examine media ownership and the ways in which this complicates the national ownership of cultural material. At the core of the chapter is a case study of transnational Chinese cinema as a complex network of translocal and regional industries that make up what we consider 'Chinese cinema'. The final aspect of this chapter, something that looks ahead to the final two chapters, is the global flow of cultural material and the manner in which certain texts or types of texts are produced, appropriated or circulated on local and global levels, or 'glocally', as strategies that encompass the local and global have also been described.

Transnational directors

One of the key aspects of globalisation and transnationalism that we've considered throughout the book so far has been the circulation of individuals across borders. We've seen examples of how this has been expressed on a textual level, in border narratives and by diasporic and intercultural filmmakers, but we turn in this section to cover the movement of key production personnel, directors and stars and how this engages with aspects of transnationalism. As we've seen, cinema encouraged filmmakers to cross borders almost as soon as it was invented. In the 1920s, renowned filmmakers like F.W. Murnau, Ernst Lubitsch, Charlie Chaplin and Alfred Hitchcock were already working in other countries. When the Nazis came to power in Germany, this produced a wave of migration, and directors such as Fritz Lang, Billy Wilder and Otto Preminger moved to Hollywood. The term émigré has long been used to refer to directors such as these, although they might now be seen through a prism of diaspora, since their work retained distinctive qualities associated with their identities, such as the expressionist style, or, as Vincent Brook shows in *Driven to Darkness: Jewish Emigre Directors and the Rise of Film Noir* (2009), their Jewishness. Deborah Shaw argues that, simply, transnational directors are those 'who work and seek funding in a range of national contexts, while they have their films distributed in the global market' (2013, pp. 60–61). Her examples include Luis Buñuel, Alfonso Cuarón, Alejandro González Iñárritu, Guillermo del Toro, Lars von Trier, Michael Haneke, Alejandro Amenábar, Ang Lee, Fernando Meirelles, Walter Salles, Baz Luhrmann although the list might go on and on. Ezra and Rowden point out that *auteurs* have long been held to be representatives of national film cultures, but also 'bearer[s] of national and/or ethnic identity' (2006, p. 3). In contemporary cinema, directors have 'hybridized and cosmopolitan identities' that make oppositional relations obsolete 'in the complex interconnected world-system with which even the most marginalized of [filmmakers] must now contend', even making terms such as 'Third World' and 'Third Cinema' seem old-fashioned and out of step with a world order that isn't so easily defined by different coloured parts of a map (p. 4).

In the last chapter, we looked at Atom Egoyan and Fatih Akin's filmmaking as examples of diasporic directors whose authorship engages with their own condition of being across borders, or negotiating identities across borders. Other examples we've mentioned have done so, such as Trinh Minh-ha, Gurinder Chadha, Alex Rivera, Iñárritu, Saadi Yacef and Meirelles, and we'll hear more about transnational directors, like Ang Lee or Martin Campbell, during the course of this chapter as we explore how globalised film production engages with and challenges what we think of as national film culture. Therefore, at this point, it seems redundant to explore further directors as case studies as their authorship relates to transnational cultures; we've done this in other chapters and will do so as we proceed. What we should acknowledge is that directors hold a privileged place in film discourse – we wouldn't expect to spend as much time discussing how cinematographers travel across borders (although many do, and take aesthetics with them) because of the primacy still placed upon the role of the *auteur* in cinema cultures.

While successful internationally, directors who are seen as transnational can often be placed into categories that complicate their standing as representatives of a national culture. Directors such as Guillermo del Toro can sometimes be considered problematic as transnational filmmakers. Del Toro's work straddles Hollywood, Mexican and Spanish cinema, from the arthouse success of Spanish civil war-set *Pan's Labyrinth* (*El laberinto del Fauno*, 2006) to major blockbusters like *Hellboy* (2004), its sequel *Hellboy II: The Golden Army* (2008), *Blade 2* (2002) and *Pacific Rim* (2013). Antonio Lázaro-Reboll has noted how this has placed del Toro in a marginal position in relation to official Mexican cinema policy: 'With the international critical success of *Cronos* and his work in Hollywood, ... his industrial modus operandi and his hybrid cultural texts still pose problems for Mexican critical praxis' (Lázaro-Reboll, 2007, p. 43). Lázaro-Reboll notes how del Toro's *The Devil's Backbone* (*El espinazo del diablo*, 2001), alongside Alfonso Cuarón's *Y tu mamá también* (released widely with its Spanish title, which translates as *And Your Mother Too*, 2001) were not recognised officially as products of a national cinema by Mexican cultural institutions, and were both excluded from being Mexico's entry for the foreign language film Academy Award. Their genres – horror and road movie respectively – as well as del Toro's use of the Spanish civil war setting did not conform with notions of what constitutes national cinema. In the film's Mexican reception, Lázaro-Reboll finds negative responses to del Toro's international cinema and the Spanishness of the film, including the participation of noted Spanish *auteur* Pedro Almodóvar, citing one review that referred to del Toro as 'chico Almodóvar' (Almodóvar boy) (Lázaro-Reboll, 2007, p. 45). Ann Davies has noted a parallel between del Toro, the national cinema misfit, and Hellboy, 'who attempts to save New York but who receives no healing and nurture from it in return' (2014, p. 41). Keith McDonald and Roger Clark (2014) have seen del Toro's work in the context of Naficy's notion of an accented cinema. They argue that he is a filmmaker in exile – following his father's kidnap in 1998 – and that his films use tropes of multivocality, rupture, trauma and the transcultural bases (Mexico, Spain and America) that give his films much of their fantasy. It is also frequently remarked that del Toro's work is a product of a range of production and distribution sources, across the mainstream and interstitial trans-Atlantic Latino cinema. Issues such as these – including the divergent readings dependent on the location of the critic – can complicate how film directors, as *auteurs*, can find themselves positioned in reception as negotiating different national contexts, and how this can be perceived as a negative in relation to their standing as validated by different forms of nationalist discourse.

Transnational stardom

Unlike directors, transnational stars offer quite different forms of negotiation between the national and transnational. In her book, *Jet Li: Chinese Masculinity and Transnational Film Stardom* (2012), Sabrina Qiong Yu makes a significant distinction between international and transnational film stardoms. An international film star will be a star within a particular nation, and those films and the star will circulate outside that country, regionally or internationally, perhaps never making a film outside that local industry. Transnational stars on the other hand will move from one country to another. But while transnational stars will generally cross from the film industry of a 'home' country to another, the defining factor of that stardom will be the ability to make films in different languages, a translingual stardom. Hence, we think about Spanish Penélope Cruz and French Juliette Binoche as transnational stars, both having made their names in their first languages and then transferred successfully to English-speaking cinema, but we won't necessarily think of Nicole Kidman or Kate Winslet as transnational stars due to them only appearing in in films in English. As Yu argues, the 'typical trajectory for a transnational star involves gaining fame in one's own country, attracting the attention of American producers and then being invited to make films in Hollywood' (p. 2). Hollywood cinema though does not generally export its own stars. Yu notes that this is part of Hollywood's globalised distribution strategy to extend its reach into foreign markets. As we'll see later in the chapter, this is typical of glocal approaches to the mass market and more targeted production in local markets, and the strategy of using stars to make films that have simultaneous local and global appeal. This approach testifies to Yu's conclusion regarding the travel of transnational stars, that it is 'one-way traffic' that demonstrates the imbalance of transnational flows: 'Hollywood's assimilation of and control over foreign talents' (p. 2).

Ezra and Rowden have similarly problematised this notion of transnational stardom with reference to a number of border-crossing stars who demonstrate the 'homogenizing dynamic' of Hollywood, 'through forms of cultural and ideological cleansing': Russell Crowe (they contend that he is Australian, but he was born in New Zealand, raised in Australia yet denied citizenship in 2006); Colin Farrell (from the Republic of Ireland); Winslet and Jude Law (both from England); Binoche; Catherine Zeta-Jones (Welsh); and the Spanish Cruz and Antonio Banderas. In most cases, Ezra and Rowden stress, these performers will perform an Americanness that becomes a universal feature of international cinema: 'national identity has been jettisoned as a marker of cultural specificity to an extent that goes beyond what might be necessary for the demands of a particular role' (p. 2). Donna Peberdy (2014) questions this in her introduction to a special issue of the *Transnational Cinemas* journal about performance and what makes performances universal or American. She wonders what it is that makes it possible for some performers to cross boundaries, between nations and different national cinemas, while that mobility is denied to others. Meanwhile, in the same issue, Martin Shingler draws a similar conclusion regarding Aishwarya Rai Bachchan. Rai is a former Miss World and model (her position as the face of L'Oreal's skin whitening cream, Shingler points out, made her an aspirational figure for middle-class Indian women due to her cosmopolitan looks and ambiguous ethnicity), whose performances in Hindi and Tamil cinema made her the highest-paid female star in India. Shingler draws attention to her performances in five films that she made outside India: *Bride & Prejudice*; *The Mistress of Spices* (Paul Mayeda Berger, 2005); *Provoked: A True Story* (Jag Mundhra, 2006); *The Last Legion* (Doug Lefler, 2007); and *The Pink Panther 2* (Harald Zwatt, 2009). The first three were co-productions involving British companies, while the last two are multinational productions, one European, the other Hollywood. What Shingler observes in Rai's five transnational productions is a greater focus on her acting ability than her beauty, unlike her work in India. *Bride & Prejudice* utilised her Bollywood appeal to draw attention to her globally, although it didn't turn her into a major global star but allowed her to produce a further series of films that enabled her to become an icon of modern India. However, in this, Shingler has a reservation:

> for all her beauty, versatility, talent and charm, Rai's transnational films have neither earned her awards nor a series of commercially successful Hollywood star vehicles. If Rai has been unable to achieve these with her abundant star qualities, what is the likelihood that another Bollywood star might do so? (2014, p. 108)

Few ethnic transnational stars have made major breakthroughs as Hollywood stars. The Hindi actor Irrfan Khan has appeared in numerous Hollywood films, such as Oscar-winners *Slumdog Millionaire* (Danny Boyle, 2008) and *Life of Pi* (Ang Lee, 2012), and major films like *The Amazing Spider-Man* (Marc Webb, 2012), but often in supporting roles, as a character actor rather than a lead. For a time, Jackie Chan crossed over, albeit in sidekick roles, in the *Rush Hour* films (Brett Ratner, 1998, 2001 and 2007) with Chris Tucker, and *Shanghai Noon* (Tom Dey, 2000) and *Shanghai Knights* (David Dobkin, 2003) with Owen Wilson. Chan has continued to make films in Hong Kong, China and the US, but with more leading roles coming in Chinese-language films.

The approach to stardom in Russell Meeuf and Raphael Raphael's collection *Transnational Stardom: International Celebrity in Film and Popular Culture* (2013) utilises a cultural studies method that is less focused on the binary divide between the co-optation of Hollywood (its mining of local stars, and hollowing out of their star personas) and the peripheral cinemas that provide those stars. Following Hjort, Ďurovičová and Newman, they follow an understanding of transnational cinema 'as a contact zone [that] explains the ability of cinema and other transnational media to forge connections (even if only momentarily) between peoples and localities that may reflect global inequalities but yet also transcend them' (Meeuf & Raphael, 2013, p. 3). Their collection historicises transnational stardom, including chapters on John Wayne's transnational masculinity and its relationship with assumptions of US imperialism, and Jane Fonda's mobility in the 1960s and her opposition to the war in Vietnam, her time in French cinema and the multiplicity of her transnational personas. Their collection is as much focused on issues of celebrity as it is stardom, and there is a strong emphasis on reception studies, as well as fan discourses. Charlie Henniker's chapter 'Pink Rupees or Gay Icons? Accounting for the Camp Appropriation of Male Bollywood Stars' (2013, originally published in 2010) investigates the 'queer slippages' in the performances of Shah Rukh Khan that have become appropriated not just by gay Indian and South Asian diasporic audiences, but broadly, where camp appropriation and readings become meaningful acts of pleasure for those audiences. Khan is one of the biggest film stars in the world, but in some of the terms we've explored so far in this section, he'd be considered an international film star. His work crosses borders, but he does not – he hasn't made a Hollywood film, for instance. The approach of Henniker, and across Meeuf and Raphael's collection, looks much more closely at the construction of star images for audiences and across media, as opposed to looking closely just at performances or the production histories of the performers. They discuss the multiplicity of contact zones between different regions, nations and subjectivities in which the 'transnational circulation and popularity of media celebrities help[s] mediate and articulate the social, cultural, and political transformation of a rapidly changing world' (Meeuf & Raphael,

2013, p. 8). There are significant consequences here for the ways in which gender, ethnicity, race and sexuality intersect both for stars themselves and for audiences.

In her article on Chow Yun-fat's transnational stardom in *Pirates of the Caribbean 3: At World's End* (Gore Verbinski, 2007), Feng Lin explores the range of uses of international, global and transnational in discourses surrounding film stardom. She argues that the terms have a fluid and overlapping interrelationship. Transnational stars, she contends, 'are those whose images are constantly adjusted to cater for different market specifications' (Lin, 2011, p. 78). Whereas global processes tend to create a totalising or universalising dimension to the star's image, transnational stars have multiple personas that are refined and articulated in ways that fit the demands and tastes of local markets – she refers to this as 'glocalising a star's image'; the star has global stature but is adapted as needed to fit the requirements of local markets. Lin notes how Chow's presence in the film was given only minimal promotion in the English-language marketing for his role in *At World's End*, but that he played a very substantial role in the marketing of the film in Chinese-language markets. For Lin, this an example of Sheldon Lu's notion that identity has weakened its roots in a defined nationhood, supplanted by a transnational culture in which there is local participation within a global imaginary. While Lin's argument focuses on the promotion of star images through publicity and the function of a film market promoting particular stars depending on their locality, we see a similar process at work in Henniker's reading of the queering of Khan's stardom in its appropriation by diasporic and global audiences, something also explored in Hrithik Roshan's homoerotic spectatorial pleasures by Nandana Bose (2013, p. 159).

This is witnessed in a different form in the reception of Weng Weng, the 'Filipino midget James Bond', star of films such as *For Y'ur Height Only* (Eddie Nicart, 1981) and *Agent 00* (Eddie Nicart, 1981), whose cult stardom, Iain Robert Smith has argued, 'relies precisely on [the] productive tension between celebration and mockery of difference' (2013, p. 237). The appropriation of Weng Weng by audiences has different consequences from that of Shah Rukh Khan, whereby the simultaneous celebration of the badness of the film's text alongside the mockery of the star's difference from perceived norms, his Otherness, ethnically and physically, highlight important factors in how cultural power is articulated in fans' responses. The text is celebrated from a position of superior laughter, its makers seemingly unaware of its campy qualities, and for its perceived act of mimicking a western text, something that only highlights its difference. Cultural power is articulated through the western audience's adoption of the cult text as a means of rejecting western norms, but the adoption is filtered through a lens that sees it, and its star, as Othered through those same mechanisms, as the fan appropriates the very difference they simultaneously identity with and mock. These dimensions of cultural power are articulated in the transnational reception of star images, something that is also highlighted in the following case study of Assayas's *Irma Vep* (1996), a film that self-reflexively explores the construction of star images along gendered, ethnic and sexual lines, and their problematic articulation within local, national industries.

Case study: Maggie Cheung in *Irma Vep* (Olivier Assayas, 1996)

Maggie Cheung's appearance in Olivier Assayas's comedy *Irma Vep* self-reflexively uncovers many issues pertaining to the transnational movement of stars across borders. The film raises questions about national cinema, the gendering of stardoms and the ways in which culture is globally mobile. Playing a partly fictionalised version of herself, Cheung arrives in Paris to star in a remake of Louis Feuillade's 1915 silent serial *Les Vampires*. Cast as the cat burglar Irma Vep (an anagram of 'vampire'), she steps into a role originally played by the French cultural icon, Musidora. The director, René Vidal (played by Jean-Pierre Léaud, best known as François Truffaut's alter ego Antoine Doinel), casts Maggie after seeing her performance in *The Heroic Trio* (*Dung fong saam hap*, Jonnie To, 1992). Entranced by her balletic action performance, Vidal believes Maggie has a star quality like Musidora, and embodies Irma, despite the obvious ethnic and national difference. Cheung finds herself an object of scrutiny and debate amongst the crew, 'une Chinoise.' After a late-night screening of dailies, the crew even forgets about her, leaving while she makes a phone call. The costume designer, Zoé (Nathalie Richard), takes Cheung under her wing. Zoé is one of several characters in the film to act as a mouthpiece to vocalise opinions regarding the current status of French and global cinema. Vidal has asked her to style Maggie's costume on that worn by Michelle Pfeiffer in *Batman Returns* (Tim Burton, 1992), which Zoé realises in latex with outfits from a sex shop. Zoé tells Maggie that she finds Hollywood cinema superficial, that they achieve little despite their astronomical costs. Later, finding Maggie outside the laboratory after the dailies, Zoé takes her to a dinner party with other members of the crew. She complains that French cinema is no longer political in the vein of a '*cinéma militante*' – an excerpt from Chris Marker's 1969 film *Class Struggle* (*Classe de lute*) plays on the television (although it fills the cinema screen). A French journalist who interviews Maggie tells her of his disdain for French cinema, its repetitive and unpopular state-funded navel gazing. When Maggie expresses interest in Vidal's films, which she has seen on video because they aren't available in Hong Kong, he tells her she's being 'polite,' and that the true *auteurs* of world cinema are Schwarzenegger, van Damme and John Woo. Woo's 'choreography of extreme violence' is more alive and vital than the French cinema, he explains. Uncomfortable,

Maggie says she finds Woo's films 'too masculine', just as she earlier tells members of the crew that her previous film in Hong Kong was 'too violent'.

The film descends into chaos as the crew bickers and infights. Vidal struggles with the responsibility of producing a remake of Feuillade's classic, while Maggie struggles to get into the role of Irma Vep. He tells her simply 'play yourself', something she attempts by getting into costume and wandering the corridors and roof of her hotel, sneaking into another guest's room, eavesdropping on the occupant (a naked Arsinée Khanjian) having a phone conversation with her boyfriend, and stealing a necklace. Vidal is eventually fired from the film and replaced with a contemporary, the 'resting' Murano, who accepts the job just as his welfare is about to run out. Murano's first act is to fire Maggie, with barely concealed racism; he says the film is Feuillade, not 'Fu Manchu'. Maggie leaves the film behind, the crew gossiping about her next destination: New York or Los Angeles? To meet Ridley Scott or her agent? At the end of Assayas's film, we see Vidal's version of *Les Vampire*, a confusing avant-garde construction, with images of Maggie as Irma scratched around, with superimposed black spots and bars covering eyes and faces. Maggie's eyes shoot lines of film scratches. There is no semblance of narrative. The film collapses under the weight of attempting to remake such a national classic (Figure 6.1).

At the time of the film's production, Maggie Cheung was a well-respected star of Hong Kong cinema. A former Miss Hong Kong, she was

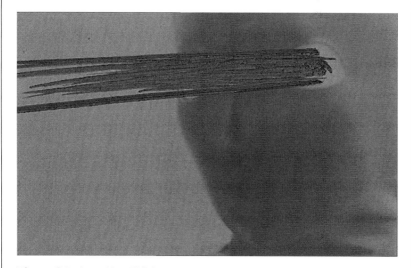

Figure 6.1 *Irma Vep* (Olivier Assayas, 1996): Vidal's version of Irma Vep is an experimental mess; the scratches on the film seem to draw attention to Maggie's eyes, a sign of her ethnicity (Dacia Films)

known globally to cult audiences for her work with Jackie Chan, as the girlfriend of the protagonist of the *Police Story* films (*Ging chaat gu sih*, 1985, 1988 and 1992) and from numerous *wuxia* films, including Raymond Lee's *New Dragon Gate Inn* (*Sun lung moon hak chan*, 1992) and *The Heroic Trio*. While these are the films most referenced in *Irma Vep* (Murano dismissively refers to her work with 'Jack Chan'), Cheung was also heavily associated with filmmakers from the Hong Kong new wave. By 1996, she had collaborated three times with Wong Kar-wai, in *As Tears Go By* (*Wong gok ka moon*, 1988), *Days of Being Wild* (*Ah fei zing zyun*, 1990) and *Ashes of Time* (*Dung che sai duk*, 1994), and twice with Stanley Kwan, in *Full Moon in New York* (*Ren zai Niu Yue*, 1989) and *Centre Stage* (*Yun ling yuk*, AKA *Actress*, 1992). *Centre Stage*, a self-reflexive biopic about tragic silent film star Ruan Ling yu, had been an international festival hit, earning Cheung the Silver Bear for best actress at the Berlin Film Festival in 1992. Cheung reached higher levels of global prominence for her work in the early 2000s, particularly her roles in Wong's *In the Mood for Love* (*Fa yeung nin wa*, 2000), Zhang Yimou's blockbuster *Hero* (*Ying xiong*, 2002) and another film with Assayas (to whom she was married for three years), *Clean* (2004), for which she won a best actress award at the Cannes Film Festival. She has acted little since then, however, while a role she filmed for Quentin Tarantino's *Inglourious Basterds* (2009) was left out of the film's final cut.

Cheung's stardom in *Irma Vep* is presented as a cosmopolitan one, one at odds with the insularity of the French crew with which she works. Unlike most of the crew, Maggie speaks perfect English (a consequence of having been raised for much of her childhood in Kent), although she speaks little to no French, which forces the crew to speak to her in broken English. At one moment in the film, she attempts to speak to a crew member whose only language is German, and without a common language their communication is very abrupt. Maggie's presence, however, testifies to the permeability of borders in transnational stardom. She flies into Paris late after her Hong Kong film goes over schedule, and leaves for the US following the end of her time on the film. Her ethnicity is at odds with the protectionism and insularity of the French film industry, though. Vidal's choice to shoot the film as a silent overcomes the language barriers for Maggie, although the costume still draws attention to her ethnicity, the mask of her cat burglar costume accenting her oval eyes, as does her make-up. Maggie is repeatedly objectified – Zoé refers to her as a 'plastic doll', a reference to her sexual desire for Maggie, but also to reinforce a cultural stereotype onto her, as she is likened to an exotic, Orientalised Chinese doll, both in her onscreen appearance as Irma and in discourse.

As Dale Hudson (2006) contends about *Irma Vep's* deconstruction of transnational stardom and national cinema, 'Transnational stardom complicates discussions of conventional gendered patterns of audience identification of stars with national identity' (p. 224). Just as Meeuf and Raphael point out that transnational stars function as 'dynamic and effective sources of ideological negotiation' (2013, p. 5), Maggie's Orientalised Othering by the crew of the film betrays a colonial gaze at the star from East Asia. Other film stars are mentioned, such as the journalist's outpouring of admiration for Schwarzenegger, van Damme and Steven Seagal, or Maggie's own praise for Alain Delon, but none of those references are gendered in the same way Maggie experiences, nor viewed through a similar lens of Otherness; indeed they are valorised as universal. Certainly, none of those allusions are racialised in the same way as Murano's overtly racist reference to Cheung as 'Fu Manchu'. The reference to Sax Rohmer's fictional 'yellow peril' character resurrects a long-held stereotype of the Far East. An invention of the American author in the early twentieth century, Dr. Manchu was an invader set on 'Oriental' colonisation of the Occident by miscegenation. As Jachinson Chan has noted, Rohmer's fiction, by 'perpetuating the dominant culture's fear and fascination with the Chinese, ... satisfies the need of British and American societies to interpret Chinese immigration as an invader' (2001, p. 35). Here, that interpretation is read as a cultural one, a miscegenation of a French cultural icon. Murano's reference to Arletty, the star of Marcel Carné's *Children of Paradise* (*Les Enfants du Paradis*, 1945), a French star and cultural icon on a par with Musidora, expresses a need for cultural nostalgia, a return to an earlier stage of national cinema. However, *Irma Vep* expresses the impossibility of a purely national cinema under globalisation; the cinema is at once national and transnational.

Right from the outset, *Irma Vep* presents a film culture that is it at once international in its outlook. In the first scene, there are signifiers present that attest to global film culture: one member of the crew wears a T-shirt depicting a poster for *Terminator 2: Judgment Day* (James Cameron, 1991), while a production assistant wears a Looney Tunes T-shirt. Maggie enters this environment dressed in a shirt patterned with international flags (Figure 6.2). This acts as a signifier of her cosmopolitanism, her ability to hop boundaries comfortably. Vidal's conceptualisation of the modern Irma Vep as Catwoman, despite the condescending attitudes of both Zoé and Maggie, demonstrate transnational influences on cinema. Likewise, the casting of Maggie from a viewing of *The Heroic Trio* speaks to the ways in which films are received transnationally. Although Maggie attempts to distance herself from Hong Kong genre films, as 'too violent' or 'masculine', her star image is constructed through Vidal's engagement with these films. Just as the journalist elevates John Woo's films to the highest level of artistic expression, Vidal has also done this with Maggie. He commends her grace and skill in the *wuxia*, to which she replies that it was all the work

Figure 6.2 *Irma Vep* (Olivier Assayas, 1996): Maggie's cosmopolitanism is emphasised through her costuming, with the many international flags, when she arrives in France (Dacia Films)

of stunt performers. This emphasises the constructedness and multiplicity of star images, especially on a transnational basis. What is received as trash or low culture, or representative of popular cultural trends, in one country can often be received as high art or validated through means such as film festivals or criticism to a higher level of cultural capital abroad. Transnational audiences, including those with agency like Vidal or the film journalist, can also often use those works to express cultural or subcultural capital through their engagement with different kinds of global cinema, just like the characters dressed in images from American popular culture. As Vidal, Léaud also interrogates his own star image. As a critique of auteurist trends in French cinema (the film journalist is as dismissive of French cinema as Truffaut was of the 'tradition of quality' in the article (1976) that stimulated the original wave of auteurist criticism), Léaud's presence as Vidal is a reminder of the primacy of *la nouvelle vague* as a globally influential film movement, one now consigned to nostalgia. The reference to Maggie as 'une Chinoise' also cites Jean-Luc Godard's *La Chinoise* (1967), about a group of Maoist students, itself the kind of film Zoé laments the absence of in modern French cinema. So, while the presence of one star, Cheung, demonstrates the problematic attitudes expressed towards transnational stardom and the movement of individuals across borders, the presence of another, Léaud, is more inward looking, reflective of a crisis in national cinema, and insular attitudes towards race, ethnicity, culture and national identity in France in the 1990s.

Recommended further reading:

Amelio, Maria Elena (2014), 'The Hybrid Star: Steve Reeves, Hercules and the Politics of Transnational Whiteness', *Journal of Italian Cinema and Media Studies* 2(2): pp. 259–277.

Fujiki, Hideaki (2013), *Making Personas: Transnational Film Stardom in Modern Japan*. Cambridge, Mass.: Harvard University Asia Center.

Li, Eva Cheuk-yin (2015), 'Approaching Transnational Chinese Queer Stardom as Zhongxing ("Neutral Sex/Gender") Sensibility', *East Asian Journal of Popular Culture* 1(1): pp. 75–95.

Miyao, Daisuke (2007), *Sessue Hayakawa: Silent Cinema and Transnational Stardom*. Durham and London: Duke University Press.

Palmer, Landon (2015), '"And introducing Elvis Presley": Industrial Convergence and Transmedia Stardom in the Rock 'n' Roll Movie', *Music, Sound, and the Moving Image* 2: pp. 177–190.

Park, JaeYoon (2009), 'Asia's Beloved Sassy Girl: Jun Ji-Hyun's Star Image and Her Transnational Stardom', Jump Cut: A Review of Contemporary Media 51. Available online: http://ejumpcut.org/archive/jc51.2009/SassyGirl/index.html. Accessed 19 September 2017.

Peberdy, Donna, ed. (2014), Special Issue: Acting and Performance, *Transnational Cinemas* 5(2).

Rivera-Velázquez, Celiany, and Tanya L. Saunders (2009), 'Canta Como Celia y Baila Como Juana: La Prima and the Queer Transnational (Re)Enactment of Black Female Cuban Stardom', *Feminist Media Studies* 9(2): pp. 259–262.

Sutton, Paul (1999), 'Remaking the Remake: Olivier Assayas' *Irma Vep* (1996)', in ed. Phil Powrie, *French Cinema in the 1990s: Continuity and Difference*. Oxford: Oxford University Press, pp. 69–80.

Tsika, Noah (2014), 'From Yorùbá to YouTube: Studying Nollywood's Star System', *Black Camera: An International Film Journal* 5(2): pp. 95–115.

Wang, Yiman (2012), 'The Palimpsest Body and the S(h)ifting Border: On Maggie Cheung's Two Crossover Films', *Positions: East Asia Cultures Critique* 20(4): pp. 953–981.

Globalised film production and co-productions

In Chapter 3, we considered Mette Hjort's categorisation of different kinds of transnationalism. We used those categories to look particularly at ideas relating to migrant, diasporic and exilic cinema in which we saw epiphanic and affinitive transnationalisms in the way shared cultural and national belonging were uncovered. Her other categories of transnationalism lean heavily towards how films are produced across borders, mainly through her focus on Danish cinema and the work of Lars von Trier's Zentropa films, and its collaborations across regional borders in Scandinavia and with other small nations, such as Scotland. Throughout this chapter, we'll engage with aspects of these other categories – opportunistic, globalising, modernising and cosmopolitan transnationalisms – that explore aspects of the flow of individuals and capital in transnational film production.

Earlier in the book, we heard briefly about the British Film Institute's Cultural Test that certifies films as British to qualify for tax relief of up to 25 per cent. The legislation was made even more favourable in 2014 with the reduction of total UK spend from 25 per cent to 10 per cent of the film's overall budget being spent in the UK. In many respects, this provides a means for opportunistic transnationalisms for many productions that wouldn't necessarily be considered as British. For example, due to being designated British, Disney's *Star Wars: Episode VII: The Force Awakens* (JJ Abrams, 2015) was eligible to reclaim 25 per cent of UK budgetary spend from the local tax office. The tax credit was reported to be in the region of £31.6 million (Spence, 2016), and the co-operation of the British government lead to George Osborne, Chancellor of the Exchequer at the time, being thanked in the closing credits. Tax relief schemes such as these are intended to boost local production and incentivise international productions to shoot in particular nations, or to complete post-production work, such as visual effects, there. There has been a boom in visual effects companies moving to different countries to capitalise on tax breaks to court business from Hollywood studios. Companies such as the Motion Picture Company (MPC) have set up offices in Canada, India, China, Mexico, France, the Netherlands and Britain as means of qualifying for tax breaks – this stimulates employment, but also creates a transitory work force who move from country to country (the short documentary *Life After Pi* (Scott Leberecht, 2014) about the bankruptcy of Rhythm & Hues Studios immediately before their 2013 Oscar win for *Life of Pi* covers this subject). This is largely an example of opportunistic transnationalism that benefits major productions while attempting to support local industry. While a film like *Star Wars* will qualify for the tax break, so do many low-budget productions. Andy Goddard's *Set Fire to the Stars* (2014), about Dylan Thomas's visit to New York in 1950, was an entirely British production, aside from the casting of Elijah Wood. Produced on a budget of £500,000, the production reclaimed 25 per cent of its budget from tax relief.

In 2012, 200 films passed the cultural test to gain official national film status (thereby demonstrating the problematic issues around that term); only 13 were official UK co-productions. The tax rebate on the investment in 2012 was £214 million, a figure that shows how lucrative official national film status can be, especially for transnational productions that are not officially co-productions (Follows, 2013). Huw David Jones (2016) has argued this tends to skew British film policy towards America rather than Europe, as this has produced much higher levels of inward investment, but at the expense of co-productions, which have been on a downward trend. But what criteria do a production have to fulfil to become 'British'? The cultural test is structured around several criteria: cultural content, cultural contribution, cultural hubs and cultural practitioners. There are a total of 35 points available and 18 points are required to qualify as British. 18 points are available for cultural content, although a third of this (six points) is given to films mainly in the English language, or another UK or EEA (European Economic Area) language. Four points each are given to films either set in Britain or the EEA, principal characters who are British or EEA residents, or if the film is based on British or EEA subject matter. With a third of the points required overall, there is a heavy weighting towards films that are principally in English, and therefore this captures many of the Hollywood productions that have been filmed in Britain. For a lower budget film like *Set Fire to the Stars*, there is a stronger focus on British lead characters, although the film wasn't set in Britain but in New York (yet shot entirely in Swansea), and based on British subject matter. Likewise, the film qualifies under the cultural contribution (four points), demonstrating British creativity, heritage or diversity with its story about Thomas, a celebrated Welsh poet. The film also qualified strongly under the cultural hubs criteria, with more than 50 per cent of principal photography or special effects taking place in the UK (two points) and 50 per cent of visual effects work being done in the UK (two points), along with an additional two points' incentive for 80 per cent of principal photography or effects work taking place in the UK. Post-production work, including music recording, contributes another point. Up to eight points are available for cultural practitioners who are UK or EEA residents/citizens, including directors, writers, producers, composers, lead actors, the majority of the rest of the cast, key department heads and the majority of the crew. Therefore, the cultural test provides strong support for low-budget British and EU features but also sets the benchmark for opportunistic transnationalism, where major Hollywood productions can capitalise upon incentives to base productions in the UK (this is also supported by national and regional cultural sector agencies such as the public Creative England or privately run Screen Yorkshire, which was a public agency until 2010). On a national level, tax breaks bring investment, utilise studio space, employ local practitioners and technicians, and develop local talent (the casting of Daisy Ridley and John Boyega in *Star Wars* fulfilled part of the cultural test). They also provide the conditions for opportunistic transnationalism, not only in the UK but internationally, with production companies facilitating cosmopolitan travel by film workers moving production-by-production across borders. Cheaper labour in countries like India, Mexico and China is also exploited alongside First World labour to produce major blockbusters.

This isn't to say, though, that all transnational film production is opportunistic. Other means of co-production are more geared towards milieu-building. Tax breaks are available for films that qualify under other terms, in the UK and other countries. Co-production agreements are treaties between governments that afford the same rights given to national films for officially recognised co-productions. Under these terms, regardless of their textual content, transnational films are legally and economically equal with those of national films. The UK has treaties with a number of countries, including Australia, Canada, China, France, India, Israel, Jamaica, Morocco, New Zealand, Occupied Palestinian Territories, South Africa and Brazil, that specify the proportion of budget (between 20 and 80 per cent) that each country's producers are required to contribute to gain official co-production status and therefore to acquire the equal standing with national films in both territories, which gives access to things like tax breaks, preferential treatment in terms of distribution and access to assistance with import controls. The same conditions are extended through the European Convention of Cinematographic Co-Production, signed by most members of the Council of Europe. Like co-production agreements, this treaty (initially signed in 1992) extends the rights available to national films to co-productions that involve producers from three countries that are signatories to the convention, 'to safeguard creation and freedom of expression and defend the cultural diversity of the various European countries' (Council of Europe, 2016). Like the BFI Cultural Test, there is also a points scale through which a film can be determined to be European, in particular its personnel, director, writer, composer, key cast, editor, sound recordist, art director and director of photography, as well as its shooting and post-production locations; if the production doesn't meet these requirements, it can still be designated as European if it reflects a European identity. The Council of Europe's body for supporting the audiovisual arts, Eurimages, provides support and funding for European co-productions; in 2015 it provided support for 92 co-productions of over €22.5 million, as well as support for distribution and theatrical exhibition. Eurimages-backed films have included consecutive foreign language Oscar winners Michael Haneke's *Amour* (2012), *The Great Beauty* (*La grande bellezza*, Paulo Sorrentino, 2013) and *Ida* (Paweł Pawlikowski, 2013). The need for milieu-building transnational co-productions has long been a focus of discourse surrounding responses by European cinema in the face of growing Hollywood competition. In the 1994 book *Border Crossing: Film in Ireland, Britain and Europe*, John Hill discussed the then European Community's MEDIA programme to develop 'a pan-European industry capable of competing with Hollywood' and 'the potential for national industries to pool resources' (p. 67). Transnational co-productions in Europe tend to be in the form of traditional auteurist art cinema, rather than a move towards what might be seen as a pan-European blockbuster or entertainment cinema in the vein of Hollywood. As Hill argued, 'it is through the mobilisation of trans-national resources in support of national and regional cinemas rooted in specific cultures that the cause of genuinely European cinema would be most successfully advanced' (p. 68). Products of the cross-Europe industry tend to be rooted in a single culture (*Ida* is very much a Polish film, for instance), but produced through transnational means, facilitated by co-production treaties that grant co-productions the same rights as national productions, just as the cultural tests provide the same access through points-based systems or a commitment to identity politics, and therefore tend to benefit from tax breaks and local and regional co-ordination even if that film might not be representative of a culturally national cinema.

If we take a selection of films that Andrew Higson has termed 'culturally English', we'll see how the transnational movement of individuals, capital and culture has helped facilitate a transnational cinema. Following Hjort, Higson contends: 'English cinema has been hybrid from the very start ... caught up in a complicated transnational exchange of films and filmmakers.' In an age of globalisation, however, this condition has become *accelerated*, 'as a complex amalgam of often competing local, national and international forces' (2011, pp. 4–5. Taking a series of films produced over the last 20 years, we see a range of ways in which films are subject to accelerated forces of transnationalisation. As a Jane Austen adaptation, *Sense and Sensibility* (1995) might seem to be what Higson describes as an 'established, iconic and canonical English brand' (p. 251), and the text of the film would seem to support this, with a historical English setting and an adaptation by Emma Thompson, who is also a member of the largely English cast (including Kate Winslet and Hugh Grant). However, the film was produced by an American company, Columbia Pictures, which is owned by a Japanese electronics firm, Sony. The two producers of the film are American, James Schamus and Sydney Pollack, and the film's director, Ang Lee, is Taiwanese (he would describe his later *wuxia pain Crouching Tiger, Hidden Dragon* (*Wo hu cang long*, 2000) as '*Sense and Sensibility* with martial arts'). Likewise, the slightly later *Elizabeth* (1998) is another culturally English production with a heav-ily transnational production background. As a biography of Elizabeth I, it is a historical biopic, a typical British heritage film. Its locations were British and often historical, including York Minster. Its star is the Australian Cate Blanchett, while other members of the cast were Australian (Geoffrey Rush), British (including Christopher Eccleston, Joseph Fiennes and John Gielgud) and French (Fanny Ardant, Eric Cantona and Vincent Cassell). The film was directed by Shekhar Kapur, an Indian director, whose previous film *Bandit Queen* (1994), about the Indian outlaw Phoolan Devi, was an Indian-British co-production, involving Channel Four, the company behind *Elizabeth*.

Channel Four produced the film in co-operation with British company Working Title, part of Canadian-owned Polygram (which had initially been a Dutch/German company prior to its buyout by Seagram, better known as a distillery). We find the same thing when we look at other films: *Match Point* (2005), a film set at Wimbledon, with a mostly British cast, but an American star (Scarlett Johansson) and writer-director (Woody Allen), that is a British-Russian-Irish-American-Luxembourgian co-production; *Bright Star* (2009), a biography of beloved eighteenth-/nineteenth-century British poet John Keats, that is a British-French-Australian co-production, written and directed by a New Zealander (Jane Campion), with a British-Australian-New Zealand cast, shot partly in Italy; even a major Hollywood production such as *Harry Potter and the Prisoner of Azkaban* (2004), that is strongly culturally English, is heavily transnational, as an adaptation of a British novel that is set in Britain with a mostly British cast, but made by an American production company (Warner Bros.), produced by a Brit (David Heyman), directed by a Mexican (Alfonso Cuarón), with a screenplay by an American (Steve Kloves) and shot by a New Zealander (Michael Seresin). None of these are strongly marked transnational films – they don't encourage us to think about transnationalism (although Elizabeth might make us think about the relationship between England and France) – but they are strongly products of transnational film-making. At first glance, each of these films might initially seem strongly English, even British, if we view that through a very limited focus, until we lift the veil of the text to see below to the level of production and how transnational even seemingly very national films might be. Here, we see generally privileged cosmopolitan citizens crossing borders as film labourers, alongside the flexibility of transnational co-production and media ownership.

Case study: James Bond's national roots and transnational foundations

The James Bond films have been part of the British imaginary for over 50 years. Over 25 films (including the non-Eon Production *Never Say Never Again* (Irvin Kershner, 1983)) the series has grossed a worldwide box office of over $7 billion (The Numbers, 2016) and become what James Chapman describes as 'nothing less than a cultural phenomenon' (2007, p. 4). The films have a key place in British cultural identity, especially for the generations for whom Bond films were a fixture of Christmas Day viewing on ITV from 1975 onwards, as Tony Bennett and Janet Woollacott (2003) have noted. The Bond films demonstrate particular British attitudes towards masculinity, class, Empire and ideological tensions, often through an ironic or parodic perspective. Andrew Spicer has referred to Bond as 'incarnating both the unwavering patriotism of the traditional British gentleman hero and the guiltless sexual philandering of the international playboy who embodied the "swinging" sixties' (2001, p. 75). Yet, while Ian Fleming's novels and aspects of the films might be seen as very British, as Chapman notes:

> Bond has outgrown his origins [like Sherlock Holmes] at a historically specific point of British culture ... The transformation of Bond from relatively modest origins into a global brand-name and multi-media "franchise" is a complex process that involves both Britain and America. (2007, p. 22)

Chapman argues that the Bond films arose from a combination of the conditions in the British and American film industries towards the end of the 1950s: 'The Bond films represent a unique marriage between British cultural capital and American dollars that is rooted in the historical circumstances of their original production arrangements' (p. 39). Hollywood's tendency towards quality higher budget productions with more runaway production (Chapman notes that by the 1960s almost half of all American film production was happening outside the US) met with favourable conditions in British cinema, with tax breaks for resident overseas artists and the Film Production Fund that provided funding for British-shot films. While the initial films arose from transnational collaboration – and more than a little opportunism – they (and the novels) engaged with what we might see as transnational concerns. In many respects, they fit Deborah's Shaw's definition of transnational films with multiple international locations, and thematically, they meshed with international concerns surrounding cold war tensions. As Bennett and Woollacott argue:

> Bond effects an ideologically loaded imaginary resolution of the real historical contradictions of the period, a resolution in which all the values associated with Bond, and, thereby, the West – notably, freedom and individualism – gain ascendancy over those associated with the villain and, thereby, communist Russia, such as totalitarianism and bureaucratic rigidity. (2003, p. 18)

This interconnectivity of national and transnational production (where we might see a lens of purely national cinema as limiting) becomes more complicated with more recent Bond films, where Bond becomes more of a transnational product than ever before. As Chapman argues in his postscript to the second edition of *Licence to Thrill*, the revision of Bond in 2006 was not just about the need to revitalise the series (which had hardly been mothballed, given that only four years had passed since *Die Another Day*

(Lee Tamahori) in 2002) but it was facilitated through the choice to adapt *Casino Royale*, the only one of Fleming's novels not to have been given a serious cinematic adaptation (despite a 1950s American TV version, and a spoof film of the same name from 1967). Chapman also argues that it would too easy to see the added complexity of the film as a consequence of its release at a similar time as competitors like Jason Bourne or Jack Bauer, but that many of the ingredients in the more serious, adult Bond film came directly from the source material. The new films are products of an international consortium supported by Sony Entertainment, who owned Columbia studios, and Chapman sees this as a return to some of the origins of the series, and the renewed prominence of runaway productions, with *Casino Royale's* production largely being based in Prague. He quotes Martin Campbell, the film's New Zealander director, who quipped that 'Like everyone, we're heading off to where we can get a good exchange rate' (Chapman, 2007, p. 243). Productions of this kind are so lucrative for local economies that in 2012 overall investment in UK film production dropped by 30 per cent from the previous year, an impact credited to the shooting of the 50th anniversary Bond *Skyfall* during 2011 (Cookson, 2013). Therefore, on one level, border-crossing productions are an attempt to keep costs down and exploit cheaper labour, but they also sometimes allow producers to take advantage of laxer health and safety regulations. As we've seen above, Hollywood studios generally move across borders to take advantage of tax breaks while the Bond films have always taken advantage of exotic locations, from former colonial locations, such as Jamaica (*Dr. No*, 1963, Figure 6.3), to the Orientalised East (*You Only Live Twice*, 1967). As Deborah Shaw

Figure 6.3 The border-crossing of Bond films is presented as an apolitical exotic spectacle, as in *Dr. No* (Guy Hamilton, 1963) (Eon Productions)

has noted, such films rarely make critical points about border-crossings, but use transnational movement as a narrative feature and an aesthetic spectacle, their 'commercial success [depending] on harnessing a tourist gaze... they are often not used predominantly to make social and political points about the nature of globalisation' (2013, p. 55). In many respects they are more the products of globalisation than they are comments on the conditions that produced them, unlike the films we examined in earlier chapters that explored the violence, politics and consequences for identity of border-crossing.

While there might be a perception that Bond is a typically British property, the productions have never been technically 'British' but all produced by Hollywood studios. The four Columbia co-produced films have been products of a transnational corporation with diverse interests. Since the 1970s, the biggest studios have often been owned by multinational corporations. As we've already mentioned, Columbia Pictures has been owned by the Japanese electronics company Sony since 1989 (it had formerly been owned by Coca-Cola), and is part of Sony Pictures Entertainment, which also includes Tristar Pictures and Sony Pictures Classics, their indie-arthouse specialty wing. Sony's diversification is typical of convergent and synergistic media practices, where they produce both hardware and content for those devices. Sony developed the Blu-ray high definition disc and packaged a player in the PlayStation 3 in 2006, an action that is credited with winning the format war with Toshiba's HD-DVD. Sony's acquisition of MGM in 2005 secured a sizeable back catalogue for Blu-ray releases, and the distribution deal for Bond films, which expired with *SPECTRE* (2015), meant these were secured along with the rest of the MGM catalogue (the pre-1968 portion of which was already owned by Turner Entertainment).

However, this convergence goes further in terms of how the films are products of late capitalist commodity production. In 2015, Sony launched a campaign for their Xperia Z5 smartphone that was 'Made for Bond' and the campaign featured the film's stars Daniel Craig and Naomie Harris (who plays Moneypenny). The phone features in *SPECTRE*, alongside other Sony products, such as TVs, Blu-ray players and other smart technology (as has been the case since *Casino Royale*). The film also featured multiple product placements for German and Italian cars, Polish vodka, Dutch beer, and other high-end consumer goods, such as champagne, luggage and designer suits. While these are products that help define the 'quality' and aspirational features of Bond and the film series (such brands were also features of Fleming's novels), they demonstrate how global brands work with film production to define textual features and how they are products of complex global finance, ownership and convergence alongside their border-crossing film cast and crew. This is before we even begin to explore how the texts of the films incorporate other national art forms, such as the extended parkour sequence in *Casino Royale*, a trend within which Leon Hunt (2008) has traced transnational connections between French action cinema and Hong Kong martial arts films.

Transnational Chinese cinema

So far, we've looked solely at mostly western examples of how industries might be transnational, collaborating across borders or exploiting the conditions of globalisation to produce major blockbusters, or how regional resources are pooled to create transnational milieus that challenge Hollywood hegemony. Following on from this, we'll now turn to look at what Chris Berry has termed 'the Chinese situation'. In his article 'What is Transnational Cinema? Thinking from the Chinese Situation' (2010), he articulates several criticisms of the notion of the transnational, the theorisation of which he criticises in a later rewrite of the article as 'woolly and ill-defined' (2011, p. 9). This is partly down to some of the aspects of transnational cinema that we've explored already in the book, that it covers many facets of border-crossing that are sometimes viewed as conflicting or problematic. For Berry, this is too much an acceptance of the values of post-Fordist neoliberal free trade and the economic conditions of globalisation. In the context of Chinese cinema, he argues that the term '"transnational" is most commonly used to talk about Asian martial arts blockbusters and other Hollywood-style productions' (2010, p. 113). We'll engage with some of those films later in the chapter, but it's important first to provide an overview of Chinese cinema, following Berry's work, that defines how the term 'transnational' might be applied to 'the Chinese situation'. The term has come into usage almost as a default way of talking about Chinese cinema, something that Berry traces to Sheldon Hsiao-peng Lu's book *Transnational Chinese Cinemas: Identity, Nationhood, Gender* (1997). Lu asserted that 1896 brought the advent of a Chinese transnational cinema in terms of consumption and distribution, whereas a national production context developed later, somewhere between the first Chinese film in 1905 and its first narrative feature in 1913. For Berry, this classification is problematic, since it sees globalisation as a trigger for transnationalism but a transnational cinema predates globalisation. In some regards, however, Lu's comments do chime with those of Higson in this chapter, about the historical transnational dimension of British cinema. Higson saw globalisation as a catalyst for the *acceleration* of transnationalism, not as a starting point but as a means of intensifying and further hybridising what may have always been hybridised.

This comparison here is worth offering with a caveat that not all transnationalisms are the same, nor all relationships balanced, and the ways in which national cinemas and institutions interact at a transnational level are not equal. British and Chinese cinemas are different, as national cinemas and in their transnational connections.

Because of the segmentation of Chinese cinema into a set of previously assumed national cinemas – the People's Republic of China (PRC), Hong Kong and Taiwan – it has been easy for scholars to adopt a notion of transnationalism in exploring Chinese cinema. For Berry, this is problematised by the quasi-national status bestowed upon both Hong Kong (a former British colony now part of the PRC) and Taiwan (a contested province formed following civil war and creation of the PRC in 1949). *The Encyclopedia of Chinese Film*, published in 1998, lists transnational cinema as a separate entity to three normally recognised branches of Chinese cinema. Following historical entries for each of Chinese, Hong Kong and Taiwanese cinemas, Yingjin Zhang's short chapter on transnational cinema describes it as 'a long tradition of communication and cooperation between China and Hong Kong, between Hong Kong and Taiwan, and between Taiwan and the mainland' (1998, p. 63).

Berry cites Zhang's later criticism of the term transnational as a key aspect of his thinking, but Zhang's earlier distinction of a transnational Chinese cinema as a series of cross-border projects situates transnational Chinese cinema as a regional practice. In another article, Zhang refers to the 'translocal' dimensions of Chinese cinema, across borders that might have been designated as national, such as between Hong Kong and Shanghai, with regular migration of filmmakers between those nodes of production (2011). For Berry, this is an important aspect of the territories that make up Chinese cinema, and thinking of them as separate national cinemas that then collaborate not transregionally, but transnationally, is problematic. The 'increasing levels of cross-border activities limit how meaningful territory-based output statistics are, but also ... those statistics obscure and confuse the transnational reality of the contemporary situation' (Berry, 2010, p. 119). Berry therefore suggests that we define transnationalism as a concept *and* as a practice. Following Anna Tsing's anthropology, Berry 'suggests we use "globalization" as part of the ideological rhetoric of globalism, whereas we use "transnational" to refer to the specific "transborder projects" that actually constitute the growth of the transnational on the ground' (p. 122). This gives us a means of avoiding looking at the transnational solely through the logic of the neoliberal market and the 'fantasy of globalization' but also how projects operate across borders outside that logic. Therefore, by understanding how a transnational world order has emerged from a previous international order we can avoid simply analogising transnational cinema purely along lines of globalisation (p. 124).

In her book, *From Tian'anmen Square to Times Square: Transnational China and the Chinese Diaspora on Global Screens, 1989–1997* (2006), Gina Marchetti discusses the ways in which China, between the student uprising in Tian'anmen Square in 1989 and the handover of Hong Kong to Chinese rule in 1997, found itself 'at a crossroads within a shifting global culture' and within the '"scattered hegemonies" [Grewal & Kaplan, 1994]' 'that characterize postmodern, transnational culture' (p. 18). Marchetti looks broadly across Chinese cinema: from the genre films of transnational directors like John Woo, and martials arts films featuring stars such as Michelle Yeoh, Brigitte Lin and Maggie Cheung, to films with themes of shifting gender, as in Hui's *Song of the Exile*, and sexual identities, some of which had strongly allegorical dimensions. Ang Lee's *The Wedding Banquet* (*Xi yan*, 1993) tells the story of a gay landlord and his female tenant who enter a marriage of convenience, allegorising Taiwan's 'unrecognised' relationship with the PRC; *Happy Together* (*Chun gwong cha sit*, Wong Kar-wai, 1997) is a 'can't live with him, can't live without him' story that depicts the dynamic of Hong Kong's relationship with China prior to the 1997 handover. Martial arts films also engage with aspects of queered gender and sexuality, such as *Swordsman II* (*Xiao ao jiang hu: dong fang bu bai*, Tsiu Hark, 1992), in which the film's title character, Invincible Asia (Brigitte Lin), leader of a cult sect, castrates himself to achieve great power (Figure 6.4). The self-castration can be seen either as a figure of anxiety surrounding Hong Kong's impending return to Chinese power, or a sign of a self-Orientalising submission to the west's idea of a global market. Marchetti also defines a transnational Chinese cinema beyond the borders of

Figure 6.4 Brigitte Lin's Invincible Asia castrates himself as a self-orientalising feminisation that acts as a queered sign of anxiety about Hong Kong return's to Chinese rule in *Swordsman II* (Tsiu Hark, 1992) (Film Workshop/Long Shong Pictures)

the PRC, Hong Kong and Taiwan (Greater China) in particular diasporic film-makers, such as: Evans Chan, a cosmopolitan transnational filmmaker; Yau Ching, an exiled experimental filmmaker whose work includes the epistolary experimental film *Is There Anything Specific You Want Me to Tell You About?* (1991), a film that Marks described as intercultural, featuring 'a wry suspicion of the images that already contain her (Chinese) culture in the west' (Marks, 2000, p. 136); and Chinese-American filmmakers such as Wayne Wang. Marchetti's notion of a Chinese cinema during this time spans global cinema, across cultural and national boundaries: the films it produces:

> not only show the marks of circulation within a transnational economy, with international crews, casts, funding, and distribution, they also cross cultural borders to comment on the diversity contained within Greater China, based on national, linguistic, political, class, gender, generational, sexual, and other differences. As the films display the hybridity accrued from very different histories of colonialism, socialism, capitalism, migration, exile, and diaspora, they present no singular Chinese way of life but a cultural cornucopia associated with the ethnic Chinese globally. (2006, p. 26)

Marchetti's vision here draws on Naficy's definitions of an independent transnational film genre, and also his work on exilic and diasporic cinema, as Marchetti sets this in the context of a global Chinese diaspora depicted on-screen. Her definition of a transnational Chinese cinema echoes that of Berry, in that it connects the efficacy of global marketplaces and how they are trans-forming national cinemas, but also in the way that it engages more critically with identities and the multiplicity of historical and political concerns that have little concern with the marketplace, although they might be facilitated through the movement of people and capital via transnational flows.

One of the most significant ways in which Chinese cinema has been dis-cussed as a transnational cinema, something to which Berry and Marchetti allude, concerns the growth of a blockbuster culture. Berry's article '"What's Big About the Big Film?" "De-westernizing" the blockbuster in Korea and China' (2003) argues that 'the blockbuster is no longer American owned'. He points out that the term 'blockbuster' has been adopted by local critics and filmmakers to describe not just Hollywood products distributed in South Korea and China, but local filmmaking practice. While the concept:

> may be borrowed and translated, ... this should not be understood in terms of the original and the copy, where divergence from the original marks failure of authenticity. Instead, in the postcolonial politics and globalized economics of blockbusters, borrowing and translation are only the first step on the road toward agency and creativity. (p. 218)

'[B]lockbusters today are global and plural', he contends (p. 218). The block-buster has been localised through different responses in both countries. In South Korea, local versions of the blockbuster have been produced. Berry notes the examples of two films produced at the turn of the twenty-first century that defined the Korean blockbuster: *Shiri* (Kang Je-gyu, 1999) and *Joint Security Area* (Park Chan-wook, 2000), that both engaged with ongoing tensions surrounding the Korean division (Park's film is very much a border narrative, about a military shooting along the Demilitarised Zone on the 38th Parallel) and defined the success of the Korean blockbuster, as both films out-grossed *Titanic* (James Cameron, 1997) at the South Korean box office. Unlike the longer availability of big-budget American films in South Korea, in China it was only after 1995 that such films hit the market en masse. Berry notes that in both countries there was a critical observation that local films were unable to compete with such films, in terms of scope, drama and spectacle. But in China the discourse around the 'big film' (*dapian*) is filtered through a historical focus on epics, or 'giant films' (*jupain*) that had a didactic, educational quality. There was an attempt to emulate Hollywood in 1997 with *The Opium War* (*Yapian zhanzheng*, Jin Xie), at the time the highest budgeted Chinese blockbuster. Berry sees the film as an attempt to produce a fusion between the seriousness of the 'giant film' and the produc-tion values of the 'big film' as a means of distinguishing it as 'a qualitatively different and superior Chinese blockbuster' (p. 223). Nevertheless, Berry sees this attempt as one that provides agency for filmmakers through the produc-tion of blockbusters, even if those films don't challenge the domination of Hollywood blockbusters.

Since the publication of Berry's article in 2003, there has been a greater flow of big-budget Chinese blockbusters that have used strategies normally reserved for Hollywood films: spectacle, stars, star directors and genre, as well as higher budgets. Some of those films have been produced in collabo-ration with Hollywood studios, giving them a greater global reach, beyond arthouses, cult or diasporic audiences, while also providing access to those higher budgets. The film that initiated this trend was *Crouching Tiger, Hidden Dragon* (Ang Lee, 2000), a production that Darrell William Davis and Emilie Yueh-yu Yeh refer to as 'a beacon of cultural China' (2008, p. 25). In an important article that looks at the film as a key example of a transnational production, Christina Klein has defined it as:

> embedded within a network of transnational flows – of people, capital, texts, and ideas – that muddy the distinction between the global and the local. The film emerged not out of any neatly bounded national and cultural space called 'China,' 'Taiwan,' 'Hong Kong,' 'Hollywood,' or even 'the East' or 'the West' but from the boundary-crossing processes

of war, migration, capitalist exchange, aesthetic appropriations, and memory. (2004, p. 21)

She notes how the film is a product of companies based in five different countries (China, Taiwan, Hong Kong, the US, and the British Virgin Islands, where Ang Lee's United China Vision incorporated a subsidiary); the script was written back and forth in translation between writers in America (James Schamus) and Taiwan (Wang Hui Ling); the content is strongly Chinese in origin, as an adaptation of Wang Du Lu's novel, never translated in English, about *jiang hu* bandits and outlaws during the Qing Dynasty (1644–1911). The cast drew on major East Asian ethnic-Chinese stars, Malaysian Michelle Yeoh (known outside the region for her role in 1997 Bond film *Tomorrow Never Dies* (Roger Spottiswoode)), Chow Yun-fat (best known for Hong Kong action films made with John Woo, such as *The Killer* (*Dip huet seung hung*, 1989) and *Hard Boiled* (*Lat sau san taam*, 1992), but who had also made films in Hollywood, including the action film *The Replacement Killers* (Antoine Fuqua, 1998) and drama *Anna and the King* (Andy Tennant, 1999)), and provided breakthrough roles for Chinese Zhang Ziyi and Taiwanese Chang Chen. The film also nostalgically harked back to the martial arts films of the 1960s with the casting of Cheng Pei-pei as the film's principal antagonist; her role as Golden Swallow in King Hu's *Come Drink with Me* (*Da zui xia*, 1966) and sequel *Golden Swallow* (*Jin yan zi*, Chang Cheh, 1968) made her a prominent star of Shaw Brothers' martial arts extravaganzas. Klein notes how the film's release (and success) was met with mixed responses globally – some critics saw it as a sumptuous and distinctively Asian film that finally challenged Hollywood's dominance in the blockbuster field, while others saw it as a co-optation of Asian material, rendering it palatable for a western gaze, and erasing the legacy of more 'authentic' filmmakers in the genre, like King Hu (Hu's *Touch of Zen* (*Xia nü*, 1971) has been held as a key influence on *Crouching Tiger*, with its strong female protagonist and spectacular locations). Genre fans were quick to spot the actors' lack of martial arts skills, while others commented on their poor Mandarin pronunciation and the inauthenticity of historical settings. Klein argues, though, that seeing the film purely through monocultural points of view is unhelpful in defining it, and she sees it strongly as an example of a diasporic film, signalled by Lee's diasporic roots, and how it sits within a triangular arrangement of 'Lee's ties to his Chinese homeland, to other members of the Chinese diaspora, and to the culture of his American hostland' (p. 21). For Klein, Lee retains a strong connection with his Taiwanese homeland as a member of the Chinese diaspora, culturally and economically.

The film's choice of genre, martial arts, Klein notes, is central to its core presentation of Lee's nostalgic '"dream" of old China' (p. 36), a place he visited for the first time during production. For Klein, the genre is already diasporic, as Hong Kong cinema had been since waves of migration in the mid-twentieth century produced a dual-language cinema, in Cantonese, the local dialect, and the northern Mandarin language. The Mandarin-speaking cinema was exported to diasporic audiences across South-East Asia and globally, and this is echoed in *Crouching Tiger*'s choice of Mandarin as its main language as a diasporic signifier. Klein also highlights how the film benefits from a range of diasporic talents, such as its cast from across the region and its fight choreographer, Yuen Wo-ping (whose previous work included *The Matrix* (The Wachowskis, 1999)), who provides significant visual pleasures in its fight sequences. The third dimension of the film's 'cross-cultural dialogue and creolization' (a term that refers to the ways in which colonisation created diasporic cultures with cultural identities that are a mixture of home and host cultures) is its adoption of a Hollywood generic trait as a means of integrating spectacle and narrative (p. 31). Martial arts films could often exhibit a weak relationship between the overarching narrative and fight sequences, where the narrative might simply be a flimsy pretext to string fights together. The Hollywood musical forms the template through which the two are fused in *Crouching Tiger*.

Finally, Klein notes the ways in which critics grasped the poor box office performance of the film in China as a sign of its cultural inauthenticity. Conversely, she highlights how the film became embroiled in a battle between Asia Union Film and Entertainment, who owned 80 per cent of its distribution rights, and the state-owned China Film Co-Production Corporation who wanted a bigger cut. The legal struggle kept the film from screens for three-and-a-half months, and once it returned, the market was flooded with pirated DVDs and video CDs, and the film had already shown on television. So, while it ostensibly flopped at the box office, it was, in Schamus's terms, 'probably [China's] most watched movie of the year' (Klein, 2004, p. 36). Klein calls *Crouching Tiger* 'an exemplary instance of transnational cinema' that muddies 'the distinction between Hollywood and "foreign" cinema' with 'aesthetic affiliations [that] cross multiple cultural boundaries' (p. 37). We can't simply see it as an example of the 'colonial mimicry' that Berry observed in the Chinese blockbuster, as a copy of the blockbuster, but nor does it qualify simply as a Hollywoodisation of the martial arts film either; instead, as Klein strongly argues, it is a diasporic blockbuster, produced by a diasporic cast and crew, with multiple sources of transnational funding that targeted a predominantly diasporic audience.

Davis and Yeh stress that *Crouching Tiger* set a benchmark for Chinese blockbuster cinema, and that its success led to a wave of Chinese state-backed blockbusters, including *Hero* (*Ying xiong*, Zhang Yimou, 2002), *House of Flying Daggers* (*Shimian maifu*, Zhang Yimou, 2004), *The Emperor and the*

Assassin (*Jing Ke ci Qin Wang*, Chen Kaige, 1998), and *Kung Fu Hustle* (*Gongfu*, Stephen Chow, 2004) (2008, pp. 27–28). As we've already heard from Hjort, films such as *Hero* are strong examples of globalising transnationalism, as works that access international distribution through the adoption of popular cinema traits such as stardom, genre and Hollywood-style production values. Like *Crouching Tiger*, they adopt a blend of national concerns, such as historical subject matter: *Hero* and *The Emperor and the Assassin* are both based on the same story, about the third-century plot to assassinate the king of the Qin state, who later became China's first emperor. Jenny Lau has referred to *Hero* as 'China's response to Hollywood globalization' (2007), the culmination of a process of developing a popular Chinese cinema that sought to end the decline in production and distribution revenue in the face of increased competition from imported films in China. Following the end of their monopoly of film distribution, the Chinese Film Bureau focused more on popular film production than on the kind of artisanal film production that had been popular with international festivals. This produced three strands of filmmaking: 'the artisan/cultural films, usually banned; the state-sponsored films (old mainstream), usually not popular; and the new mainstream entertainment, commercial and stylistically imitating Hollywood' (Lau, 2007). Some films in the artisanal mode, such as *Suzhou River* (*Suzhou he*, Lou Ye, 1999) or *The Missing Gun* (*Xun qiang*, Lu Chuan, 2002) (which uses a missing gun trope that is shared with Akira Kurosawa's *Stray Dog* (*Nora inu*, 1949) and Johnnie To's slightly later Hong Kong film *PTU* (2003)) were international festival hits, but not strong box office successes in China. The development of the new mainstream film production was largely an attempt to secure success with the local box office, although it drew in stylistic features and commercial production strategies from global Hollywood. *Hero* was caught in a bind, however, pitched somewhere between the local and global dimensions of this policy, as Lau contends:

> *Hero* is caught in the contradictions between narrow nationalism (security and unity) and self-conscious cosmopolitanism (world peace – 'Tian xia' peace). This confusion, perhaps, can also be seen as a reflection of China's own situation since the country is still in the process of balancing its semi-dictatorial feudalism with modern global internationalism.

Leon Hunt, in *Kung Fu Cult Masters* (2003), also argues that the film has a strong blending of international and local dimensions, that it 'seems packaged to replicate *Crouching Tiger's* Western success', but that it is 'more Sinicist in outlook' (p. 183). This Sinicist outlook is also noted by Lau in the ways in which the film, with its 'All Under Heaven' message, can be read as advocating China's one-state policy and its desire to unify China, Hong

Kong and Taiwan, and this was controversial when the film was released in China. Despite Hunt's comment that the film seemed designed to replicate *Crouching Tiger*'s success in the west, the film was released slowly around the globe after its Chinese release in December 2002; the film wasn't released in the US and UK until late summer in 2004. By the time the film was released in most territories, it had long been available on DVD in China, and the film's distributors, Miramax, had to fight to stop these being sold in its territories. The film was only released uncut and in a subtitled version following the intervention of Quentin Tarantino, with the headline 'Quentin Tarantino Presents' above the title on posters. This reminds us of Berry's comments about the lack of a level playing field for international blockbusters (despite this, it grossed almost $54 million in the US (Box Office Mojo, 2016), making it the third highest grossing foreign language film of all time); while the film seemed strongly designed to be global, its nationalist themes were an impediment that aren't necessarily a blockage for films that have transnational or diasporic bases. Nevertheless, as Berry and Farquhar have argued, 'the need for a global audience does not preclude reproducing territorial nation-state nationalism in' the global martial arts blockbuster (2006, p. 49).

Klein has argued that questions about production are an important factor in thinking about the transnational dimensions of Chinese cinema: 'More attention needs to be paid to transnational Chinese-language films as products of industries that are in historically specific states of flux, and as regionally and globally circulating commodities' (2007, p. 190). Just as she did with *Crouching Tiger* in her earlier article, she also looked at how Stephen Chow's *Kung Fu Hustle* is a product of transnational production, as 'a complex form of transnationalism' (p. 190). She sees the film as an example of the convergence of the film industries of Hong Kong, Hollywood and China. Chow was a major star in Hong Kong at the time, and had been since the 1980s. Because of the complexities of his verbal humour in Cantonese, and since comedy is often the least mobile of film genres, his films didn't travel well. He came to international recognition in 2001 with the release of *Shaolin Soccer* (*Shaolin zuqiu*), a mixture of comedy, kung fu and CGI-enhanced aesthetics that was a massive hit in Hong Kong. It was also handily timed to benefit from the hype surrounding the 2002 FIFA World Cup that was due to take place in South-East Asia. The film's potential was limited due to its effective banning in China (due to the use of the Shaolin name without permission), and a hackneyed release in the US, where distributors Miramax cut 23 minutes and released it in a dubbed version. The film brought Chow to the attention of a wider global audience, in spite of the limited exposure the film received officially.

Chow produced *Kung Fu Hustle* in collaboration with Columbia Pictures Film Production Asia, one of the companies involved in *Crouching Tiger*'s production, something Klein notes is part of the company's strategy of 'glocalisation' (global localisation). This combines two strategies: one that targets films at the broad mass entertainment audience, such as the Bond films; and another one that produces films with fewer resources targeted at local markets. In combination, the two strategies 'embody the homogenizing and localizing tendencies of corporate-led globalization: while the blockbusters treat the globe as a single mass audience, the local-language films cater to multiple discrete audiences with culturally specific tastes and histories' (Klein, 2007, p. 197). For Sony (Columbia's parent company), Chow provided an opportunity to target audiences in Chinese-speaking markets, while Sony afforded an opportunity for Chow to reach a global audience. Klein attributes the film's high production values, wide release and formalised production process (rather than the more improvisational style more typical of Hong Kong directors) to the involvement of Sony, while the Chinese co-producers granted access to the Chinese market that had previously been denied to Chow's films. The two companies who collaborated on the film – the private firm Huayi Brothers and the state-run China Film Group – meant the film took on all the rights of a Chinese national film, and this helped to navigate state censorship. This support was crucial, Klein argues, for the Hong Kong film industry, in the face of a shrinking industry and the loss of their traditional export markets. Therefore:

[While] *Kung Fu Hustle* is emblematic of the Hong Kong industry's transformation under the pressures of globalization, the film is likewise a marker of the Chinese film industry's efforts to transform itself from a state-run instrument of education and propaganda into a viable commercial industry. (p. 202–203)

The film is therefore a model for mapping global flows in different directions:

[F]lows out of Hollywood (in the form of capital, mode of production, stylistic conventions) into Hong Kong; reverse flows out of Hong Kong (in the form of the film itself and Chow's star persona and comic sensibility) into the United States; and regional flows out of Hong Kong (in the form of its film workers and expertise) into China. (p. 204)

This final point is important because it emphasises the importance of cross-border flows in unidirectional ways. While we can't simply see all those flows as equal, it does show how transregional and transnational production has become an integral part of Chinese cinema, across the three regions of PRC, Taiwan and Hong Kong. Since the production of *Kung Fu Hustle*, China Film Group have intensified their co-production policy with credits on over 100 films, some of which have combined international stars with Chinese genres: *The Myth* (*San wa*, Stanley Tong, 2005), with Jackie Chan; the starry two-part epic *Red Cliff* (*Chi bi* and *Chi bi Part II: Jue zhan tian xia*, John Woo, 2008 and 2009), based on a historical third-century battle that marked the end of the Han dynasty; and *Crouching Tiger, Hidden Dragon: Sword of Destiny* (Yuen Wo-ping, 2016), which caused controversy when its distribution rights were sold to Netflix, meaning it largely bypassed theatrical distribution in the west (an IMAX version was released but boycotted by some exhibitors). However, it was a hit in China, where it grossed more than twice the first film due to being granted local status by the involvement of China Film Group (Tartaglione, 2016).

The China Film Group were also involved in the production of the 2010 remake of *The Karate Kid* (Harald Zwart), starring Jackie Chan and Jaden Smith. The remake relocates the story from Los Angeles to Beijing, and karate is replaced with kung fu; in China the film was released as *Gongfu meng*, literally *Kung Fu Kid*. The Japanese *sensei* Mr. Miyagi (played in the 1984 original by the Japanese-American actor Pat Morita) is replaced with *shifu* Mr. Han, played by Chan. This recasting necessitates some changes. Miyagi's family, we're told, died during the Second World War while he served honourably in infantry; while he was away, his pregnant wife was placed in an internment camp, as many Japanese-Americans were following the Japanese attack on Pearl Harbour. The remake steers away from politicisation, something Rachel Mizsei-Ward, in her review in the journal *Scope*, attributes to the involvement of the China Film Group (2011). She points out that the absence of politics in the film – the absence testified to by the presence of statues and images of Mao and noted Communist Party members – are overwhelmed by the film's emphasis on tourist images of China. Han and Dre, the title character, visit the Great Wall, with little narrative motivation, to train, while we're also treated to views of the Forbidden Palace, the Bird's Nest Olympic Stadium (Figure 6.5), and the Wudang mountains alongside spectacular countryside and images of Beijing's vibrant cultural festivals. Miszei-Ward argues that the film makes China look like 'an exciting holiday destination'. In *Remaking Chinese Cinema: Through the Prism of Shanghai, Hong Kong, and Hollywood* (2013), Yiman Wang attributes the changes made in remaking the film to the convergence of three factors:

1. The transnational (re)emergence of kung fu and martials arts following the landslide success of *Crouching Tiger, Hidden Dragon*.
2. Hollywood's outsourcing from southern California to China (and other low-cost areas).
3. The increasing number of Americans losing jobs during the current economic depression and finding themselves landed in countries like China for work opportunities (p. 145).

Figure 6.5 *The Karate Kid* (Harald Zwart, 2010): Dre and friend run through Beijing's Olympic Park with the Bird's Nest Stadium in the background, in one of many scenes in *The Karate Kid* that present a touristic China to audiences (Overbrook Entertainment/China Film Group/Jerry Weintraub Productions)

This final point, which frames the film's narrative, about Dre's mother moving from Detroit to Beijing for work purposes, helps define how the film engages with globalisation on a textual level, although others demonstrate how the film is a product of globalisation and the need to compete in challenging global markets. Wang also notes how the film is a literal expression of outsourcing, as the film's Detroit scenes were also shot in Beijing. Like Mizsei-Ward, though, she describes the film as 'an all-out attempt to sell the post-Olympics kung fu China to Western as well as Chinese audiences' (p. 145).

This extended case study of transnational Chinese cinema has sought to spell out some of the ways in which China has been conceived as a transborder cinema, as well as how the Chinese cinema industry has responded to globalisation. Looking at China has allowed us to consider how globalisation has required cinemas to look outwards and engage with different kinds of filmmaking, both commercial and diasporic, and how cosmopolitan filmmakers have been able to straddle different industries, across China, Taiwan, Hong Kong and Hollywood. During this chapter, the emphasis has been on considering issues of production, some of which have been expressed onscreen, and in subsequent chapters we'll consider these issues more from a textual perspective, as we look at global flows of culture.

Recommended further reading:

Aquilia, Pieter (2006), 'Westernizing Southeast Asian Cinema: Co-productions for "Transnational" Markets', *Continuum: Journal of Media & Cultural Studies* 20(4): pp. 433–445.

Chan, Kenneth (2004), 'The Global Return of the Wu Xia Pian (Chinese Sword-Fighting Movie): Ang Lee's *Crouching Tiger, Hidden Dragon*', *Cinema Journal* 43(4): pp. 3–17.

—— (2009), *Remade in Hollywood: The Global Chinese Presence in Transnational Cinemas.* Hong Kong: Hong Kong University Press.

Provencher, Ken (2016), 'Transnational Wong', in ed. Martha P. Nochimson, *A Companion to Wong Kar-wai.* Oxford: Wiley Blackwell, pp. 23–46.

Raju, Zakir Hossain (2008), 'Filmic imaginations of the Malaysian Chinese: "Mahua cinema" as a Transnational Chinese Cinema', *Journal of Chinese Cinemas* 2(1): pp. 67–79.

Rawnsley, Ming-Yeh T. (2013), 'Taiwanese-Language Cinema: State versus Market, National versus Transnational', *Oriental Archive* 81(3): pp. 1–22.

Sun, Yi (2015), 'Shaping Hong Kong Cinema's New Icon: Milkyway Image at International Film Festivals', *Transnational Cinemas* 6(1): pp. 67–83.

Taylor, Jeremy E. (2008), 'From Transnationalism to Nativism? The Rise, Decline and Reinvention of a Regional Hokkien Entertainment Industry', *Inter-Asia Cultural Studies* 9(1): pp. 62–81.

—— (2011), *Rethinking Transnational Chinese Cinemas: The Amoy-dialect Film Industry in Cold War Asia.* London: Routledge.

Zhang, Yingjin (2010), *Cinema, Space, and Polylocality in a Globalizing China.* Honolulu: University of Hawai'i Press.

—— (2010), 'Transnationalism and Translocality in Chinese Cinema', *Cinema Journal* 49(3): pp. 135–139.

Discussion questions:

- If there has always been a transnational dimension to the circulation of production personnel and films, why do you think we have only recently seen film studies adopt the term 'transnational'?
- How do transnational film industries like Hollywood and China complicate our understanding of what makes a film 'national'?
- How might the study of transnational film industries tend to favour bigger nations and obscure more marginal films and filmmakers?
- Which other global actors can you think of who have become transnational stars? Can you think of any examples who have had their star images subverted by fans?

CHAPTER 7

Remaking Transnational Culture

Arjun Appadurai, responding to Pico Iyer's book *Video Night in Kathmandu: And Other Reports from the Not-so-Far East*, first published in 1988, suggests that, 'if *a* global cultural system is emerging, it is filled with ironies and resistances, sometimes camouflaged as passivity and a bottomless appetite in the Asian world for things Western' (1996, p. 29). In his travels around South and South-East Asia, Iyer had seen the adoption of American cultural products around China, Thailand, The Philippines, India and Japan. He witnessed the adoption of American music, such as the anti-establishment anthem 'Born in the USA' by Bruce Springsteen & The E Street Band, and a mania for John Rambo. One of the things he noted was that as soon as *First Blood* (Ted Kotcheff, 1982) had been released in India, five remakes went into production, 'one of them recasting the macho superman as a sari-clad woman' (Iyer, 1989, p. 3). Appadurai reflects on Iyer's observations as a way of responding to the casting of globalisation as a process of homogenisation and particularly of Americanisation. He argues that Americanisation is a 'pallid term' for the processes witnessed by Iyer. He argues (although this is the opening of his original article, 'Disjuncture and Difference in the Global Cultural Economy' – Iyer is not mentioned in that version):

> The central problem of today's global interactions is the tension between cultural homogenization and cultural heterogenization ... Most often, the homogenization argument subspeciates into either an argument about Americanization or an argument about commoditization, and very often the two arguments are closely linked. What these arguments fail to consider is that at least as rapidly as forces from various metropolises are brought into new societies they tend to become indigenized in one way or another. (Appadurai, 1996, p. 32)

For some societies, other nationalisms may pose a greater concern: 'Japanization ... for Koreans, Indianization for Sri Lankans, Vietnamization for the Cambodians' (p. 32). Nearby nations, especially those with legacies of colonialism, may be more threatening than Americanisation. 'One man's imagined community is another man's political prison', Appadurai contends, referencing Benedict Anderson. Hence, this 'global cultural economy has to be seen as a complex, overlapping, disjunctive order that cannot any longer be understood in terms of existing center-periphery models (even those that might account for multiple centers and peripheries)' (p. 32).

Appadurai's concept of mediascapes, the 'image-centered, narrative-based accounts or strips of reality' (1990, p. 299), will largely be a focus of this and the next chapter. In the 'global flow of people and things' (1996, p. 29), we move from people towards texts and cultural influence. We also return to Tom O'Regan's processes of cultural exchange, as ever-present mechanisms in the transnational movement of film and filmmaking across national and cultural borders, and even translocally within states:

> They facilitate the lending and redisposition of cultural materials from one filmmaking and cultural tradition to another. A powerful force for innovation in filmmaking and the development of international under-standing and misunderstanding alike, cultural exchange is a critical component of wider processes of cultural identity formation and cultural development. (1999, p. 262)

In this chapter, we will explore how these issues relate to transnational remakes, how cultural production in transnational cinemas is subject to appropriation, cultural revisionism and the flow and drift of ideas, concepts and stories. As Appadurai argues, this sees a process of homogenisation and heterogeneity, and the tension between Hollywood's co-optation of global material, its remakes of films from around the world, from Japan to South Korea to France, Germany, Italy, Sweden, Norway and Spain to Thailand and South Africa, and the appropriation of Hollywood cinema by a number of global cinemas, not just as imitation but through processes of localisation, irony or parody. In so doing, remakes reflect significant issues of cultural power and how culture circulates globally and is adopted or appropriated by other nations through the heterogenisation noted by Appadurai.

Remaking world cinema

The film industry analyst Stephen Follows has quantified the trend in Hollywood for remakes: between 2005 and 2014, of the top 100 grossing films of each year just under 10 per cent were remakes (his definition of remake is generous, and doesn't include new adaptations of source litera-ture or remakes of TV shows). But he sees it as a declining trend. In 2005, 17 per cent were remakes, while just 5 per cent were remakes in 2014.

Instead, he charts a rising trend towards sequels, prequels or spin-offs (Follows, 2015). While the selection of just the top 100 grossing films will inevitably be an incomplete picture of how many films Hollywood remakes, it speaks to a trend that has long been an element of production of previously made films from other nations. French cinema has long been a focus of Hollywood remake strategies: *Pépé-le-Moko*, which we encountered in an earlier chapter, was remade in 1938, a year after the original, as *Algiers* (John Cromwell); Jean-Luc Godard's *A bout de souffle* (1960) was remade under its English title, *Breathless* (Jim McBride, 1983), starring Richard Gere; *Three Men and a Baby* (Frank Oz, 1987) was a remake of the popular comedy *Trois hommes et un couffin* (*Three Men and a Cradle*, Coline Serreau, 1985); *La Totale!* (Claude Zizi, 1991) provided the basis for James Cameron's Arnold Schwarzenegger action comedy *True Lies* (1994); and the romantic comedy *Neuf mois* (Patrick Braoudé, 1994) was swiftly remade as *Nine Months* (Chris Columbus, 1995) with Hugh Grant and Julianne Moore. Other films from Europe have been remade by Hollywood studios, such as the Norwegian *Insomnia* (Erik Skjoldbjærg, 1997), with the same title, starring Al Pacino (Christopher Nolan, 2002); the Hungarian football war film *Two Half-Times in Hell* (*Két félidö a pokolban*, Zoltán Fábri, 1961) as the star-studded *Escape to Victory* (John Huston, 1981); and the Spanish *Open Your Eyes* (*Abre los Ojos*, Alejandro Amenábar, 1997), as *Vanilla Sky* (Cameron Crowe, 2001), with Penélope Cruz reprising her role from the original. Hindi films have also been remade, such as the US-Sri Lankan co-production *A Common Man* (Chandran Rutnam, 2013), a remake of *A Wednesday!* (Neeraj Pandey, 2008). There has also been a trend towards remaking films from East Asia, especially Japan and South Korea, but also Hong Kong: The Oscar-winning *The Departed* (Martin Scorsese, 2006) was a remake of Hong Kong film *Infernal Affairs* (*Mou gaan dou*, translated as Uninterrupted Road, a shortening of a translation of the Sanskrit Buddhist term *avīci-nakara*, 'the endless Hell'); South Korean film *Il Mare* (*Siworae*, Lee Hyun-seung, 2000) was remade as *The Lake House* (Alejandro Agresti, 2006); Japanese film *Shall We Dance?* (Masayuki Suo, 1996) became an American film of the same title starring Richard Gere (Peter Chelsom, 2004). Much of the academic focus on remakes of East Asian films have focused on the cycle of genre films that were produced in the wake of the J-horror cycle in the early 2000s, and we'll return to those in more detail later in the chapter.

The argument surrounding Hollywood's interest in foreign cinemas has tended towards the homogenising side of Appadurai's argument about globalisation. Where films are pre-sold in foreign markets, popular hits provide American cinema with proven properties: they have been market-tested, often have a form of brand-name recognition with audiences, and they come with fully developed scripts and stories. It is then assumed that the film will be stripped of culturally specific, local features to be universalised for the Hollywood market (which may include the film's original territory). Constantine Verevis describes this assumption as being where foreign films are 'dispossessed of local detail to exploit (English language) markets' (2004, p. 88). Likewise, Linda Hutcheon argues that the adaptation of films on a global level tends towards the nonspecific determination of certain culturally located meaning, 'because Hollywood films are increasingly being made for international audiences ... [T]he adaptation might end up not only altering characters' nationalities, but on the contrary, actually deemphasising any national, regional, or historical specificities' (2006, p. 147). The universalising argument sees this as an act of cultural imperialism, a sign of the ongoing dominance of Hollywood in global markets in which 'local' products are reconfigured and co-opted by Hollywood.

Verevis gives us three different ways in which we can explore and critically evaluate remakes:

> the first, *remaking as industrial category*, deals with issues of production, including industry (commerce) and authors (intention); the second, *remaking as textual category*, considers texts (plots and structures) and taxonomies; and the third, *remaking as critical category*, deals with issues of reception, including audiences (recognition) and institutions (discourse). (2004, pp. 87–88)

Like genres, remakes deal in repetition and difference. Some remakes are signalled, legally through copyright attribution, while others are unacknowledged or unrecognised. Audiences are often aware of the intertextual connections between films, as they are with genres, and the ways in which one plot or structure refers to another. Therefore, Verevis argues that the study of the field of film remakes is one 'of endlessly proliferating patterns of repetition and difference' (p. 100). When we consider the remaking of films across borders and cultures, there are a range of nationally specific issues that come into play, as well as how films are positioned for international markets (made to be transnational products) before they are remade. They call into question how audiences relate to issues of national cinema, as well as how national cinemas relate to one another.

In her book on Hollywood remakes of French cinema, Lucy Mazdon offers a rebuttal to this argument that 'French source films are often described as intrinsically "national" products enabling condemnation of the remake as an act of violence against the "national" culture' (2000, p. 88). Her analysis of a number of films demonstrates how problematic the national becomes as a category to understand how films are subject to global cultural influence and that what emerges 'is a negotiation of identity which undermines any attempt to position [the original and the remake] in the fixed binaries of France/Hollywood, art/popular, original/copy' (p. 88). Mazdon looks at two examples of French originals with Hollywood remakes that problematise the purity of a nationally specific cinematic identity: *The Return of Martin Guerre* (*La Retour de Martin Guerre*, Daniel Vigne, 1982), a heritage costume drama based on a sixteenth-century folk tale about the return of a man who had previously abandoned his family whose identity is called into questions by locals, and Godard's *Breathless*. The remakes of both films starred Richard Gere, the former as *Sommersby* (Jon Amiel, 1993), set just after the American civil war, while, as we've mentioned, *Breathless* was remade by Jim McBride in 1983, although it was released in France under the title *A bout de souffle made in USA* (Figure 7.1), a reference to Godard's 1966 film *Made in U.S.A.*. Mazdon uses the two films and their remakes to call into question the specificity of national identity and a national cinema. The French version of *Martin Guerre* came at the time of a series of popular historical dramas across the 1970s and 1980s that achieved some international success (the film's star Gérard Depardieu is a key representative of this cycle, with his international award success for this film and the later *Cyrano de Bergerac* (Jean-Paul Rappeneau, 1990)). Mazdon notes that the historical drama calls into question the articulation of national identity, both hegemonic and otherwise (she actually sees this film as contrary to a hegemonic national identity), something shared across the genre, which cannot be claimed to be specifically French:

> the heritage film reveals the problematic nature of definitions of the national. The development of the heritage film in France was mirrored by the production of similar types of film in Britain and elsewhere ... In other words, like the remake the heritage film reveals a tension between articulations of the national and its location in a transnational film industry. (p. 73)

Whereas other films in the heritage cycle offered a cosy, nostalgic vision of national identity in the face of an uncertain present, this particular example presents its instability and constructedness, the protagonist at once familiar, yet unknowable and forgetful. This, Mazdon argues, is a metaphor for a national culture that at once presents a familiar and stable identity, but that is always undergoing a process of construction and reconstruction. While the remake, she explains, offers a different negotiation of national identity in a time of change, 'both [*Martin Guerre* and its Hollywood remake] can be seen to articulate concerns about the national present through their representations of the national past'. Therefore:

> [It] does then seem that in the case of the cinematic remake, reworking and adaptation within another national context can be seen as an

Figure 7.1 *A bout de souffle made in USA* poster: This poster for the American remake *Breathless* (Jim McBride, 1983) highlights its links with Godard's films, along with the film's generic basis, shared with the original (UGC)

extension, an addition to the source film rather than as an explicit threat to its identity and the identity of its country of production. (p. 78)

In the case of Godard's film and its remake, Mazdon notes how central the original film is to conceptions of a distinctively French, high art, national cinema. As one of the foundational films of the *nouvelle vague, A bout de souffle* sits at the intersection of art, commercial and experimental cinemas. Yet, as Mazdon points out, the homogeneity of focus on the *nouvelle vague* as a high art movement tended to diminish the range of work and the interests of the filmmakers whose work is considered part of that movement. This problematises the 'Frenchness' of a film like *A bout de souffle*, its experimentation and intertextuality key to its standing as an art film, but for Mazdon it is Godard's repeated intertextual referencing of American cinema, particularly the Hollywood cinema of the 1930s and 1940s, that undermines its claims solely to a French national identity. With a plot borrowed from B-movie thrillers and a protagonist obsessed with American popular culture and the image of Humphrey Bogart, the film 'overtly borrows from and imitates cinematic genres that are neither French nor a part of high culture', and 'these "Americanisms" problematise attempts to locate Godard's film with a specifically French art cinema' (p. 81). Its remake therefore cannot simply be defined as an example of Hollywood appropriation of the high cultural capital of French cinema, set within a broader tradition of the European art cinema tradition. McBride's version re-appropriates Godard's own rewriting of Hollywood cinema. Mazdon argues that the film articulates the logic of the simulacrum, as a copy of a copy; it is a pastiche of the 'original' film, itself a parody. Thus, it 'is possible to see *A bout de souffle* as part of a European (local) modernism and *Breathless* as part of a globalised postmodernism' and therefore to see them both 'as products of a specific national aesthetic is highly problematic'. The films might more suitably sit in the local/global relationship of theories of postmodernism, one claimed as art cinema where the other must be assumed to be a pale, commercialised commodity, where both of these designations could be called into question (p. 87). Mazdon's exploration of these two examples demonstrates how transnational remakes within a global cinematic industry call into question assumptions about how film articulates national identity and the ways in which Hollywood remakes, more than just emptying out the films of their cultural specificity to co-opt those products. Instead, she demonstrates how the distinctions between remakes and their originals demonstrate 'the varying forms of exchange and interaction which identify the remake process'. Whereas critical discourse still tends to prioritise notions of the 'national' as a core concept, 'tropes of intertextuality and the hybrid nature of the products of an increasingly globalised cinema industry undermine national identities' (p. 67).

Gary G. Xu reflects differently on the issue of the increasingly globalised film industry in the very last paragraph of the postscript of *Sinascape: Contemporary Chinese Cinema*, where he contends that 'Hollywoodization is irreversible' (2007, p. 158). Consequently, Xu, taking 'sides' in the argument, offers a critique of the problems of investing too much stock in transnational cinemas, an '[o]veremphasis on multidirectional ... flows of cultural production', his conclusion that 'If all cultural productions were interconnected, deterritorialized, and freely exchanged, then Hollywood would have been dispersed and would have lost its special interests deeply rooted in American hegemony'. Thus, the 'biggest irony is that the more transnational national cinemas become, the more dominant Hollywood is' (p. 151). As

Figure 7.2 *A bout de souffle* (Jean-Luc Godard, 1960) intertextually references American cinema, as Belmondo identifies with the image of Humphrey Bogart (Les Films Impéria/Les Productions Georges de Beauregard/Société Nouvelle de Cinématographie (SNC))

we've already seen, Hollywood has long been a product of transnational capital, and has local interests in a host of national markets (as we saw with the examples of Bond and *Kung Fu Hustle* in the last chapter), as well as a cultural influence that might be considered as imperialist, colonialist and/ or as Americanisation. Xu offers a much more pertinent argument when he contends that remake trends:

> correspon[d] to East Asia's new status as the world's production center. As much as computer chips, flat-panel screens, automobile parts, DVD players, and almost entire Wal-Mart inventories are increasingly being produced out of Taiwan, China, South Korea, and Japan, the film industry is slowly but steadily shifting its production to East Asia. (p. 156)

This defines the issue of transnational remakes as more complex than a simple predator/prey relationship, just as Mazdon argued, but places the remake within the flow of globalisation more generally. Xu sees remaking as a form of outsourcing for Hollywood. Just as many companies in the United States and Europe have shifted production and service centres to South and South-East Asia, Hollywood is outsourcing the labour of development, a trend which, for Xu, continues to entrench the power of Hollywood in a global marketplace. Films are market-tested in Asia, meaning development comes at a reduced cost, as well as delivering the pre-sold product demanded by Hollywood's modern economics. Consequently, this places filmmakers on both sides of the Pacific in a symbiotic position: filmmakers in East Asia have exploited the remake trend to fund production through the sale of remake rights, just as filmmakers rely on the sale of distribution rights to fund production (p. 156). Through a series of significant intermediaries, such as Roy Lee's Vertigo Entertainment, the transnational remake market has become particularly lucrative for both sides of the equation – the remakes and the originals – where rights and development are supported by transnational capital and distribution. Lee's company has worked as a very prominent exponent in the sale of East Asian remake rights, and Lee has taken producer and executive producer credits on a number of high profile films, including *The Ring* (Gore Verbinski, 2002), *The Grudge* (Shimizu Takashi, 2004), *The Departed*, *Shutter* (Ochiai Masayuki, 2008), *The Lake House*, the long-in-development *Oldboy* (Spike Lee, 2013), and was involved in developing *Godzilla* (Gareth Edwards, 2014) before was acrimoniously fired; he has also been involved in non-Asian remakes, such as *Quarantine* (John Eric Dowdle, 2008), a remake of the Spanish horror film *REC* (Jaume Balagueró and Paco Plaza, 2007) and the 2015 *Poltergeist* remake (Gil Kenan). His company has also been behind long-delayed projects including the adaptation of the manga *Death Note* (*Desu Nōto*), based on the 2006 Japanese adaptation (directed by Shūsuke Kaneko) and finally released on Netflix in 2017 (directed by Adam Wingard), and the unsuccessful attempt to produce an American version of *Battle Royale* (*Batoru Rowaiaru*, Kinji Fukasaku, 2000) that was cancelled due to the similarities the story holds with *The Hunger Games* series. Vertigo act as brokers for remake rights, the sale of which can often determine the profit/loss margins of Asian films, where remake rights sales can cover production costs prior to release. In some cases, this is simply an attempt to exploit popular properties for other markets (English-speaking audiences in the US and UK can be resistant to practices of both dubbing and subtitling, which minimise mass market appeal), as well as using common practices such as stardom, auteurism and genre. This continues to be an important contextual issue, where we place content to one side to consider how film remakes fit with broader industrial issues of globalisation. Again, though, we're reminded of the imbalance of global cultural flows, but that there are mutual benefits for local and global producers in co-operation. Nevertheless, as Xu argues, the films that are remade have generic roots that are 'ethnically specific, albeit Hollywoodized, representations, [while] the remakes are completely severed from the original ethnic soil and become solely the product of Hollywood' (p. 155). Here, we need to see the balance between looking at the films contextually, as products of globalised industries, and as texts that often mingle local and global flavours.

Daniel Varndell has situated transnational remakes within 'contact zones', drawing on Mary Louise Pratt's notion that such contact zones are the areas where different cultures collide, tussle, and encounter each other in a range of hierarchised ways (Varndell, 2014, p. 57). He points out that often in the case of transnational remakes there can be a disappearance of the original version, as the Othered 'foreign' text can be made to disappear where the rights are purchased but the original film is not released. This has been the case with some of the films in this chapter, particularly the French comedies mentioned earlier, and *Ring* (Hideo Nakata, 1998), which wasn't released in the US until the remake had been released. The DVD release of *Ring* promoted the remake, of which this was 'the original version'; that pattern wasn't repeated around the world, as the film had already been an arthouse hit in Britain, as part of the Tartan Asia Extreme wave. This partly testifies to some of the imbalances, however, and we also run the risk of seeing this flow of culture from world cinema to Hollywood as the only flow, whereas there are often more regional flows, as films are remade more locally, or there are Hollywood films that are unofficially (without legal permission) remade in other countries, where we began this chapter, which is where we encounter Appadurai's heterogenising argument surrounding globalisation.

Global flows

There are multiple centres in global flows. Remakes are made across many borders and culture is co-opted in multidirectional ways. To return to examples from East Asia, we see the establishment of multiple centres of influence, between which culture can flow. Hence, we have examples of South Korea remaking Japanese films and vice versa, as we'll explore in just a moment. As we saw in Chapter 1, global products are often likely to be localised and indigenised through local frames of reference – as Taiwanese or Japanese youngsters might see McDonald's as local rather than as a sign of Americanisation. Remaking is one process of localisation, part of a global strategy of appropriating cultural material, alongside translation, such as dubbing or subtitling, including producing local frames of reference of cultural signifiers, names, products, texts, or the wholesale reproduction of narratives, characters or culturally specific codes of identity, such as gender, sexuality, ethnicity or race.

Koichi Iwabuchi describes Asian and Japanese transnationalisms developed by the growth of consumer capitalist modernity as a 'subtle cultural mixing of "the local" and "the foreign" (the West)', something he argues is 'a common feature in the formation of non-western modernity' (2002, pp. 17–18). Offering a different perspective to that of Xu, who sees a 'becoming-American' in the growth of East Asian engagement with cultural products, especially cinema, and the spread of Hollywood remakes of East Asian films, Iwabuchi, in *Recentering Globalization*, argues that cultural products are subject to ongoing processes of re-localisation in their movements across borders:

> the age of 'Americanization'[,] in which cross-cultural consumption was predominantly discussed in terms of the production of a sense of 'yearning' for a way of life and ideas of a dominant country, seems to be over. Global cultural power does not disappear but is now highly dispersed. (p. 45)

Iwabuchi argues that the transnational avoids binaristic conceptions of cultural hegemony, imperialism and colonial cultural power, but that 'the term transnational draws attention in a more locally contextualized manner to the interconnections and asymmetries that are promoted by the multi-directional flow of information and images, and by the ongoing cultural mixing and infiltration of these messages' (p. 17). Flows of culture might be uneven, or asymmetrical, even if, as Iwabuchi discusses, they are perceived as contemporaneous in terms of the growth of non-western modernity, but he argues that transnational flows are not subject simply to forces of imperialism, Americanisation or Japanisation (in Japan's historic position of being in, but above, 'Asia'), wherein indigenised cultural products exhibit a culturally specific odour or reject global or hybridised odours in favour of more domestic ones. In this, cultural dominance is becoming 'highly dispersed'. At the heart of this tendency, for Japanese texts, Iwabuchi places the concept of *mukokuseki*: 'the mixing of elements of multiple cultural origins, and [the implication of] the erasure of visible ethnic and cultural characteristics' (p. 71). Long held as a necessity for Japanese cultural projects to become successful or portable across national boundaries, particularly in anime, the erasure of a local or distinctive odour comes with the diminishment of national or cultural distinctiveness in design, sensibility, tradition or meaning (something common with successful Japanese imports in the consumer electronics sphere). This is something which might also be understood as a form of aura, or authenticity, of a definable national origin, something graspable for international audiences, for whom the odour of Othered national products might be a necessary part of the experience of the Asian text, as a form of Orientalist gaze.

Case study: Rings, remakes and reception

We could initially point to the overabundance of remakes of Japanese films in the horror genre – itself a highly international genre – that came along in the 2000s. Hollywood remakes of Japanese films were nothing new, beginning prominently in the 1960s with Kurosawa's *Seven Samurai* (*Shichinin no Samurai*, 1954) remade as the Western *The Magnificent Seven* (John Sturges, 1960), and later as a science fiction film, *Battle Beyond the Stars* (Jimmy T. Murakami, 1980), and subsequently as Pixar's *A Bug's Life* (John Lasseter and Andrew Stanton, 1998). A 2008 Japanese remake, directed by Hiroyuki Nakano, was released only on pachinko machines in Japan, while a steampunk anime series, *Samurai 7*, was produced in 2004. Unlike the samurai film, which is highly contingent upon myths and histories of feudal Japan (despite its similarities with the American Western), some of the films that have been remade have been transnational in their adoption of global cultural features, such as *Shall We Dance?*, which takes its title from a song in the Rodgers and Hammerstein musical *The King and I* (not the similarly titled (without question mark) Fred Astaire-Ginger Rogers film (Mark Sandrich, 1937)). The template for the cycle of horror remakes was undoubtedly *Ring*, which initiated the trend, following the release of its remake *The Ring* in 2002. Rather than focus solely on differences between the original and its remake, on narrative and aesthetic levels (something done in detail elsewhere, see below), this case study will explore some of the issues behind transnational remakes and relationships between national and transnational cinemas, covering the Japanese and US versions, but also the South Korean version, known internationally as *The Ring Virus* (Kim Dong-bin, 1999) although its Korean title translates literally as *Ring*.

Xu argues that, with the minimisation of psychological and sexual ambiguity in the original version of *Ring*, the film was 'already Hollywoodised before it was remade as *The Ring*' (2008, p. 193). Xu's points here are extremely pertinent about the ways in which genre norms have been implemented in Nakata's version (a television movie adaptation had already been produced in Japan in 1995): 'American suburban life style, the strong-minded yet vulnerable female as the "final girl", unambiguous sexuality, and thrilling yet non-threatening horror' (p. 192). Xu's comment regarding the 'final girl', a trope identified by Carol Clover in her seminal work on gender in the horror film, *Men, Women and Chainsaws: Gender in the Modern Horror Film* (1992), is particularly noteworthy in the ways we can think about the already internationalised features of the Japanese *Ring*. The final girl is the ambiguously gendered heroine of the horror film who takes on the phallic power of the monster to defeat it. What makes this worthy of comment is the film's relationship with its source material, Koji Suzuki's 1991 novel of the same name, in which the protagonist is male (other character details are retained, such as their occupation – journalist – and relationship to one of the original victims – uncle/aunt). As Xu also contends, the problematic sexual dimension of the novel's story is minimised – in the novel, the ghost Sadako is revealed to have been intersex, with both female and male genitalia, and her rape and death at the hands of a doctor was as a result of his discovery of this (the novel also implies that Sadako has willed her murder, telepathically manipulating the doctor). Her sexual identity is absent from Nakata's version, as is her rape, with her murder coming at the hands of the doctor who identified her terrifying psychic abilities. The Korean version is the only one that retains this aspect of the novel, although it too adopts the final girl trope introduced in Nakata's version.

Ring foregrounds the supernatural aspects of its story, with the implication that Sadako has been fathered by a sea demon. In the cursed video in the film, we hear a line of dialogue in an Oshima (an Island to the south of Japan's main island, Honshu) dialect that says, '*Shoumon bakkari, boukon ga kuru zo*', something translated differently in subtitled versions of the film: as 'If you keep playing with water, monsters will come' or as the more poetic, 'frolic in brine, goblins be thine'. The Oshima dialect is also something used to locate the volcano into which Sadako's mother threw herself. By highlighting the rural Otherness through the use of the Oshima dialect, this emphasises other aspects of Nakata's film that were highly congruent with globalisation, cosmopolitanism and technology: as Mitsuyo Wada-Marciano argues, the 'appeal of J-horror films can be seen in their textual elements drawn from the urban topography and the pervasive use of technology, elements which are at once, particular and universal' (2009, p. 18) (Figure 7.3). She argues that

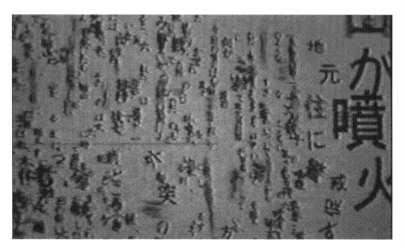

Figure 7.3 The Japanese *Ring* (Hideo Nakata, 1998) emphasises the blending of technology and local cultural content in its use of kanji in the cursed video (Imagica/Asmik Ace Entertainment)

there is a significant transformation in the use of locale between the original and remake: Tokyo, Izu peninsula and Oshima island in Japan (the latter both popular leisure spots for Tokyo residents), and their contrasting urbanity and pre-modern cultures; *The Ring* re-sets the film in Seattle (but was actually shot in Vancouver), but uses fictional spaces to evoke the same geographical contrast in the original. The original use of space, with its mixture of rational and irrational locales, reflects an external sense of Japan as a land of mystery, the exoticism of Orientalism.

The films also share a focus on technology that runs through all variants of the narrative, something that Daniel Herbert has seen as intrinsic to what he calls '*The Ring* intertext', 'a circuit of economic, semiotic, and cultural exchange ... [that] maps a transnational and macroregional space' (2010, p. 154). His notion of an intertext is one that spans these three countries (Japan, South Korea and the US) and 'a constellation of texts' and 'their industrial and cultural connections ... in a distinctly transnational formation' (p. 169). Herbert's analysis reveals problematic imbalances in economic and discursive flows. As he argues, the global financial success of *The Ring* encouraged further patterns of cultural exchange in the flood of remakes of East Asian films that followed. These asymmetries of economic and cultural influence might threaten 'to reinforce certain cultural boundaries and relations of power' (p. 166), although they also shift those boundaries in ways that are 'producing new forms and conditions in a continual process of struggle and change' (p. 169). This transnational space criss-crosses national boundaries, albeit in different and often fundamentally imbalanced ways, and transcends the binaries of inside and out that often characterise national cinemas, especially in their relationship with Hollywood. In a similar fashion to Xu and Wada-Marciano, Herbert implicates technology within this transference.

Similarly, Julian Stringer has demonstrated how 'the *Ring* phenomenon constitutes one of the cross-cultural, cross-media sensations of contemporary global pop culture' (2007, p. 298). This phenomenon crosses several cultures, as we've noted, but also crosses media, with television, film, manga and games, as well as the original novels and its two sequels, produced over the past two decades as well as the 2016 release *Sadako vs. Kayako* (Kôji Shiraishi, Figure 7.4). In this production, Sadako takes on the female ghost from *The Grudge* films (itself a cross-media franchise of seven Japanese films across cinema and television, an American remake with two sequels, novelisations, comics and games), following two 3D films in 2012 and 2013 directed by Tsutomu Hanabusa. Stringer, however, brings to attention the problematic issue of an original and copy in the *Ring* cycle. He questions the importance of issues of fidelity in the remaking process – where, in this case, the question of adaptation is all but eliminated from the equation – and the argument that the remake represents

Figure 7.4 The poster for *Sadako vs. Kayako* (Kôji Shiraishi, 2016) emphasises its mash-up of iconography from the *Ring* and *Grudge* series (Kadokawa Daiei)

the cannibalisation of the film by the US is limiting. Stringer stresses that this 'media recycling and remaking also point to the very many narratives of repetition, circularity, and endless return that, as Aaron Gerow (2002) perceptively notes, are a hallmark of modern Japanese cinema' (p. 304). The confining nature of this discourse is perhaps down to some of the transnational reception of the film. At one level, when *Ring* was released internationally, it was initially circulated with its original title, *Ring*. Following the release of the remake, the film became universally known by its transliterated title, *Ringu*, highlighting its foreignness. In his exploration of the film's British critical reception, Daniel Martin identified a tendency to familiarise the film, which critics did through local norms as often happens when films cross national borders: 'Rather than trying to understand the film in terms of its specific Japanese-ness, or its universality, these critics (mostly) understood the film simply in terms of *Western* traditions' (2009, p. 49). The film, he argues, isn't presented solely through a sense of difference from Hollywood norms, but 'is presented as different from a certain kind of US commercial cinema, a "bad" Hollywood, while simultaneously being renationalised and aligned with positive and virtuous examples of a "quality" Western cinema' (p. 50). Matt Hills has looked at the ways in which cult fans of *Ring* and *The Ring* and US fans have discussed readings and interpretations of the Japanese film and its remake – he defines this as a kind of 'techno-occidentalism', a strategy of 'reading-for-cultural-difference' and how these viewers and their 'reading positions outside "the mainstream" are based on their identification with, and of, Japanese cultural identities and aesthetics' (2005, p. 171). Like the critics observed by Martin, these fans position themselves in opposition to mainstream tastes, adopting the Japanese text as a way of rejecting the norms of mainstream Hollywood cinema, as represented by the remake. As Hills quotes one commenter: 'The remake is more "westernised" and to make money it has to be more mainstream, and as such has to give more answers'. Hills describes this tendency as a 'focus on differences between western "rationalism" and what is construed as a broader acceptance of the supernatural in Japanese culture' (p. 168). What is at stake here is the ways in which transnational remakes articulate cultural difference, how that cultural difference is received in transnational fandom and critical reception and the ways in which film remakes highlight core issues about film production, national specificity, and genre, and the different flows involved in capital, production, narrative and distribution. Remakes are particular texts that highlight how material is transformed, how national contexts are understood and distributed and the ways in which some remakes are modelled on texts that are already designed to suit the international market. We can't simply take a view of the purity of the original versus the spoiled remake – as Stringer highlighted, this would be to ignore the ways in which Japanese cultural texts are produced, as well as the ways in which they circulate, and where those discourses are manifest.

Recommended viewing:

American remakes of world cinema:
Rashomon (Akira Kurosawa, 1950)/*The Outrage* (Martin Ritt, 1964)
Two Times Lotte (*Das doppelte Lottchen*, Josef von Báky, 1950)/*The Parent Trap* (David Swift, 1961)
Hachiko monogatari (Seijirō Kōyama, 1987)/*Hachi: A Dog's Tale* (Lasse Hallström, 2010)
The Vanishing (*Spoorloos*, George Sluizer, 1988)/*The Vanishing* (George Sluizer, 1993)
Funny Games (Michael Haneke, 1997)/*Funny Games* (Michael Haneke, 2007)
Dark Water (*Honogurai Mizu no soko kara*, Hideo Nakata, 2002)/*Dark Water* (Walter Salles, 2005)
The Eye (*Gin gwai*, Pang Brothers, 2002)/*The Eye* (David Moreau, Xavier Palud, 2008)
A Tale of Two Sisters (*Janghwa, Hongryeon*, Kim Jee-woon, 2003)/*The Uninvited* (The Guard Brothers, 2009)
Premonition (*Yogen*, Tsuruta Norio, 2004)/*Premonition* (Mennan Yapo, 2007)
Shutter (Banjong Pisanthanakun, Parkpoom Wongpoom, 2004)/*Shutter* (Masayuki Ochiai, 2008)
Let the Right One In (*Låt den rätte komma in*, Thomas Alfredson, 2008)/*Let Me In* (Matt Reeves, 2010)

Recommended further reading:

Balmain, Colette (2006), 'Inside the Well of Loneliness: Towards a Definition of the Japanese Horror Film', *Electronic Journal of Contemporary Japanese Studies*, 2 May. Available online: www.japanesestudies.org.uk/discussionpapers/2006/Balmain.html. Accessed 19 September 2017.

Durham, Carolyn A. (1998), *Double Takes: Culture and Gender in French Films and their American Remakes*. Hanover, NH: University Press of New England.

Forrest, Jennifer, and Leonard R. Koos, eds (2002), *Dead Ringers: The Remake in Theory and Practice*. New York: State University of New York.

Goldberg, Ruth (2004), 'Demons in the Family: Tracking the Japanese "Uncanny Mother Film" from *A Page of Madness* to *Ringu*', in eds Barry Keith Grant and Christopher Sharrett, *Planks of Reason: Essays on the Horror Film*, Lanham, Toronto and Oxford: Scarecrow Press, pp. 370–386.

Lim, Bliss Cua (2007), 'Generic Ghosts: Remaking the New "Asian Horror Film"', in eds Gina Marchetti and Tan See Kam, *Hong Kong Film, Hollywood And The New Global Cinema*. London and New York: Routledge, pp. 109–125.

Messier, Vartan (2014), 'Game Over? The (Re)play of Horror in Michael Haneke's Funny Games U.S.', *New Cinemas: Journal of Contemporary Film* 12(1–2): pp. 59–77.

Posadas, Baryon Tensor (2014), 'Remaking Yamato, Remaking Japan', *Science Fiction Film & Television* 7(3): pp. 315–342.

Rawle, Steven (2010), 'Video Killed the Movie: Cultural Translation in *Ringu* and *The Ring*', in ed. Kristen Lacefield, *The Scary Screen: Media Anxiety in The Ring*, Farnham and Burlington, VT: Ashgate, pp. 97–113.

—— (2015), 'Ringing One Missed Call: Franchising, Transnational Flows and Genre Production', *East Asian Journal of Popular Culture* 1(1): pp. 97–112.

Shriver-Rice, Meryl (2011), 'Adapting National Identity: Ethical Borders Made Suspect in the Hollywood Version of Susanne Bier's *Brothers*', *Film International* 9(2): pp. 8–19.

Wee, Valerie (2010), 'Visual Aesthetics and Ways of Seeing: Comparing Video Images from Ringu and The Ring', *Cinema Journal* 50(2): pp. 41–60.

—— (2011), 'Patriarchy and the Horror of the Monstrous Feminine: A Comparative Study of *Ringu* and *The Ring*', *Feminist Media Studies* 11(2): pp. 151–165.

—— (2014), *Japanese Horror Films and the American Remakes: Translating Fear, Adapting Culture*. New York: Routledge.

White, Eric (2005), 'Case Study: Nakata Hideo's *Ringu* and *Ringu 2*', in ed. Jay McRoy, *Japanese Horror Cinema*, Edinburgh: Edinburgh University Press, pp. 38–47.

Global remakes

Considering a cycle as well explored in film studies as the *Ring* films and their remakes, spin-offs and reception highlights many issues surrounding national specificity, regional flows and the imbalance of transnational relationships, for producers as well as for viewers. The case of *Ring* and its South Korean remake is not an isolated one, and there are numerous examples of remakes of films between the two countries. One prominent example is Kim Jee-woon's *The Quiet Family* (*Joyonghan Gajok*, 1998). The film tells the story of a family whose move to the mountains to open a bed and breakfast is fraught with problems. When they finally receive their first guest, he fails to survive the night after committing suicide. Fearing bad publicity and the possible involvement of his son Young-min (Song Kang-ho), a former petty criminal, the owner Dae-goo (Park In-Hwan) buries the body. An escalating series of deaths, some accidental, some intentional, forces the family to work together – to be quiet and maintain their silence. When the film was remade in Japan as *The Happiness of the Katakuris* (*Katakuri-ke no Kōfuku*, Takashi Miike, 2001), the remake bore little resemblance to the original version. First, the title is changed, which fails to acknowledge the source text. Second, the action is transplanted from South Korea to Japan. Third, the remake is a genre mash-up of the musical, romantic comedy, crime thriller and zombie film and is also part animated. Chi-Yun Shin (2012) has argued that the case of the two films represents 'a unique case of cross-cultural remaking' since it avoids repetition (Figure 7.5). The case of the 'excessive' remake, she argues, reveals aspects of cultural difference, as well as the ways it speaks about directors'

Figure 7.5 The super-happy musical finale of *The Happiness of the Katakuris* (Takashi Miike, 2001) shares thematic similarities with its original, but the familial concept is bound in specifically national concerns (Shochiku)

aesthetic choices, socio-historical changes, and aspects of genre (2012, p. 78). Film remakes usually, in Constantine Verevis's terms, utilise intertextual structures that 'are highly particular in their repetition of *narrative units*, and these repetitions most often (though certainly not always) relate to the content ... rather than to the form ... of the film' (2006, p. 21). With the *Ring* films, this is easy to see, as both Nakata and Verbinski's versions revolve around the repetition of five discrete narrative units (from the opening with two teenage girls discussing the urban legend of the cursed video, through the investigation narrative, to the iconic final death of the protagonist's ex-husband at the hands of the ghost as she crawls out from the television), but this is much harder to factor with Miike's remake of Kim's film. Shin argues that this trans-Asian remake is different on many levels, from their different interpretations of genre conventions to *Katakuris'* use of a 4-year-old child as a narrator, as well as its reference to nationally specific pop culture and socio-economic contexts.

Shin notes how, in this case, the remake is much better known than the original (she even refers to one case of a critic describing Kim's film as a rip-off of Miike's, despite having being made three years previously), something she attributes to a number of factors: first, the lack of linearity in the ways in which viewers access films on DVD (in the UK, Tartan's release of *Katakuris* came two years before Tai Seng Entertainment released a DVD version of *The Quiet Family*); second, the reputation of the *auteur*, Miike, whose work was prominent in the Asia Extreme phenomenon, while this was Kim's first film; third, the production of *The Quiet Family* prior to the emergence of New Korean Cinema in 1999, as well as the growth in popularity of J-horror films and their remakes. Hence these factors, which relate both to perceptions of national cinema and transnational patterns of distribution and reception, mean the remake is better known than the original. As I've shown in an article on Miike's film (Rawle, 2014), the remake is a hybrid transnational cult film where the reception of the film was preceded by the *auteur*'s reputation, something that was reductive in terms of seeing its status as a remake, but also as a hybrid work that references specific Japanese cultural contexts, such as the collapse of the economic bubble in the late 1990s (Shin notes how this is more relevant to the remake than the original, since Kim's film was produced prior to the collapse), and the 'senior staff shock' (*kanri shoku*) that led to Masao Katakuri losing his job as a shoe salesman (a period in the 1990s in which major Japanese enterprise reduced its staffing by 15 to 30 per cent, with senior staff hit most strongly). Some of its casting also refers to specific aspects of Japanese popular culture: Kenji Sawada, the actor who plays Masao, was a major pop icon in Japan in the 1960s, while Kiyoshiro Imawano, who plays a hustler posing as an American nephew of Queen Elizabeth II, was a prominent rock star at the time of the film's production. These factors demonstrate the transnational repositioning of the film – as Shin notes, *The Quiet Family*, while it shares themes of family restoration, features a more socially detached narrative, and emotionally distant nuclear (rather than extended Japanese) family (2012, p. 77).

Katakuris is rooted in its generic hybridity, where multiple genres are intertextually referenced or culled from a transnational economy (*The Sound of Music* (Robert Wise, 1965), *The Rocky Horror Picture Show* (Jim Sharman, 1975), *Night of the Living Dead* (George Romero, 1968), as well as *The Quiet Family*). The cultural positioning of the film, especially its perceived Japanese 'strangeness', and transgressive excess, all means it spills over the boundaries of genre and national/transnational meaning. Shin also notes that both films share their intertextual referencing, albeit differently, of genre. As highlighted above, the hybridity of *Katakuris* is rooted in its invocation of musicals and the horror genre, whereas Shin highlights how *The Quiet Family* references the floating, subjective point of view of the slasher film and the crane shots of Sam Raimi's *Evil Dead* (1982), as well as the absurdity of the Coen Brothers' work. As such, this trans-Asian remake demonstrates how issues of cultural exchange function – the lack of repetition in the remake makes it difficult to form a direct comparison (therefore it's also not possible to make an argument that positions the impure remake against the unpolluted original) – but shows how cultural material can be appropriated across national borders and localised politically and ideologically, as well as stylistically. Through the intertextuality of genre tropes, both films indigenise and mix the local and the foreign, in Iwabuchi's terms, and demonstrate how global power is more dispersed – these aren't examples of peripheral cinemas in Japan and South Korea (although neither film represents the mainstream, at their time of production, of their respective countries) imitating Hollywood, but co-opting transnational aspects of genre and reworking them. While other aspects of film remakes point towards cultural homogenisation, as we saw in the case of the *Ring* cycle, we can also see how cultural heterogenisation is produced through this process of the global flow of cultural material and how it is used. That's still not to say that all power is equitable and evenly distributed, but that flow works in multiple directions. We'll also see elements of this in the next chapter when we turn to look more specifically at genre.

How do we account for the influence of Hollywood on peripheral cinemas? How do we understand diverse phenomena such as the Ugandan remake of *The Expendables* (Sylvester Stallone, 2010), *Operation Kakongoliro!* (Nabwana I.G.G., 2016), or *O.K. Connery* (AKA *Operation Kid Brother*, Alberto De Martino, 1967), an Italian James Bond film starring Sean Connery's brother, Neil, as James Bond's brother, and stars from the series, including Bernard Lee (M) and Lois Maxwell (Miss Moneypenny)? Iain Robert Smith's book *The Hollywood Meme: Transnational Adaptations in World Cinema* (2017), explores these issues of 'cross-cultural borrowings and syncretism'. (Syncretism concerns the merging of different thought systems or of different linguistic functions in a single word.) Smith argues that 'scholarship on world cinema tends to neglect the transnational influence of Hollywood', and that film studies 'needs to address this interrelationship in order to better interrogate the complex cultural dynamics underpinning the transnational circulation of cinema' (p. 3). He draws attention to a range of different borrowings from Hollywood – many of them without attribution of copyright (unofficial or unacknowledged remakes) – including a Nigerian remake of *Titanic* (1997), *My Beloved* (*Masoyiyata*, 2003), an Indonesian version of *The Terminator* (James Cameron, 1984) called *Revenge of the South Seas Queen* (*Pembalasan ratu pantai selatan*, 1989) and a Mexican version of *Batwoman* (*La Mujer Murcielago, The Batwoman*, 1968), as well as a Brazilian parody of *Jaws* titled *Codfish* (*Bacalhau*, 1975). On this last film, Smith refers to the work of Robert Stam and João Luiz Vieira, and their argument regarding the film, a soft-core porn parody, alongside *Costinha e o King Mong* (1977), a lampoon of *King Kong* (John Guillermin, 1976). They argue that the parodies activate the transgressive power of the carnivalesque, as conceptualised by Mikhail Bakhtin in *Rabelais and His World* (1984), that has the power to resist – albeit temporarily – and subvert a dominant ideology. In Stam and Vieira's view, parody in this manner is a legitimate tool through which to resist the power of domination in a neo-colonial context (harking back to the traditions of Third Cinema), in the ways that it 'is well suited to the needs of the oppressed and powerless' because it uses 'the force of dominant discourse' contrary to its intended goals, to subvert that discourse rather than to imitate it and therefore to be dominated by it (Stam & Vieira, 1990, p. 84). In the case of *Bacalhau*, though, they contend that it fails to live up to the potential power of the carnivalesque parody. They see no 'devastating critique of the shallow factitiousness ultimately conveyed by the increasingly sophisticated mimesis of contemporary dominant cinema' (p. 95), only the film's 'uncritical admiration' of the 'foreign model' (p. 93). In response to Stam and Vieira, Smith argues that their argument 'is certainly politically attractive' but that seeing the appropriation of Hollywood material through a focus on dominance and resistance 'can actually neglect the much more ambivalent nature of many of these borrowings' (Smith, 2017, p. 27). Smith describes his model of cultural transmission as a form of 'vernacular postmodernism'. Here he is drawing on Miriam Hansen's concept of vernacular modernism, 'a transnational and translatable resonance' that played 'a key role in mediating competing cultural discourses on modernity and modernization, because it articulated, multiplied, and globalized a particular historical experience' rather than because it created 'universal templates' (1999, p. 67). In this sense of how Hollywood circulated historically and globally, Hansen shows how it helps us understand the role of Hollywood, not to produce standardisation in its adoption by world cinemas but in how it is transmitted, localised and helps to negotiate the experience of multiple modernities.

Smith also adopts the metaphor of the meme from Richard Dawkins' evolutionary biology, as 'a unit of culture which spreads and replicates' (Smith, 2017, p. 31), moulding itself to its new environment as it travels. The concept of the meme, Smith argues, allows us to break away from the core principle of fidelity (to an 'original' source) that dominates adaptation and remake studies. In their more common form, memes refer to the borrowing, reworking and circulation of online images and media shared through a variety of means, something that Smith argues accounts for the ways in which the concept of the meme is invested with human agency, unlike in the term's biological sense where the mutation and transmission is automatic. He explores how Hollywood provides a multiplicity of memes, beginning in the form of a single film, which can then be broken into smaller memes, and those units can then be followed through processes of appropriation and adaptation. This, he contends, allows us to see Hollywood as a huge catalogue of memes that make up its film industry as a whole, the mechanisms through which its influence is circulated and adopted around the world, and also how micro-level analysis can help us understand how particular memes – like a character or extract of musical score – are spread and adapted:

> This allows for a comparative model to be developed that maps the proliferation of a meme from one context, and then traces how it spreads and mutates as it travels to other contexts. In this way, the model helps us to consider which memes are flourishing in which locations, how they are being adapted for local (or indeed global) audiences, and to what purpose. (p. 32)

Smith's comparative model is applied to three case studies in his book: borrowings from Hollywood cinema in Turkey, India and the Philippines. His analysis is highly contextual, looking at how transnational adaptations in popular cinema (which he notes have often been written out of scholarly accounts of national cinemas in favour of the focus on more marginal art cinemas) draw on specific socio-historical contexts, articulating 'the dynamics of transnational flows of media and culture' (p. 42). In the case of Turkey, he explores the 1973 film *Üç Dev Adam* (*Three Mighty Men*), which combined Captain America, Spider-Man and the Mexican wrestler El Santo in an action crime drama, and *Turist Ömer Uzay Yolunda* (*Tourist Omer in Star Trek*, 1974) in which the popular character Turist Ömer was inserted into the iconography of *Star Trek* (Figure 7.6), which had only begun airing in Turkey in 1973 (despite ending the US in 1969). The fundamental revisions of the

Figure 7.6 The recreation of *Star Trek* in *Tourist Omer in Star Trek* (Hulki Saner, 1974) appropriates a range of the show's features to be overwritten by the Turkish film (Renkli/Saner Film)

recognisable Spider-Man (as a psychotic mask-wearing villain) and Captain America (as a crime fighter without powers who adopts the mask in order to catch Spider-Man), as well as the wholesale recreation of the Starship Enterprise as a means of using the Ömer character's sudden intrusion into the fictional world of the TV show (a specific episode at that: the 1966 series premiere 'The Man Trap') in order to 'comment upon the American popular culture that was entering the country at the time' (p. 53), all draw attention to the differing regimes of international copyright:

> international treaties on copyright protection tend to serve the purposes of those who are exporters of content rather than those who are primarily importing content from elsewhere. In the case of 1970s Turkey, a net-importer of such assets, the incentive was not there to expand copyright protection to the media texts entering the country and this contributed to the cultural climate in which *Turist Ömer Uzay Yolunda* was able to replicate much of the *Star Trek* episode. (p. 55)

With the use of the show's opening titles and theme tune – over which the film's own titles are superimposed – the text becomes a palimpsest ('an ancient scroll that has been written on, scraped off, and then written on again') and the Turkish film is overwritten on top of the American *Star Trek*. Smith's other cases studies include: *Dünyayı Kurtaran Adam* (1982), a Turkish science fiction film that doesn't rework a narrative but appropriates footage from *Star Wars* (George Lucas, 1977), alongside music from *Raiders of the Lost Ark* (Steven Spielberg, 1981); the hybrid commercial cinema of the Philippines that Smith argues is less a reflection of the country's post-colonial status than an industry model reworking global texts for export, including *Dynamite Johnson*, a 1979 reworking of *The Six Million Dollar Man*, and *Alyas Batman en Robin* (1993) that capitalised on the release of the Tim Burton Batman films of the late 1980s and early 1990s; Indian reworkings of localised Hollywood plots ('chutneyed' in Sheila Nayar's terms) that often disguise the source material, such as *Koi... Mil Gaya* (*I've Found Someone*, 2003), a big budget science fiction film modelled on Spielberg's *E.T.* (1982), amongst others; *Sarkar* (2005), which appropriates the plot of *The Godfather* (Francis Coppola, 1972); *Heyy Babyy* (2007), a remake of *Three Men and a Baby* (which as we saw above was already a remake); and *Ghajini* (2008), a reworking of Christopher Nolan's *Memento* (2000) that was claimed to have been no such thing (it didn't use the film's trademark reverse narration) but a remake of a Tamil film of the same name (as a means of navigating copyright legalities). The figure of the meme allows Smith, through these case studies, to explore the ways in which Hollywood is appropriated, reworked and localised in other cinemas, often through the creative agency of local (sometimes glocal) filmmakers. As he concludes:

> a comparative analysis of transnational adaptation can tell us a great deal about the way texts circulate internationally and the specific circumstances in which they are received and reworked. Rather than see the global circulation of Hollywood in terms of blanket Americanisation, I have argued for a more nuanced model of cultural exchange which pays attention to the tensions and ambivalences in these processes of globalisation. These borrowings should be understood less through the prism of cultural domination and resistance than through the lens of agency and creativity. (p. 148)

Smith's contribution to the field of transnational remake studies is significant in that it demonstrates how processes of localisation, socio-historical positioning (he notes that trends for Hollywood remakes and appropriation are now all but things of the past in Turkey and the Philippines), issues of international copyright and local agency demonstrate how Hollywood products circulate and are used globally. While Smith sees Hollywood as the centre of the global film industry, his analyses of cultural borrowings and the heterogenisation of globalisation and cultural flows help us move beyond oppositional viewpoints in relation to the co-optation, use and exploitation of cinema. There any many reasons for and consequences of the global remaking of cinema: where Hollywood does capitalise upon popular works in national cinema markets, it also enables production in those industries, whereas creative agency gives filmmakers the means to diversify our understanding of reception and appropriation in response to globalisation, rather than simply viewing it as Americanisation. Hence we see examples of both homogenisation and heterogenisation in global cultural flows.

Recommended viewing:

Non-Hollywood remakes/appropriations
Hindi remakes:
Reservoir Dogs (Quentin Tarantino, 1992)/*Kaante* (Sanjay Gupta, 2002)
Mrs Doubtfire (Chris Columbus, 1993)/*Chachi 420* (Kamal Hassan, 1997)
My Sassy Girl (*Yeopgijeogin Geunyeo*, Kwak Jae-yong, 2001)/*Ugly Aur Pagli* (Sachin Khot, 2008)
The Eye (*Gin gwai*, Pang Brothers, 2002)/*Naina* (Shirpal Morakhai, 2005)
Oldboy (Park Chan-wook, 2003)/*Zinda* (Sanjay Gupta, 2006)

Turkish remakes:

The Exorcist (William Friedkin, 1973)/*Şeytan* (Metin Erksan, 1974)

Star Wars (George Lucas, 1977)/*Dünyayı Kurtaran Adam* (Çetin Inanç, 1982)

Rambo: First Blood Part Two (George P. Cosmatos, 1985)/*Korkusuz* (Çetin Inanç, 1986)

Japanese remakes:

Make Way for Tomorrow (Leo McCarey, 1937)/*Tokyo Monogatari* (Yasujiro Ozu, 1953)

Ghost (Jerry Zucker, 1990)/*Ghost: Mouichido Dakishimetai* (Taro Otani, 2010)

Unforgiven (Clint Eastwood, 1992)/*Yurusarezaru mono* (Lee Sang-il, 2013)

Korean remakes:

A Better Tomorrow (*Ying hung boon sik*, John Woo, 1986)/*A Better Tomorrow* (*Moo-jeok-ja*, Song Hae-sung, 2010)

Eye in the Sky (*Gun Chung*, Yau Nai-Hoi, 2007)/*Cold Eyes* (*Gamsijadeul*, Jo Ui-seok and Kim Byeong-seo, 2013)

Recommended further reading:

Alessio, Dominic, and Jessica Langer (2007), 'Nationalism and Postcolonialism in Indian Science Fiction: Bollywood's *Koi Mil Gaya* (2003)', *New Cinemas: Journal of Contemporary Film* 5(3): pp. 217–229.

Aufderheide, Patricia (1998), 'Made in Hong Kong: Translation and Transmutation', in eds Andrew Horton and Stuart Y. McDougal, *Play It Again, Sam: Retakes on Remakes*. Berkeley: University of California Press, pp. 191–199.

Banerjee, Suparno (2014), 'Melodrama, Mimicry, and Menace: Reinventing Hollywood in Indian Science Fiction Films', *South Asian Popular Culture* 12(1): pp. 15–28.

Evans, Jonathan (2014), 'Zhang Yimou's *Blood Simple*: Cannibalism, Remaking and Translation in World Cinema', *Journal of Adaptation In Film & Performance* 7(3): pp. 283–297.

Griffin, Jeffrey L. (2014), 'Turning Japanese: From *Sideways* to *Saidoweizu*: An Examination of the Japanese Remake of a Hollywood Film', *Film International* 12(4): pp. 84–98.

Gürata, Ahmet (2006), 'Translating Modernity: Remakes in Turkish Cinema', in eds Dimitri Eleftheoritis and Gary Needham, *Asian Cinemas: A Reader and Guide*. Edinburgh: Edinburgh University Press, pp. 242–254.

Horton, Andrew (1998), 'Cinematic Makeovers and Cultural Border Crossings: Kusturica's *Time of the Gypsies* and Coppola's *Godfather* and *Godfather II*', in Horton and McDougal, pp. 177–190.

Krämer, Lúcia (2015), 'The End of the Hollywood 'Rip-Off'? Changes in the Bollywood Politics of Copyright', in eds Dan Hassler-Forest and Pascal Nicklas, *The Politics of Adaptation: Media Convergence and Ideology*. London: Palgrave Macmillan, pp. 143–157.

Nayar, Sheila J. (2003), 'Dreams, Dharma and Mrs. Doubtfire: Exploring Hindi Popular Cinema via its "Chutneyed" Western Scripts', *Journal of Popular Film and Television* 31(2): pp. 73–82.

Siddiqui, Gohar (2013), '"Behind Her Laughter...Is Fear!" Domestic Abuse and Transnational Feminism in Bollywood Remakes', *Jump Cut: A Review of Contemporary Media* 55(4). Available online: www.ejumpcut.org/archive/jc55.2013/SiddiquiDomesAbuseIndia/text.html. Accessed 19 September 2017.

Smith, Iain Robert (2008), '"Beam Me up, Ömer": Transnational Media Flow and the Cultural Politics of the Turkish *Star Trek* Remake', *Velvet Light Trap* 61: pp. 3–13.

―――― (2013), '*Oldboy* Goes to Bollywood: *Zinda* and the Transnational Appropriation of South Korean "Extreme" Cinema', in eds Alison Pierse and Daniel Martin, *Korean Horror Cinema*. Edinburgh: Edinburgh University Press, pp. 187–198.

Wright, Neelam Sidhar (2009), '"Tom Cruise? Tarantino? *E.T.*? ...Indian!": Innovation through Imitation in the Cross-cultural Bollywood Remake', *Scope: Journal of Film and Television Studies* 15. Available online: www.nottingham.ac.uk/scope/documents/2009/culturalborrowingsebook.pdf. Accessed 19 September 2017.

Discussion questions:

- How valid do you think arguments are regarding cultural imperialism and Hollywood's 'borrowings' of material from other national cinemas?
- How can comparative studies of remakes and their originals help us to better understand cultural difference?
- Why do you think so many filmmakers around the world are remaking Hollywood films within their own local frames of reference? Are they resisting or demonstrating cultural homogenisation?
- What consequences does Smith's placement of Hollywood in a central position have for centre/margins models? Does it move us closer to the world of interconnected cinemas that Nagib suggested (see Chapter 1), or towards one where Hollywood is culturally dominant?

CHAPTER 8

Globalised Genres

In the last chapter, we explored how cultural exchange and the homogenising and heterogenising potentials of globalisation functioned in the field of film remakes, and we considered how Hollywood tends to act as a centre of global production, cherry-picking the most popular local hits from around the globe to remake, or how more peripheral (and not so peripheral) world cinemas take content from Hollywood or neighbouring countries to rework. Ultimately, we were considering the flow of culture globally, and how it demonstrated dynamics of power and how cinema responds creatively and industrially to those flows. In this final chapter, we'll continue that exploration, looking more specifically at genre. During the previous chapter, we briefly considered how genre production often has an international dimension. Some of the films we encountered, like *Ring*, were considered to have been produced to more easily cross international borders, with cultural odours, to use Iwabuchi's notion, that could sometimes be weaker, or be tainted with odours reminiscent of other countries' cultures. Genres have often had an international dimension, with many genres appropriated locally, such as horror, science fiction, the monster movie, film noir or the Western, and circulated internationally. Genre criticism, however, has long had a focus on Hollywood production, especially within the classical studio system, as a Fordist system of mass production, but this has been addressed in the growing context of transnational cinema. As Annette Kuhn and Guy Westwell have summarised in *A Dictionary of Film Studies* (2012), contemporary genre scholarship 'is now more inclined to adopt approaches embracing historical and contemporary social, industrial, and reception issues, as well as to consider genre and genres in the context of national cinemas, transnational cinema, and World cinema' (p. 196). Throughout this chapter, we'll consider some of these issues, across historical and contemporary approaches to genre, as well as exploring how audiences and distribution have been understood as essential for the transnational spread and adoption of genres globally.

Genre and national cinema

When it comes to the connections between world cinema and genre, there is a tendency for nation to be heavily promoted by certain genre definitions: we can often speak of *Japanese* samurai films, *Chinese* kung fu films, *Italian* sex comedies, *Australian* horror films. Some cinemas take on a generic quality of their own, such as Bollywood (normally associated with the musical) or Nollywood (with the video melodrama). Genre traditions might highlight their national distinctiveness through the adoption of linguistic terms in their original languages, like Italian *giallo* (thrillers from the 1970s and 1980s, the term describing the yellow spines of pulp novels), Japanese *kaijū eiga* (literally, monster stories), or Mexican *fronterizo* films (concerning the Mexican borderlands, something we looked at in an earlier chapter). Sometimes those genre distinctions are more regional than national, though, such as Nordic (or Scandi) noir, thrillers made in Denmark, Sweden and Norway.

As Elena Caoduro and Beth Carroll argue in the introduction to their special issue of *Frames Cinema Journal* entitled 'MondoPop: Rethinking Genre Beyond Hollywood' (2014), the tendency to link world cinema traditions with a particular kind of artistic rather than commercial practice has tended to overshadow the consideration of genres:

> the theorisation of world cinema has often privileged the realist tradition and expressions of art cinema, building a canon of world cinema auteurs and mapping styles of filmmaking from different corners of the globe, often overlooking the role of genres, the popular and the vernacular.

Genre has often been constituted in a Hollywood context, while the theorisation of genre has also tended to concentrate largely on Hollywood. This has, as Caoduro and Carroll note, been at the expense of thinking of specifically non-Hollywood genres in their respective national contexts. Even the genres that have been widely discussed have been those that have circulated internationally successfully, critically and financially (they refer to *giallo*, J-horror and French heritage cinema as their key examples of these trends). In the same issue, Stefano Baschiera explores the ways in which streaming online offers new potentials for world cinema genre films and niche cinema:

> From Asian horrors to Finnish romantic comedies, specialised films, in particular belonging to genres and subgenre categories, are now available on different online markets, from Video-On-Demand to catch up services, to the extent that each independent production can virtually reach millions of viewers through hosting websites such as Vimeo and YouTube. (2014)

Due to the cataloguing of world cinema genre films, Baschiera argues, online streaming services produce a 'geographical indeterminacy' through the cross-categorisation of films: cerebral films, exciting foreign films or cult films, for instance. Hence, this means 'several world cinema products "mingle" in the catalogue, finding places under different classifications and genres'. Baschiera contends that this has two consequences: one, that it is dissociated from the tendency to categorise foreign films as arthouse cinema, and two, that it creates more connections between mainstream generic products and world cinema due to the generation of new categories and recommendations for further viewing: thus, it 'is not uncommon to receive recommendations for *Oldboy* (Park Chan-wook, 2003) or other Korean and Scandinavian films as "what to watch next" at the end of a Hollywood mainstream thriller or drama'. Ultimately, Baschiera sees a 'new place' for world cinema within generic categories generated online by services such as Netflix or Amazon Prime. This does produce a primacy for international genres, as he notes, that films classified as horror or crime are those that find it most easy to travel internationally. Baschiera cites Roman Lobato and Mark Ryan (2011) here, and their contention that those films that highlight their national specificity are often those that travel most comfortably in global distribution. Because streaming services rely on the depth of their catalogue as their prime source of value for the consumer, instead of offering particular films that the viewer wants to see, niche cinema becomes of significant benefit, and the availability of world genre cinema has become more widespread beyond the very specialised exhibition and distribution sectors within which they would sit in cinemas or on VHS/DVD.

While Baschiera has noted this tendency to dissociate world genre cinema specifically from its national contexts while simultaneously making them more available in the broader genre canon developing in the streaming age, an earlier article by Tim Bergfelder problematised the reading of popular genre texts purely through a mono-national viewpoint. In 'The Nation Vanishes: European Co-Productions and Popular Genre Formula in the 1950s and 1960s' (2005), Bergfelder argued that pan-European genre production in the 1950s and 1960s was a 'culturally and economically viable strategy' of cross-Europe co-operation (p. 141). Nevertheless, he points out that the 'economic failure of these pan-European endeavours has strengthened the argument for the national specificity of filmic texts, and reinforced an emphasis on culturally and nationally defined film industries' (p. 132). Unlike the kind of adherence to clear structures and blueprints of genre that were more familiar from Hollywood (or from genre theory), the European co-productions Bergfelder explores had a tendency to be less rigidly defined in terms of their formulas: 'producers and audiences alike seem to have been guided instead by fairly general and broad categories'. This tends to demonstrate a different kind of model from the producer-audience contract defined more classically by genre theory, one that was more hybridised, or subject to parody.

> 'Adventure films', for instance, a term commonly used by producers, distributors and exhibitors during the 1960s, constituted a rather fluid definition, and referred in turn to more or less short-lived cycles of

Westerns, historical 'swashbuckler' movies, peplum films [Greco-Roman epics], biblical epics and exotic adventure films in a contemporary setting. With regard to the latter variant, the 'adventure' film would frequently overlap with spy thrillers, equally set in exotic locations. Crime films, horror, costume melodrama and, later on in the decade, the sex film also rarely defined 'pure' genres, and were often used as narrational components in hybrid combinations. (p. 147)

Such generic classification, eclectic, stylish, eventually sexually explicit, provided a clear alternative to the more rigidly classified and realist Hollywood approach to genre, where these European co-productions often offered an experience that privileged visual stylisation above a coherent narrative experience. The cross-border collaborations, within which Bergfelder includes the James Bond films, achieved 'a remarkable degree of standardisation' despite the need to cater to a broad sweep of film markets with the involvement of several national industries. In critical discourse, though, Bergfelder notes that there is still a tendency to 'contain these genres' within the recognisable limits of a national cultural context (he points to studies of the Spaghetti Western and exploitation cinema that are explored solely in the context of Italian national cinema). 'What such an approach ignores,' he argues, 'is that the success of these genres, and indeed the primary motivation for their production, rested precisely on their cross-cultural appeal.' (p. 141) We'll return to the Spaghetti Western later in the chapter, although it's important to remember here that genre can, and often does, move beyond the limits set for it by structures, blueprints or contracts supposed by genre theory, and the highly dependent Hollywood context of such theorisation means we can often impose limits on genres, as well as attempting to place genres within clearly delineated national boundaries that may obscure origins that are more transnational than national.

Genre in transnational cultures

In the introduction to *Global Genres, Local Films: The Transnational Dimension of Spanish Cinema* (2016), Elena Oliete-Aldea, Beatriz Oria and Juan Tarancón position the issue of transnational genres within the development of trajectories of national and regional connections:

films, regardless of their generic resemblances, engage in a context that is always changing as a consequence of concrete political, social and cultural forces, and genre conventions – although developed in a supranational sphere – always derive their meanings from these forces as much as from the histories and traditions they carry with them. (p. 3)

The supranational transcends the borders of any one nation, with global or regional reach. Structures and aesthetics of genre develop in this space over and above national boundaries, although, as Oliete-Aldea et al. describe here, they are contextualised (grounded might be a better term) through their contact with identifiable national contexts: 'genres evolve in a supranational exchange of recognizable narrative and aesthetic choices while engaging in and responding to specific social challenges' (p. 3). Importantly, they also contend that transnationalism is not a unified or homogeneous experience, only cohering within specific dimensions of local and global forces; likewise, globalisation is not a totalising experience. As 'both agents and expressions of globalization', films play a significant role in articulating the different experiences of transnationalism (p. 5). In this sense, the development of gen-res has been inflected with transnational flows, but that doesn't necessarily mean that it constitutes a rigid or distinct genre in itself, nor does it always represent nation in the same way. As they contend:

> generic conventions rest on international interactions that undercut any attempt to put forward a unique and distinctive account of national iden-tity. How we represent the nation to ourselves (or how we imagine our community) is inextricably linked to transnational relations ... The nation and the transnational – or the local and the global – do not designate different, mutually exclusive conditions. (p. 4)

Therefore, genres do not always articulate nation in the same way, although for Oliete-Aldea et al. they do always represent nation in some sense, weakly or strongly (in the sense that they might offer different levels of cultural odour), in their interactions with supra-, trans- or international conventions or structures, or the fact that they are made according to particular blueprints (or how they combine or deviate from those forms).

Hamid Naficy's notion of an independent transnational film genre does somewhat complicate this issue, in that his focus on an accented cinema, given its identifiable criteria, exhibits qualities of a genre. Naficy's use of the term 'genre' is close to that offered by Rick Altman, that genres rely 'on the existence of an implied contract among four parties: filmmakers/authors, film texts, individual spectators and interpretive communities, and the film industry and its practices' (2003, p. 206). The articles in the collection edited by Oliete-Aldea et al. cover a range of popular genres that are associated with filmmaking across Europe and the United States, including musicals, melo-dramas, historical epics, *banlieue* cinema and crime dramas, and sometimes how those genres are combined, and the ways in which the articulation of those genres is indicative of national and transnational issues. However, Naficy's definition of a transnational genre is, like in the case of the accented style, a case of interstitial authors rather than popular genres derived from international or supranational genre production, but rooted in what might be termed a former Third Cinema practice. It is an expression of transnationality as much as an agent of transnationality, since those filmmakers working in the genre occupy liminal spaces between and across borders in interstitial formations. In this article, Naficy explores the aesthetic and thematic conventions of the transnational genre that convey transnational, exiled experience. He links this tangentially with the melodrama in the ways that its use of space expresses 'emotional extremes'. In the transnational variant of the genre:

> it is the enclosed claustrophobic spaces, often in the form of prisons, which both express and encode the (melo)drama of transnational subjectivity. The phobic spaces are often played off of spaces of immensity. Space in transnational cinema, therefore, mediates between cosmos (order) and chaos (disorder). (2003, p. 211)

As his article's title articulates, this mediation between liminal panics and phobic spaces is one of the key generic markers of independent transnational films. In Turkish films, for instance, such as Yilmaz Güney's French-financed exilic film *The Wall (Duvar*, 1983), the phobic space is often symbolically articulated by the prison, in this case the ways in which 'structures of vision and division so necessary for coercion and control ... turn the diegetic prison into a metaphor of Turkish society itself as a total prison' (2003, p. 215). Therefore, like others, Naficy sees a genrifying function in transnational films, with the development of specific structures, conventions and themes that are shared, but rather than expressing a more local dimension they are more concerned with the articulation of transnationalism and exile in that connection between home and host cultures shared with the accented style.

Contrasting the comparative, contextual approach of Naficy and Oliete-Aldea et al., Ramon Lobato and Mark Ryan have suggested a different approach to understanding how genres develop in cross-border formations. Their article, 'Rethinking Genre Studies Through Distribution Analysis: Issues in International Horror Movie Circuits' (2011), explores how distribution, rather than textual analysis or the definition of generic categories, can provide an alternative means of demonstrating how networks of distribution mark film texts and help to communicate audience expectations. They argue that 'Thinking genre *through* distribution provides a different way of addressing some of the typical concerns of genre studies, such as patterns of generic evolution, aesthetics histories of individual genres/sub-genres, and debates around categorization and canonization'. In so doing, they argue that they shift genre away from a semiotic contractual model between producer and audience, and can demonstrate some of the ways in which genres' developments are both enabled and constrained through analysing distribution networks (p. 189). Their focus in the article is the Australian horror film, and their discussion 'advances thinking beyond a preoccupation with texts as self-contained outputs towards a better understanding of how a movie's generic identity in relation to its distribution trajectory (actual or desired) influences its content' (p. 200). Lobato and Ryan argue that a high number of horror titles are direct-to-DVD releases and rarely screen in cinemas. Digital and nontheatrical distribution are diverse and fragmented, thereby widening the distribution sphere begun during the era of VHS. This fragmentation includes both legal forms of rental streaming and purchasing files and the informal, such as BitTorrents and YouTube. In the case of low-budget Australian horror films, Lobato and Ryan witness a form of 'market-driven textual customization ... in play at the bottom end of the spectrum' where producers produce films that conform with preferences of international distributors to gain access to markets beyond the local, usually by ramping up the gore, sex and violence (p. 196). Their research perhaps produced a surprising result in that, in accessing international markets, these Australian horror films often exhibit distinctive national features and highlight their local characteristics. As they conclude: 'The flourishing of distinctively local content is one unlikely by-product of an increasingly globalized and digitized distribution landscape which affords Australian producers easier access to international long-tail markets'. This then 'allows national specificity to operate as a marker of difference' (p. 197). They also note how a number of film movements, such as J-horror, Italian *giallo*, and Indonesian cult cinema, have operated through similar processes, in 'feedback loops' between distribution and production that demonstrate how genres operate through considering distribution, as well as how those national dimensions of genre find global and local fandoms. Through a different model, therefore, Lobato and Ryan see a similar process of supranational genre and its relationship with local contexts that we've explored previously in the chapter.

Issues of transnational distribution are further discussed in Lobato's book, *Shadow Economies of Cinema: Mapping Informal Film Distribution* (2012). Throughout, Lobato explores the informal networks through which film is accessed, 'industrial architectures' that facilitate the movement of films through channels and circuits around the globe. He describes this as a 'transnational view of film culture, approaching global industries not as surfaces for US domination but as a complex of networks with their own logics, strategies and ambitions' (p. 3). Informal distribution is an inherently transnational practice, where practices such as piracy, peer-to-peer file sharing, local video clubs and halls, create a 'phantasmatic infrastructure' that 'perform a mediating function, linking economies and cultures through popular imaginaries', often for consumers who find themselves 'priced out of legal markets' (p. 46–47). Formal distribution – top-down Hollywood distribution – is alternatively a form of 'standardisation and "brand integrity"', where the viewer's experience of big-budget film is the same regardless of where they are anywhere around the globe. Informal distribution disturbs that standardisation; pirated films might have been recut, dubbed or even retitled. They might be unfinished versions, or have alternative endings. Even legal forms of distribution, such as low-budget genre films on DVD, might be just as misleading in their promises about a film's content, storylines or casts (a star with a small role might be given above-the-title recognition, for instance) (p. 44–45). These transnational processes therefore upset the standardisation associated with big-budget filmmaking, although they also reinforce practices associated with some kinds of genre-filmmaking, even while undermining the very standardisation that we might associate with the audience-producer contracts of genre. As Lobato also notes, the claims of genre theory that oppose the single-author ownership of the *auteur* theory also undermine claims to ownership of intellectual property so central to arguments surrounding piracy. As he asks, how can the use of a genre system that gleans textual codes from other works make significant claims to individual ownership of those tropes? Given the labour of audiences in authorising the prominence of certain conventions over others, how does a studio or producer claim ownership of those, when it is impossible to equitably redistribute revenue based on that proposition? Lobato cites the work of Laikwan Pang (2004) to consider how piracy might also be considered as a resistant strategy against being '(re)colonised by transnational audiovisual empires', usually those of Hollywood and the west (the two are often synonymous). In considering this argument, Lobato draws on Pang's work around Quentin Tarantino's *Kill Bill* (2003–2004), and its borrowings from East Asian cinemas: 'Hollywood has freely pilfered textual content from Asian cinemas while waging rhetorical war against copyright infringement' (Lobato, 2012, p. 81). From this perspective, piracy is a means of subverting dominant forms of power, but in so doing, Lobato also reminds us how those issues relate to discourses of global cultural flows, and their imbalance. The political value of considering piracy in relation to the broader concerns of cultural flow is in how informal transnational networks facilitate the flow of cultural material outside the processes of standardisation and authorship that allow for material to be appropriated and/or reframed, whether through further production or distribution practices.

Straight-to-video action cinema

In exploring some of these issues, I want to turn to two of Lobato's case studies: on straight-to-video genre films and on the Nollywood video industry in Nigeria. Exploring these two areas can help us see how genre functions as a category in production and distribution, and in minor transnational practice. Lobato argues that the straight-to-video (STV) film is an offshoot of the mainstream market, more closely related than the informal pirate economy, that is 'geographically dispersed' due to producers seeking out cheaper places in which to produce their work: 'STV movies are usually more likely to be made in [the] interstices of the global film economy, or to feature one location masquerading (often unsuccessfully) as another, or to feature an incoherent polyphony of accents and costumes' (Lobato, 2012, p. 24). Its labour force is culled from around the globe, from the Philippines, Thailand, Romania, Mexico or Canada. At the core of the STV trade, though, is genre. Genre must be clearly demarcated for the market and therefore sit within clear parameters: action, martial arts, erotic thrillers, or exploitative 'mockbusters', such as *Transmorphers* (Leigh Scott, 2007), *The Da Vinci Treasure* (Peter Mervis, 2006) or *AVH: Alien vs. Hunter* (Scott Harper, 2007). The action genre takes a key place in Lobato's discussion: films starring the likes of Steven Seagal or Cynthia Rothrock, that are indicative of demand in distribution markets. Most of the films in the STV sector are financed by presales to global distributors, with distribution or exhibition rights sold to TV companies or video distributors, which then allows production to be funded. The sources are transnational in origin, which then facilitate the films' transnational production in a 'fast and cheap' model, taking advantage of lower cost locations and recruiting crew locally, a transnationalism that Lobato argues is textually marked through the mixtures of locations and accents on display. The texts they produce have little cultural value, only to be disposable; he says it 'is not a field of undiscovered gems', but one that demonstrates the impact of distribution, a feedback loop of demand on production.

Meaghan Morris makes a similar point in her article, 'Transnational Imagination in Action Cinema: Hong Kong and the Making of a Global Popular Culture', which frames the genre and 'provide[s] a model of how to understand *global* cinema from a non-American but cosmopolitan local context' (2004, p. 184). She argues that the STV action film was critical in helping to develop the global action genre, from Hong Kong outwards:

> From the mid-1980s, the rapid spread of home video technology enabled a new form of production in which Western stars with real martial arts expertise and often experience in Hong Kong cinema – Chuck Norris, Jean-Claude van Damme, Cynthia Rothrock and the Australian martial

artist Richard Norton are good cases for study – made films that might have an American director, Israeli producers, finance from Luxembourg, an assistant director, crew, and supporting cast from whatever country in Asia (including Australia) the film could be cheaply and quickly made, sometimes a specialist choreographer from Hong Kong and a 'two ways ' story foregrounding a cultural or ethical conflict. (pp. 185–186)

Like Lobato, she demonstrates the transnational basis to these productions that functions as a form of emulation. For Morris, it is not a form of colonial mimicry, but a metaphorical student-teacher relationship, in which the student emulates the teacher both physically and ethically to come to embody their ideal, and empowered in the process. Following Deleuze, she describes this as a minor practice (opposed to cultural forms in a major language): small in funding; erratically distributed; informally exhibited; local/transnational in casting; shot in cheap locations, anywhere; pitched for the small screen, often addressing diasporic audiences (p. 190). As Morris argued later in the introduction to the collection *Hong Kong Connections: Transnational Imagination in Action Cinema*, 'action cinema works as a generic zone in which cross-cultural logics of contact and connection (audio-visual and socio-cultural as well as bodily and technological) are acted and tested out' (2005, p. 13). In its minor practice, it is another example of a transnational contact zone. Lobato and Morris's explorations of the STV action cinema help demonstrate how these contact zones straddle production and distribution as well as how they evoke national histories textually, but also, for our broader purposes, some of the ways we might understand how genre relates to transnationalism in different ways.

Nollywood

Moradewun Adejunmobi has taken a similarly Deleuzian take on the Nigerian video film industry. In her article, 'Nigerian Video Film As Minor Transnational Practice' (2007), she analyses 'transnational cultural practice [in order] to identify conditions that enable different types of transnational cultural practice for populations currently marginalized in the global economy' (p. 1). Echoing Appadurai's claim that globalisation produces forms of both standardisation and heterogenisation, Adejunmobi describes a form of practice distinct from global forms of distribution, technology and genre, one that she terms a 'regional popular' that is 'uncontestably transnational'. Nigerian video filmmaking – colloquially known as Nollywood – produces films in multiple languages (English, Yoruba, Igbo, Hausa) and their circulation extends across borders: Yoruba and Hausa are spoken beyond Nigeria: Yoruba in Benin and Togo, Hausa in Niger and across West Africa (spoken by approximately 40 million people). English language productions have a much broader circulation, throughout the whole continent, but also overseas with diasporic audiences (pp. 4–5). This circulation is often facilitated through informal channels of distribution. In his overview of the Nigerian video market, Lobato argues that it 'is clearly unlike other film industries. There are no formal distribution companies, just individual marketers and pirates, and in the place of cinemas there are video clubs and street markets' (2012, p. 59). More recently, he observes a push to formalise the industry, particularly in terms of governance, censorship and regimes of copyright, as well as a drive towards higher quality production, as opposed to the more standard 'fast and cheap' production model of many producers (both Adejunmobi and Lobato observe that Nollywood can release up to three films a day, although that only represents an official figure of films submitted to the Censors' Board). Nollywood films are more easily available internationally for diasporic audiences, in shops in major cities and on specialist television channels, as well as on both pirate and official video-on-demand websites. Unofficial global channels represent a challenge for producers, as they are unable to monetise these informal networks.

Matthias Krings and Onookome Okome have referred to Nollywood as the African *auteur* cinema's '*other*' (2013, p. 3), while Nikolaus Perneczky (2014) describes 'two major schools' of African production: 'the venerable celluloid tradition (mostly from Francophone countries) on the one hand, and the lowbrow video upstarts (predominantly from Anglophone countries) on the other'. Adejunmobi also draws a distinction between two forms of production, one the regional popular, and the other the 'global ethnic' that exemplifies 'responses to the major genres of dominant culture' (2007, p. 13), typified by the films of *auteurs* such as Ousmane Sembène. While the global ethnic films will be more accessible internationally, and more politically engaged, she argues that it is the more popular forms that will be valorised by local audiences, while international audiences will often see the global ethnic works as more representative of the region. With the opposition between popular and critically engaged forms comes, as Lobato and Krings and Okome have noted, an intellectual backlash against the perceived low-cultural appeal of the content of the films and their creeping 'Nigerianisation' into other nations, such as Ghana, Tanzania and the Democratic Republic of Congo.

In a sense, there is a tendency towards the term 'Nollywood' having a similar generic function to that of Bollywood, which tends to work as a metonym for the masala form rather than describing the industry. As a minor transnational practice, Adejunmobi argues that Nollywood video films 'draw upon the minor genres and minor technologies of dominant global culture, notably, in this case, melodrama, film, and video technology among others' (2007, p. 9). Like Hollywood cinemas, Nollywood has developed its own structures, blueprints and contracts with viewers regarding its generic output. Adejunmobi (2002) has argued that no single genre is dominant in Nigerian video production, but that some dominant trends have come to the fore: 'Increasingly, the industry is tending towards a diversification of style and content motivated by the emerging delineation of audiences for particular types of video film.' (p. 78) Many films in Yoruba, English and Igbo (the language of South-eastern Nigeria) are concerned with the occult, often with a preoccupation about wealth. Adejunmobi notes that they often split down ethnic lines, with Yoruba films generally dealing with specific forms of Yoruba supernatural spirits and rituals, while Igbo and English films will tend to highlight Christian forms of iconography that 'often owe more to the syncretic spirituality of urban Nigeria than to any form of traditional belief'. There is a conservative strain to many films, where the transgression of moral fortitude is punished, especially where wealth is concerned (even if characters don't resort to spiritual means to earn that wealth): 'Becoming rich means engaging in betrayal of sacred trusts, aberrant sexual acts, prostitution, armed robbery, and inevitably manipulation of occult powers.' (p. 79) The enormously popular English-language film *Glamour Girls* (Chika Onukwufor, 1994), about five wealthy women living in the country's capital Lagos, set the template for many of these films. The narrative is structured around the women's relationships, with men who either jilt or steal from them, have affairs, or blackmail powerful partners, with several raunchy sex scenes. For each of the women, their situations end badly, from emotional collapse to arrest for murder. As Paul Ugor contends, the film 'anatomizes the immense contradictions of urban life for young women in Nigerian cities' (2013, p. 162).

Hausa films, made in Nigeria's largely Islamic northern areas, tend to be romances, often with Bollywood-style singing and dancing. They are generally conservative in tone, however, and tend not to feature any kissing. Action films are popular in English and Igbo, while melodramas are common in Yoruba filmmaking. Alongside these genres, we see more indigenous forms of filmmaking that have been argued to constitute genres in themselves. For instance, Nikolaus Perneczky (2014) has explored the 'village films' of Tunde Kelani, whose video work, he argues, bridges the genre of the village film across the auteurist cinematic terrain of sub-Saharan cinema and the video work of Nollywood. These films negotiate the pre-modern traces of rural experience and the structures of African modernity. Rather than see this coalescing definitively as a genre, although it demonstrates aspects of the core principles of a genre's concern with recurring themes, Perneczky argues that Kelani's films, including *Brass Bells* (*Saworoide*, 1999) and its sequel *Agogo eewo* (2002), embrace the postcolonial aesthetics of sub-Saharan cinema from the 1960s onwards. As he contends, 'Tunde Kelani embraces the traditional beliefs marginalised in the historical context of postcolonial nation-building' although not to the same excessive degree as Nollywood's focus on spectacular magical interventions; Kelani's Yoruba films represent not a 'return of the repressed', but a 'return of the source'. A transnational regional quasi-genre, the village film exhibits an 'allegorically charged small-ness' that it shares with the sub-Saharan 35mm films that came before it in the post-colonial era, although where those films engaged in a critique of the repository of colonial images and social roles. Kelani's films, Perneczky argues, mediate the pre-modern with the modernised nation, something he links with the generic function of the American Western: 'The term "village film" thus denotes a certain construction of communality, not entirely unlike that found in the American Western of the classical period – consider the "universe-in-a-nutshell" model John Ford's *Stagecoach* (1939) brought to bear on the task of nation-building' (Perneczky, 2014).

Nollywood produces films in a range of genres, some that are identified through conventional forms of generic analysis, such as romantic musicals, action or melodrama, although they are always filtered through local cultural standards and ideologies. Occult and supernatural genres are more distinctive of the Nollywood form, as is the televisual aesthetic of many of the films, and genres cater for different audiences across national borders, and beyond for diasporic audiences. Filmmaking practice can also be linked with traditions of postcolonial filmmaking in sub-Saharan, often Francophone countries, although we should also note that the art cinema to which they belong also constitutes an international meta-genre, with its own conventions that conform to expected forms while critiquing other narrative forms. As Adejunmobi has argued, this is a type of minor transnational practice that locates how transnational cultural systems function for audiences that are marginalised by the global economy. But, as Lobato suggests, this positions Nigeria as a regional centre of film production, which has led to concerns from other neighbouring areas about the potentially negative impact Nollywood films might have where there is widespread consumption. Since there are no official distribution channels, it is considered to be more dangerous to local markets than Hollywood.

Global daikaijū

Guillermo del Toro's *Pacific Rim* (2013) is a resolutely transnational film. With a Mexican director, principal photography carried out predominantly in Canada and a cast from Britain (Charlie Hunman, Idris Elba, Burn

Gorman), Canada (Diego Klattenhoff, the Chinese-Vietnamese-descended Luu brothers), the US (Ron Perlman, Max Martini), Japan (Rinko Kikuchi) and Spain (Santiago Segura), the film is ultimately about transnational co-operation, as a group of Americans, Russians, Chinese, Japanese and British operatives from a base in Hong Kong fight off an invasion of space monsters that travel via an inter-dimensional portal at the bottom of the Pacific Ocean known as 'The Breach'. These monsters are known as *'kaijū'* in the film. In this case, we can immediately begin to see how genre is globalised, appropriated and reworked (Figure 8.1). The *daikaijū* (big monsters) in *Pacific Rim* evoke the influence of the Japanese genre to which the use of that term refers. Del Toro spoke in interviews about the influence of Godzilla and the design of the creatures in the film that aimed to evoke the classic look of the *tokusatsu* (special effects) film, even down to referencing the 'suit-mation' style of those films that would feature an actor in a suit rampaging across a miniature landscape. In *Pacific Rim*, the kaijū are fought off by giant mecha (robots), known as Jaegars, piloted by two people whose consciousness is fused to control it. Although the term mecha is never used in the film itself, it is regularly used in critical discourse about the film (such as on the *Pacific Rim Wiki*), and, like the word *kaijū*, refers quite specifically to a Japanese subgenre. As Rayna Denison notes in *Anime: A Critical Introduction* (2015), the mecha (mechanical) subgenre emerged as one of the most successful transnational exports of the anime canon. She notes that this is not without controversy, as some of early mecha series that were exported were

Figure 8.1 *Pacific Rim* (Guillermo del Toro, 2013) situates its appropriation of Japanese material through its use of iconography as well as language (Warner Bros/Legendary Pictures)

heavily edited versions of several Japanese series, such as *Robotech* (1985), *Voltron* (1984–5), and *Gundam Wing* (2000). These, and others such as *Neon Genesis Evangelion* (*Shin Seiki Evangerion*, 1995–1996), popularised the giant robot subgenre (which Denison notes is closely related to the science fiction and *shōnen* (young boys) genres) and the term has circulated broadly in *otaku* cultures with anime fans as well as the mainstream, such as in the Steven Spielberg film *A.I. Artificial Intelligence* (2001). *Pacific Rim* blends elements of these two strands that are closely linked with a specific national culture, both of which were highlighted in the film's reception.

As a transnational appropriation, this approach to genre demonstrates some of the issues regarding mediascapes and cultural flow that we've already explored. Ultimately, though, how do we identify these genres as specifically *Japanese*? If we take a historical approach to the development of the *kaijū eiga*, we can explore how the national roots of a genre might be subject to being questioned, and we might see something more transnational in its development, its own appropriation of transnational material and its global spread. It's perhaps obvious to say that the root film in this genre is *Godzilla* (*Gojira*, Ishirō Honda, 1954), a widely regarded classic of world cinema, despite the low-cultural appeal of the genre overall. This low-cultural appeal is partly down to the films' use of cheesy special effects but also the practices of translation that would tend to favour dubbing over subtitling. Dubbing, Mark Nornes reminds us, is condemned 'as the lowest form of translation'. Dubbed, a film's 'foreign language is completely extracted, replaced with sameness' (Nornes, 2007, p. 219). The Godzilla films were released in the west by exploitation film distributors, such as American International Pictures, New World Pictures and Embassy Pictures, and there were usually dubbed, often recut, sometimes retitled or had newly filmed scenes inserted into them. This often led to them achieving cult status due to their campiness, as a type of bad cinema known as 'paracinema' (Sconce, 1995). The original *Godzilla* has been canonised as a world cinema classic, though, distributed by prestige distributors such as the British Film Institute and the Criterion Collection.

Honda's *Godzilla* is strongly linked to the national imaginary. The film begins with a freighter shipwrecked at sea – something bubbles up from beneath the surface of the water, and a great explosion and wind wrecks the ship. A fishing boat picks up some survivors – either from the first vessel or the one sent to investigate – but it too is wrecked by the same mysterious force. The opening events had national precedence: in March 1954, just eight months before the film was released, the United States exploded a nuclear bomb at Bikini Atoll in the Marshall islands, over 2,000 miles from Japan. The fallout spread over 7,000 square miles. A fishing boat, the *Fukuryū*

Maru ('Lucky Dragon'), was caught in the radiation, and the crew members became sick with radiation poisoning. Godzilla became a potent symbol of the nuclear bombs dropped on Japan by the US in 1945, with the film's *mise en scène* echoing the destruction of Nagasaki and Hiroshima in the aftermath of the bombings (Figure 8.2). As William Tsutsui argues in *Godzilla on My Mind* (2004), 'association of Godzilla's attacks with the ravages of World War II on the Japanese homeland undoubtedly brought with it substantial ideological baggage' (p. 37). Likewise, Chon Noriega (1987) has argued that Godzilla, and many of the other creatures who became popular heroes in the films that came after, enact the problematic US-Japanese relation built on the post-war occupation (that ended only two years before the production of *Godzilla*), as well as metaphorising atomic warfare and the Pacific nuclear tests. Rather than just see the US as Other to Japan, Noriega argued that the Japanese identification of selfhood with the figure of the Other complicates this simple binary: Godzilla comes to symbolize Japan (self) as well as the US (Other).

The Godzilla films are therefore deeply rooted in a specific national imaginary following the Second World War. They express ambivalence towards science and towards a national scenario in which the homeland requires rebuilding,

Figure 8.2 *Godzilla* (Ishirō Honda, 1954): The aftermath of Godzilla's attacks in the series' first films utilise *mise en scène* that is highly evocative of the nuclear attacks in the Second World War (Tōhō)

but also the mistrust of US nuclear testing. As Yomota Inuhiko has argued, this involved a 'return of the repressed':

> Godzilla was horrifying precisely because he embodied the souls of those who died during the war. That is to say that the mental image of the casualties of war was placed in an abject relation to those who had survived the atrocities and who now enjoyed the prosperity and democracy of post-war life. (2007, pp. 107–108)

Generically, though, *Godzilla* shares commonalities with the American cycle of 1950s science fiction films, although the national text is different, where the blobs and giant ants of the American variant projected Otherness outwards, onto Soviets or the monsters themselves. Perhaps the most similar film to *Godzilla* is *The Beast from 20,000 Fathoms* (Eugène Lourié, 1953), in which a nuclear test in the Arctic rouses a giant reptilian rhedosaurus that finds its way to New York to wreak havoc (there are similarities here with the 1998 American version of *Godzilla* (Roland Emmerich) that took the creature to New York). While nuclear weapons created the problem, they solve them too (Figure 8.3).

Figure 8.3 In similar fashion to the fate that befalls Godzilla, the dangerous science that awakens the creature is nullified by the science used to kill *The Beast from 20,000 Fathoms* (Eugène Lourié, 1953) (Warner Bros/Jack Dietz Productions)

Curiously, the rhedosaurus has been viewed as a *kaijū*, with *Wikizilla*, the fan-run wiki, claiming it as an example of the genre, demonstrating how fluid genres can be historically. The film was also released in Japan about a month after *Godzilla*. Perhaps more formatively, the film's influences are demonstrative of how cultural material is appropriated and indigenised, conforming with Koichi Iwabuchi's contention that 'Transnationally circulated images and commodities ... tend to become culturally odorless in the sense that origins are subsumed by the local transculturation process' (2002, p. 46). As we've seen, there is a strong national text embedded within *Godzilla*. However, Eiji Tsuburaya, the special effects director of the first eight Godzilla films, until *Destroy All Monsters* (*Kaijū Sōshingeki*, Ishirō Honda, 1968), as well as many other films and the popular *tokusatsu* television series *Ultra Q* (1966, which was followed by the iconic *Ultraman* (1966–1967)), was heavily influenced by *King Kong* (Edgar Wallace and Merian C. Cooper, 1933), and this reflected in the design and name of the monster. Gojira in katakana is ゴジラ (the form used on most advertising), and this is Romanised as go-ji-ra. The word is the combination of two Japanese words, the transliteration of gorilla (as a nod to King Kong) (katakana: ゴリラ, rom: *gorira*) and the word for whale (katakana: クジラ, rom: *kujira*). As a transnationally circulated commodity, King Kong is here appropriated and indigenised, and as we've noted, this has been considered as highly Japanese in its meanings, as well as its origins, but there are transnational roots to the genre, appropriated into a national context, prior to being re-exported, where the process of appropriation and indigenisation continues.

When *Godzilla* was released in the US by producer Joseph Levine it was indigenised as *Godzilla: King of the Monsters!* (Terry O. Morse and Ishirō Honda, 1956), dubbed and re-edited with new sequences featuring Raymond Burr, as an observer character called Steve Martin, inserted into it. The anti-American sentiment of the original film was minimised, with explicit reference to Nagasaki removed. Later films in the series were turned into television staples in the Creature Double Features that helped develop the core cult audience for *kaijū* movies. The same process of dubbing, editing and inserting Raymond Burr recurred with the release of *Godzilla 1985* (R.J. Kizer and Koji Hashimoto, 1985) by New World Pictures, a reworking of *The Return of Godzilla* (simply released in Japan as *Gojira* in 1984). The film was promoted as campy excess, the trailers telling us Godzilla's 'acting technique was revolutionary. His presence ... overwhelming. He possessed more raw talent than any performer of his generation'.

As the genre developed, Tōhō's rivals produced their own *kaijū* films: Shochiku, their most direct competitor, made *The X from Outer Space* (*Uchū Daikaijū Girara*, Kazui Nihonmatsu, 1967); another major studio, Daiei (today Kadokawa-Daiei) instigated their own *kaijū* series, most notably in *Gamera* (*Daikaijū Gamera*, Noriaki Yuasa, 1965), about a giant flying space turtle awoken by a nuclear explosion in the Arctic, that has spawned eleven sequels; Daiei also produced three *Daimajin* films (Kimiyoshi Yasuda, Kenji Misumi, all 1966), about a giant stone statue that comes to life to free its worshippers from feudal oppression; low-budget studio Nikkatsu, closely associated with the *yakuza* film, produced their own *kaijū* film as well: *Gappa, The Colossal Beast* (*Daikyojû Gappa*, Haruyasu Noguchi, 1967). This final film closely resembles the plot of *Gorgo* (Eugène Lourié, 1961), a British monster movie, in which two unscrupulous sailors sell a 65ft-tall reptile to a circus in London after discovering it off the Irish coast, only for its mother to arrive to rescue it, destroying much of London in the process. *Gappa* replaced the reptile with a bird-like lizard creature, but followed a very similar plot. The genre was also appropriated around Asia, including in South Korean films *Yongary: Monster from the Deep* (*Taekoesu Yongary* Kim Ki-duk, 1967) and *Space Monster Wangwagwi* (*Ujugoe-in wangwagwi*, Hyeok-jinn Gwon, 1967). A single Hindi monster film was produced, called *Gogola* (Balwant Dave, 1966), the only remnants of which are a promotional poster for its Mumbai release that bills it as 'an action packed story of a Sea-monster with Thrills, Suspense and What Not? [sic]' and its soundtrack, which is available on YouTube. *The Mighty Peking Man* (*Goliathon*, Meng-hua-Ho, 1977) was a Hong Kong film timed to coincide with release of a remake of *King Kong* in 1976. Perhaps the most notorious *kaijū* film however is *Pulgasari* (1985), a North Korean film directed by Shin Sang-ok, a famous South Korean director who was kidnapped by Kim Jong-il, after his ex-wife, the actress Choi Eun-hee, had been abducted in Hong Kong – they were held for eight years, until they escaped while visiting Vienna for a film festival. While in captivity, Shin directed a number of films, of which *Pulgasari* is the best known (it is perhaps the best known of all North Korean films). Based on an old Korean legend, the monster is a metal-eating giant (Figure 8.4) who fights alongside a group of peasants against a corrupt feudal lord as a means of promoting the North Korean regime's *Juche* ideology, a quasi-Socialist philosophy of independence, economic self-sufficiency and military self-reliance.

Despite these flows of material in and out of Japan and around the world, there is still an argument made for the films to be considered as a particular product of Japanese popular culture and part of a national culture. As William Tsutsui argued on the release of the 2014 American *Godzilla*, the monster was being stolen by the US:

Godzilla [was] unmistakably identified as one of *wareware Nihonjin* (we Japanese): a monster that goes out of his way to protect and defend his adopted home islands. But things are very different in the 2014 version:

Figure 8.4 *Pulgasari* (Shin Sang-ok, 1985): The North Korean Pulgasari, based on a legend about a metal-eating monster, defeats the corrupt feudal lord to protect a group of farmers (Korean Film)

as Godzilla turns for the sea at the end of the new movie, we briefly see a 24-hour news network feed declaring him 'King of the Monsters – Savior of Our City.' ... And although all of the U.S. cities destroyed in the movie are real, the Japanese city ravaged by the earlier stirrings of the MUTOs, the awkwardly named Janjira, is pure fiction. (2014)

This figure of Janjira (beneath a conveniently placed Mount Fuji) is unmistakeably reminiscent of Fukushima, which suffered a nuclear disaster on 11 March 2011 after a tsunami caused by the Tōhoku earthquake triggered a power failure that shut down the cooling of three of its reactors. The disaster at the Janjira plant at the beginning of the film, caused by one of the MUTOs (Massive Unidentified Terrestrial Organisms), seems intended to evoke this disaster. As with many remakes, there can often be a problematic cultural translation, as the film's main Japanese character, Ken Watanabe's Dr. Ishiro Serizawa (a reference to Honda and to the scientist character in the original, Dr. Daisuke Serizawa), seems heavily Orientalised, spouting stereotypical wisdoms, with an almost interchangeable use of Gojira and Godzilla (the film offers no rationale for the translation, which is simply a transliteration, unlike the previous Hollywood version which put it down to a comment misheard by a news anchor). But, in contrast with Tsutsui's comments, there is a moment at the end of the film that repositions the monster as Japanese: as the beast awakes there is a minor motif in the musical score played on a Shakuhachi flute that, for want of a better term, re-orients him as he leaves. So, while the monster is the saviour of San Francisco, we are briefly reminded of its national origins, despite their transnational connections, flows and appropriations.

National/transnational Westerns

Rick Altman addresses the question of what genres can teach us about nations in the penultimate chapter of *Film/Genre*. Drawing on Benedict Anderson's notion of the imagined community of nation and Jürgen Habermas's conception of the public sphere, Altman likens the development of genres to that of discourses of nations. With a continual dialectic between the centre and margins, there is an ongoing process and system of regenrification. In this system, the fragmented margins at the periphery are subsumed within the centre, only to then be displaced by newly constituted genres within the margins. As a semantic/syntactic approach to genre, there is an ongoing 'process of cycle-making creolization, combining gypsy adjectives with established, land-owning generic substantives. Only when those previously marginalized adjectives plant their flag in the centre of the world are they transmuted into substantival genres, thus putting them on the map' (1999, p. 199). Altman uses genre as metaphor for national political change, just as politicians always find new forms of Otherness to scapegoat, or institutionalised political movements that were radical at one time, become challenged by new waves of political thought. With genre, as with nations, hyphens become a question of politics. Hyphenated identities eventually become subsumed into the masses, while new hyphenates are acknowledged on the margins. As such with genre: 'By 1910, a series of proto-generic hyphenated experiments – Western-epic, Western-drama, Western-melodrama – had precipitated the Western. By 1930, a pattern of generic miscegenation – musical-drama, musical-comedy, musical-melodrama – had produced an offspring regarded, surprisingly, as pure' (p. 204). What happens when those hyphenated genre identities are constituted across national, as well as classificatory boundaries? As Oliete-Aldea et al. argued, genre tends to develop in a supranational space that is then re-contextualised in a more local one. The *kaijū eiga*, we saw, was subject to development in a very national context, despite some supranational spread that was then recontextualised in other national cinemas, something that can make us consider issues of national power imbalances, in this case hierarchically (between the US, Japan and East Asia in particular), rather than as a binary of the west and the rest between Hollywood and everywhere else. How would this look if we considered a genre such as the martial arts film, with its popularity globally with many diasporic or ethnic communities (Prashad, 2001), or the popularity of Bollywood musicals in communities from South Asian diasporas and their subsequent integration into Hollywood cinema? Does this constitute the development of a new genre through combination? Is *The Matrix* (The Wachowskis, 1999), a martial-arts-science-fiction film, or *Slumdog Millionaire* (Danny Boyle, 2008) a post-colonial-social-realist-masala? How would the hyphenated identities of such genres relate to those transnational flows?

At the end of the chapter now, I want to turn briefly to the example of the Western, one of Altman's examples in connecting the construction of nation with regenrification. André Bazin referred to the Western as 'the American film *par excellence*', its content 'unalloyed myth' (1972, p. 143). Robert Warshow saw its main character as one of the 'two most successful creations of American movies' (2001, p. 105). Jim Kitses' seminal structural study of the Western, *Horizons West* (1969), informs us that 'the Western is American history', not because it is historically accurate, but because it romantically recounts the myths of the nation's foundations. As David Lusted discusses it, the genre 'needs to be understood as a popular form that becomes part of the cultural language by which America understands itself' (2014, p. 22), here citing Will Wright's *Sixguns and Society* and his definition of the social myth of the Western as a meaning that must 'reflect the particular social institutions and attitudes that have created and continue to nourish the myth' (Wright, 1975, p. 2). With a few exceptions, though, the genre lost its foothold as the key American genre through the 1960s, 1970s and 1980s. Despite this, there has been a continuing fascination with the Western amongst filmmakers outside America, and it has been repeatedly appropriated and revised in films from around the world. As Vivian P.Y. Lee has argued, 'film scholars have observed signs of its revival, albeit in augmented and hybridized forms in the global mediascape, noting in particular the intertwined processes of generic crossbreeding in postmodern film cultures and cross-cultural critical reception'. Filmmakers from a range of nations and cultures are not simply mimicking or imitating Hollywood, but engaging in complex 'intergeneric and intertextual dialogues between the Western' and national and regional film cultures outside Hollywood (2015, p. 147).

For many years, Westerns have been made around the world, particularly in Italy, such as *A Fistful of Dollars* (*Per un pugno di dollari*, Sergio Leone, 1964), and *Django* (Sergio Corbucci, 1966), both of which are remakes of a Japanese film, Akira Kurosawa's *Yojimbo* (1961). Like Lee, Austin Fisher has argued that the adoption of the Western by Italian filmmakers wasn't simply a case of imitating or mimicking Hollywood filmmakers, but was a process of 'negotiation and cultural blending' (2011, p. 2), whereas, in the case of *Django*, he has argued that the consideration of the flow of the film's influence and distribution in a transnational sense is problematic because 'it assumes the integrity of the "national" referent as an oppositional starting point' when 'the make-up and distribution patterns of Corbucci's film bespeak cultural identities whose attachment to regional or national imperatives was weakening' (Fisher, 2013). *Django* is rooted in an Italian context, where the uncertainty of the 1960s were reflected in the cultural blending of many of the popular genre films being made. Therefore, Fisher argues that when it was released, it was 'already transnational' at its very core. After its release, *Django* influenced the renaming of many Italian Westerns – even without making an appearance, Django's name somehow made it into the title – while it has been appropriated most recently by Quentin Tarantino, in *Django Unchained* (2012).

In terms of roots, the Italian Western had been accused of lacking 'cultural roots' (Christopher Frayling calls it the 'cultural roots controversy'), where the Westerns made in Italy were accused of being 'cheap opportunistic imitations' (Frayling, 2006, p. 121), with the genre 'assumed to have "cultural roots" in American society' (p. 27). Frayling makes a case that the Spaghetti Western, particularly Leone's films, engaged more directly with American history (something he notes has been positioned as already having European, or 'extra-American', roots), especially around issues surrounding relationships along the border with Mexico, the place of immigrants and minority groups in the west, and the neo-feudal ways in which Spanish/American towns were run (pp. 127–129). The Italian Western thus perhaps best represents Neil Campbell's observation that the west was 'always already transnational' (2008, p. 4). Leon Hunt has argued, however, that no such argument was made in the case of 'Asian Westerns', that they 'fall outside of this controversy around "roots" by finding synergies between the American and/or Italian Western and either the Japanese *chanbara* [swordplay] film or the Hong Kong kung fu film, that pose no problems for the "authenticity" of either genre' (2011, p. 101). Hunt here draws on David Desser's point that Kurosawa's *Seven Samurai* can be reworked as a Western (or more) because it shares a deeper transcultural resonance with Greek tragedy (Desser, 2008), just as *Yojimbo* had taken inspiration from Dashiell Hammett's hard-boiled American detective novel, *Red Harvest* (1929). The Asian Westerns that Hunt discusses – Thai film *Tears of the Black Tiger* (*Fah talai jone*, Wisit Sartsanatieng, 2001), the Japanese *Sukiyaki Western Django* (Takashi Miike, 2007), and South Korean *The Good, the Bad, the Weird* (*Choŭnnom, Nappŭnnom, Isanghannom*, Kim Jee-woon, 2008) – all seem 'clearly designed to travel, sometimes on the basis of the "exoticism" of their hybridized generic make-up' (2011, p. 103). The latter film is complicated by its setting in Manchuria, a former colonial space (now in Northern China above the Korean peninsula) where, during Japanese occupation, many Koreans were sent into exile to work as forced labourers, as conscripted soldiers, or as 'comfort women'. Michelle Cho argues that Kim's film is a problematic case of cultural blending, between the Spaghetti Western, shades of reference to the kung fu film's use of Japanese-occupied Shanghai as a setting, and the Korean *Manju hwalgŭk* (Manchurian action film), a nationalist genre that imagined Manchuria as a space of romantic resistance against Japanese colonial oppression that Cho notes as having been largely disavowed by contemporary Korean viewers. Thus, the use of the setting has cultural roots that are both transnational (in its response to Japanese colonialism and generically) and highly national, hence 'Kim Jee-woon's reimagination of Manchuria as a space of *adventure* rather than as a historical setting has precedent in the Korean genre-film productions of the 1960s and 1970s' (2015, p. 53). However, she also notes that the film pales in comparison with Bong Joon-ho's more commercial-critical *kaijū* family melodrama *The Host* (*Kwoemul*, 2006), against which *The Good, the Bad, the Weird* 'would seem to be a regression to the empty spectacle of genre imitation' designed 'to please the widest swathe of potential viewers' (p. 49). Its transnational blending of generic and locally specific material was also complicated by the film's distribution, in which:

> [its] international theatrical release ... was edited to efface plot elements that might confuse non-Korean viewers, removing key elements of the Manchurian action films' localization of the western to the Manchurian frontier and, most crucially, references to the geopolitical situation of the Japanese colonial period. (Cho, 2015, pp. 46–47)

Therefore, it's easy to see why the film might be considered more imitation than critical, given this disavowal. In conclusion, Cho argues that the generic combination in the film reworks conventional moral certainties in favour of ambiguity by having Good and Bad disappear through the convention of the Mexican standoff (in a direct reference to Leone's *The Good, The Bad and The Ugly* (*Il buono, il brutto, il cattivo*, 1966), metal plate and all, only this time on Weird rather than Clint Eastwood's Good) (Figures 8.5 and 8.6). As such, it resists 'genre's relentless normativity and also brings into the picture the crucial consideration of the transnational and translational aspects of genre cinemas in the numerous national sites and affective modes in which it is produced' (p. 68).

Figures 8.5 and 8.6 The generic imitation of *The Good, The Bad, The Weird* (bottom picture) (Kim Jee-woon, 2008) strongly replicates the imagery of *The Good, The Bad and The Ugly* (top picture) (Sergio Leone, 1966), although it does so in a different national context (Barunson/CJ Entertainment/Cineclick Asia/ Grimm Pictures & Produzioni Europee Associati/Arturo González Producciones Cinematográficas, S.A/Constantin Film)

Like Kim's film, *Sukiyaki Western Django* appeared in a cut international form that problematised some of its national and transnational roots, with the removal of references to homosexuality that challenge heteronormative masculinity (Rawle, 2011). The film prequelises *Django*; at the end, we're told the young Japanese boy at the heart of the standoff between two families 'made his way to Italy and was known as a man called Django'. Sukiyaki is probably the best analogy for the film, not in the sense of nationalising it as the word Spaghetti does for Italian Westerns or the use of Curry for Indian Westerns, such as *Sholay* (Ramesh Sippy, 1975) (Westerns were produced in Japan prior to the 1960s; produced predominantly by Nikkatsu, entitled 'miso westerns' (Schilling, 2007)), but as an analogy for a film that has one pot, and everything in it. The film opens by explaining that it is set a few hundred years after the battle of Dannoura. The battle of Dannoura took place in 1185, at the end of the Genpei war between the Genji (Minamoto) and Heike (Taira) clans. Miike's film picks up this conflict some time later in a town in 'Nevada' (although the architecture is Japanese). Into this pot are thrown a mélange of references to a host of generic tropes, and not just to the eponymous *Django* (the town's sheriff is skewered with a wooden cross that reads 'Mercedes Zora', the name of Django's wife). Miike's film borrows *Django's* theme song as well as the coffin that carries his famous Gatling Gun, but also quotes broadly from American films, such as *The Godfather* (Francis Coppola, 1972), *Apocalypse Now* (Francis Coppola, 1979) and *Rambo: First Blood Part Two* (George P. Cosmatos, 1985). In addition to this, the film refers to the Japanese *chanbara*; at the outset, the Gunman (Hideaki Itō) is told that he 'best not get any ideas about playing *Yojimbo*', a clear reference to Kurosawa's film of the same name. The key issue at stake in this is that the material referred to is already transnational in origin. Again, there is a temptation to see this mixing as an appropriation by a Japanese filmmaker, hybridised with elements of Japanese history and literature, as evidence of a border-less postmodernism. However, the referenced material has always been transnational in nature, as we've already explored. This process therefore reflects transnational exchange rather than appropriation of American material, thereby complicating the movement of material across national boundaries.

What is most problematised in *Sukiyaki Western* is language. The film is almost entirely in English, despite none of the actors being English speakers, as the film's production notes attested (First Look Studios, 2008). This was also one of the key features of the reception of the film; as one reviewer remarked, 'The intent must have been to approximate poorly dubbed Italian Westerns, but the effect is near gibberish' (White, 2008). However, the use of phonetic English spoken by the actors highlights a transnational flow, as well as a paradoxical realism (although the film is not technically set in the US, it must be in English because it is a Western). East Asian actors are often called upon to speak English in western films, as highlighted by films such as *Memoirs of a Geisha* (Rob Marshall, 2005), where the Asian cast (controversially mostly Chinese in Japanese roles) were required to speak English throughout, despite the film being set in Japan. Miike redresses this balance, having Quentin Tarantino recite from the *Heike monogatari* in an Oriental-accented English. In this case, English is appropriated along with the intertextual basis of the film, thereby resisting global homogenisation – Hunt calls it 'deterritorialized' (2011, p. 103) – which would have been the consequence had the film been dubbed. The use of Japanicised English problematises the use of English as the global dominant of transnational film production. While many reviewers mistook this as 'bad English', the film intervenes in the textual struggles of transnational cinemas. This reminds us of Naficy's comments about transnational cinema's mediation 'between cosmos (order) and chaos (disorder)' (Naficy, 2003, p. 211), and that, where a transnational cinema links 'genre, authorship, and transnational positioning ... [it] allows films to be read and reread not only as individual texts produced by authorial vision and generic conventions, but also as sites for intertextual, cross-cultural, and translational struggles over meanings and identities' (p. 205). The examples at which we've looked at the end of this chapter have shown how the appropriation of genre conventions across national boundaries, and their recombination or reinterpretation through national contexts, reflect a range of issues about cross-cultural appropriation and transnational responses to genre cinemas. This final example, located in the 'American film *par excellence*' shows us just how muddied the waters can get when we explore how genres become globalised not simply as imitation, but in ways that rework or join in struggles across borders.

Recommended viewing:

Old Shatterhand (Hugo Fregonese, 1964)
Kovboy Ali (Yilmaz Atadeniz, 1966)
El Topo (Alejandro Jodorowsky, 1970)
They Call Me Trinity (E.B. Clucher, 1970)
Captain Swing the Fearless (*Korkusuz Kaptan Swing*, Tunç Basaran 1971)
Takkari Donga (Jayant Paranji, 2002)
The Proposition (John Hillcoat, 2005)
The Warrior's Way (Lee Seung-moo, 2010)
The Salvation (Kristian Levring, 2014)
Far from Men (*Loin des hommes*, David Oelhoffen, 2014)
Jauja (Lisandro Alonso, 2014)
Slow West (John MacLean, 2015)

Recommended further reading:

Baschiera, Stefano, and Francesco Chiara (2010), 'Once Upon a Time in Italy: Transnational Features of Genre Production 1960s–1970s', *Film International* 8(6): pp. 30–39.

Broughton, Lee (2014), '*Captain Swing the Fearless*: A Turkish Adaptation of an Italian Western Comic Strip', in eds Lúcia Nagib and Anne Jerslev, *Impure Cinema: Intermedial and Intercultural Approaches to Film*. London: IB Tauris, pp. 102–118.

Chung, Hye-Seung, and David Scott Diffrient (2015), *Movie Migrations: Transnational Genre Flows and South Korean Cinema*. New Brunswisk: Rutgers University Press.

Cooke, Paul, ed. (2007), *World Cinema's 'Dialogues' With Hollywood*. London: Palgrave Macmillan.

Cooke, Grayson, Warwick Mules and David Baker (2014), Special Issue: The Other Western, *Transformations* 24. Available online: www.transformationsjournal.org/issue-24/. Accessed 19 September 2017.

Desser, David (2003), 'Global Noir: Genre Film in the Age of Transnationalism', in ed. Barry Keith Grant, *Film Genre Reader III*. Austin: University of Texas Press, pp. 516–536.

Esser, Andrea, Miguel Bernal-Merino and Iain Robert Smith, eds (2016), *Media Across Borders: Localizing TV, Film and Video Games*. New York and London: Routledge.

Fisher, Austin, (2009), 'A Marxist's Gotta Do What a Marxist's Gotta Do: Political Violence on the Italian Frontier' *Scope: an Online Journal of Film and Television Studies* 15. Available online: www.nottingham.ac.uk/scope/documents/2009/culturalborrowingsebook.pdf. Accessed 19 September 2017.

—— (2015), 'Spaghettis in Translation', *[in]Transition: Journal of Videographic Film & Moving Image Studies* 2(2). Available online: http://mediacommons.futureofthebook.org/intransition/2015/05/25/spaghettis-translation. Accessed 19 September 2017.

——, ed. (2016), *Spaghetti Westerns at the Crossroads: Studies in Relocation, Transition and Appropriation*. Edinburgh: Edinburgh University Press.

Gledhill, Christine (2007), 'Genre and Nation', in ed. Brian McIlroy, *Genre and Cinema: Ireland and Transnationalism*. New York and London, pp. 11–25.

Hall, Sheldon (2012), 'Carry On, Cowboy: Roast Beef Westerns', *Iluminace: Journal of Film History, Theory, and Aesthetics* 24(3): pp. 102–124.

Hutchinson, Rachael (2006), 'Orientalism or Occidentalism?: Dynamics of Appropriation in Akira Kurosawa' in eds Stephanie Dennison and Song Hwee Lim, *Remapping World Cinema: Identity, Culture and Politics in Film*. London: Wallflower Press, pp. 173–187.

Martin-Jones, David (2012), 'Transnational Allegory/Transnational History: *Se sei vivo spara/Django Kill ... If You Live, Shoot!*', *Transnational Cinemas* 2(2): pp. 179–195.

Miller, Cynthia J., and A. Bowdoin Van Riper, eds (2014), *International Westerns: Re-Locating the Frontier*. Lanham and Plymouth: Scarecrow.

Özkaracalar, Kaya (2003), 'Between Appropriation and Innovation: Turkish Horror Cinema', in ed. Steven Jay Schneider, *Fear Without Frontiers: Horror Cinema Across the Globe*. Guildford: FABPress, pp. 204–217.

Syder, Andrew, and Dolores Tierney (2005), 'Mexploitation/Exploitation: Or, How a Crime-fighting, Vampire-slaying Mexican Wrestler Almost Found Himself in an Italian Sword-and-Sandals Epic', in eds Steven Jay Schneider and Tony Williams, *Horror International*. Detroit: Wayne State University Press, pp. 32–55.

Discussion questions:

- Why do you think certain genres spread transnationally and others don't?
- How do processes of transcultural appropriation help audiences to frame genres through local referents?
- Why do you think there has tended to be a focus on Hollywood in genre studies?
- What difficulties might we encounter in attempting to study non-Hollywood genres?
- Do you think new global distribution practices are helping to make a broader range of genre films accessible?

Bibliography

Adejunmobi, Moradewun A. (2002), 'English and the Audience of an African Popular Culture: The Case of Nigerian Video Film', *Cultural Critique* 50(1): pp. 74–103.

—— (2007), 'Nigerian Video Film As Minor Transnational Practice', *Postcolonial Text* 3(2). Available online: http://postcolonial.org/index.php/pct/article/viewArticle/ 548. Accessed 23 June 2016.

Altman, Rick (1984), 'A Semantic/Syntactic Approach to Film Genre', *Cinema Journal* 23(3): pp. 6–18.

—— (1999), *Film/Genre*. London: British Film Institute.

Anderson, Benedict (1991), *Imagined Communities: Reflections on the Origin and Spread of Nationalism*. 2nd edition. London: Verso.

Andrew, Dudley (2011), 'An Atlas of World Cinema', in eds Timothy Corrigan, Patricia White and Meta Mazaj, *Critical Visions in Film Theory: Classic and Contemporary Readings*. Boston and New York: Bedford/St Martins, pp. 999–1,010.

Appadurai, Arjun (1990), 'Disjuncture and Difference in the Global Cultural Economy', *Theory, Culture & Society* 7(2): pp. 295–310.

—— (1996), *Modernity At Large: Cultural Dimensions of Globalization*. Minneapolis and London: University of Minnesota Press.

Bakhtin, Mikhail (1984), *Rabelais and His World*. Trans. Hélène Iswolsky. Bloomington: Indiana University Press.

Ballesteros, Isolina (2015), *Immigration Cinema in the New Europe*. Bristol and Chicago: Intellect.

Barthes, Roland (1978), 'Death of the Author', in ed. and trans. Stephen Heath, *Image-Music-Text*. London: Fontana, pp. 142–148.

Baschiera, Stefano (2014), 'Streaming World Genre Cinema', *Frames Cinema Journal* (6). Available online: http://framescinemajournal.com/article/streaming-world-genre-cinema/. Accessed 23 June 2016.

Bazin, André (1972a), '*Bicycle Thief*', in ed. and trans. Hugh Gray, *What is Cinema?*, Vol. 2. Berkeley: University of California Press, pp. 47–58.

—— (1972b), *The Western: Or the American Film Par Excellence*. in ed. and trans. Hugh Gray, *What is Cinema?*, Vol. 2. Berkeley: University of California Press, pp. 140–148.

—— (2002), 'An Aesthetic of Reality', in ed. Catherine Fowler, *The European Cinema Reader*. London: Routledge, pp. 56–63.

Behnken, Brian D., and Gregory D. Smithers (2015), *Racism in American Popular Media: From Aunt Jemima to the Frito Bandito*. Santa-Barbara: Praeger.

Bennett, Tony, and Janet Woollacott (2003), 'The Moments of Bond', in ed. Christoph Lindner, *The James Bond Phenomenon: A Critical Reader*. Manchester and New York: Manchester University Press, pp. 13–33.

Bergfelder, Tim (2005), 'The Nation Vanishes: European Co-Productions and Popular Genre Formula in the 1950s and 1960s', in eds Mette Hjort and Scott Mackenzie, *Cinema and Nation*. London: Routledge, pp. 131–142.

—— (2012), 'Love Beyond the Nation: Cosmopolitanism and Transnational Desire in Cinema', in eds Luisa Passerini, Jo Labanyi and Karen Diehl, *Europe and Love in Cinema*. Bristol: Intellect, pp. 59–83.

Berghahn, Daniela (2015), *Head-On (Gegen die Wand)*. London: British Film Institute.

Berghahn, Daniela, and Claudia Sternberg (2010), 'Locating Migrant and Diasporic Cinema', in *European Cinema in Motion: Migrant and Diasporic Film in Contemporary Europe*. London: Palgrave Macmillan, pp. 12–49.

Berry, Chris (2003), '"What's Big About the Big Film?" "De-westernizing" the Blockbuster in Korea and China', in ed. Julian Stringer, *Movie Blockbuster*. London and New York: Routledge, pp. 217–229.

—— (2010), 'What is Transnational Cinema? Thinking from the Chinese Situation', *Transnational Cinemas* 1(2): pp. 111–127.

—— (2011), 'Transnational Chinese Cinema Studies', in eds Song Hwee Lim and Julian Ward, *The Chinese Cinema Book*. London: British Film Institute/Palgrave Macmillan, pp. 9–16.

Berry, Chris, and Mary Farquhar (2006), *China on Screen: Cinema and Nation*. New York: Columbia University Press.

Bertellini, Giorgio (2004), 'Introduction', in *The Cinema of Italy*. London and New York: Wallflower, pp. 1–10.

Bhabha, Homi K. (1990), *Nation and Narration*. London: Routledge.

Bose, Nandana (2013), 'From Superman to Shahenshah: Stardom and the Transnational Corporeality of Hrithik Roshan', in eds Meheli Sen and Anustup Basu, *Figurations in Indian Film*. New York: Palgrave Macmillan, pp. 158–178.

Box Office Mojo (2016), 'Foreign Language Movies at the Box Office'. Available online: www.boxofficemojo.com/genres/chart/?id=foreign.htm. Accessed 7 June 2016.

Breger, Claudia (2014), 'Configuring Affect: Complex World Making in Fatih Akin's *Auf der anderen Seite (The Edge of Heaven)*', *Cinema Journal* 54(1): pp. 65–87.

Brook, Vincent (2009), *Driven to Darkness: Jewish Emigre Directors and the Rise of Film Noir*. New Brunswick and London: Rutgers University Press.

Butler, Judith (1990), *Gender Trouble: Feminism and the Subversion of Identity*. London: Routledge.

Campbell, Neil (2008), *The Rhizomatic West: Representing the American West in a Transnational, Global, Media Age*. Lincoln and London: University of Nebraska Press.

Caoduro, Elena, and Beth Carroll (2014), 'Introduction: Rethinking Genre Beyond Hollywood', *Frames Cinema Journal* (6). Available online: http://framescinema journal.com/article/introduction-rethinking-genre-beyond-hollywood/. Accessed 23 June 2016.

Carroll, Amy Sara (2014), 'From *Papapapá* to *Sleep Dealer*: Alex Rivera's Undocumentary Poetics', in eds Antonio Traverso and Kristi Wilson, *Political Documentary Cinema in Latin America*. Abingdon and New York: Routledge, pp. 211–226.

Celli, Carlo (2004), '*Ladri Di Biciclette/The Bicycle Thieves*', in ed. Giorgio Bertellini, *The Cinema of Italy*. London and New York: Wallflower, pp. 43–50.

Chan, Jachinson (2001), *Chinese American Masculinities: From Fu Manchu to Bruce Lee*. London: Routledge.

Chan, Kenneth (2011), 'The Contemporary Wuxia Revival: Genre Remaking and the Hollywood Transnational Factor', in eds Song Hwee Lim and Julian Ward, *The Chinese Cinema Book*. London: British Film Institute/Palgrave Macmillan, pp. 150–158.

Chapman, James (2007), *Licence to Thrill: A Cultural History of the James Bond Films*. 2nd edition. London and New York: IB Tauris.

Cho, Michelle (2015), 'Genre, Translation, and Transnational Cinema: Kim Jee-woon's *The Good, the Bad, the Weird*', *Cinema Journal* 54(3): pp. 44–68.

Chu, Yiu-wai (2010), 'One Country Two Cultures? Post-1997 Hong Kong Cinema and Co-productions', in Kam Louie, *Hong Kong Culture: Word and Image*. Aberdeen, HK: Hong Kong University Press, pp. 131–145.

Clover, Carol (1992), *Men, Women and Chainsaws: Gender in the Modern Horror Film*. Princeton and Oxford: Princeton University Press.

Coates, Paul (2005), *The Red and the White: The Cinema of People's Poland*. London: Wallflower.

Collins, Jim (2002), 'Genericity in the Nineties: Eclectic Irony and the New Sincerity', in ed. Graeme Turner, *The Film Cultures Reader*. London: Routledge, pp. 276–290.

Cookson, Robert (2013), 'UK film production spending falls 30%', *The Financial Times*, 31 January. Available online: www.ft.com/cms/s/0/d9cc836e-6bdb-11e2-a700-00144feab49a.html. Accessed 3 June 2016.

Council of Europe (2016), 'Details of Treaty No.147: European Convention on Cinematographic Co-Production'. Available online: www.coe.int/en/web/conventions/full-list/-/conventions/treaty/147. Accessed 2 June 2016.

Crofts, Stephen (2006), 'Reconceptualising National Cinema/s', in eds Valentina Vitali and Paul Willemen, *Theorising National Cinema*. London: BFI, pp. 44–58.

Dabashi, Hamid (2001), *Close Up: Iranian Cinema, Past, Present, and Future*. London: Verso.

Davies, Ann (2014), 'Guillermo del Toro's Monsters: Matter Out of Place', in eds Ann Davies, Deborah Shaw and Dolores Tierney, *The Transnational Fantasies of Guillermo del Toro*. New York: Palgrave Macmillan, pp. 29–43.

Davis, Darrell William, and Emilie Yueh-yu Yeh (2008), *East Asian Screen Industries*. London: British Film Institute.

Deleuze, Gilles (2000), *Cinema 2: The Time-Image*. Trans. Hugh Tomlinson and Robert Galeta. London: Athlone.

——— (2001), *Cinema 1: The Movement-Image*. Trans. Hugh Tomlinson and Barbara Habberjam. London: Continuum.

Deleuze, Gilles, and Félix Guattari (1983), *Anti-Oedipus: Capitalism and Schizophrenia*. Trans. Robert Hurley, Mark Seem and Helen R. Lane. Minneapolis: University of Minnesota Press.

———— (1987), *A Thousand Plateaus: Capitalism and Schizophrenia*. Trans. Brian Massumi. London and Minneapolis: University of Minnesota Press.

Denison, Rayna (2015), *Anime: A Critical Introduction*. London and New York: Bloomsbury.

Dennison, Stephanie, and Song Hwee Lim (2006), *Remapping World Cinema: Identity, Culture and Politics in Film*. London and New York: Wallflower.

Desser, David (2008), 'Remaking *Seven Samurai* in World Cinema', in eds Leon Hunt and Leung Wing-fai *East Asian Cinemas: Exploring Transnational Connections on Film*. London and New York: IB Tauris, pp. 17–40.

Deveney, Thomas G. (2012), *Migration in Contemporary Hispanic Cinema*. Lanham and Plymouth: Scarecrow.

Dodds, Klaus (2013), '"I'm Still Not Crossing That": Borders, Dispossession, and Sovereignty in *Frozen River* (2008)', *Geopolitics* 18(3): pp. 560–583.

Doughty, Ruth, and Deborah Shaw (2016), 'Teaching "the World" Through Film: Possibilities and Limitations', in eds Katarzyna Marciniak and Bruce Bennett, *Teaching Transnational Cinema: Politics and Pedagogy*. New York and London: Routledge, pp. 96–104.

Ďurovičová, Nataša (2010a), 'Preface', in (eds) Nataša Ďurovičová and Kathleen Newman, *World Cinemas, Transnational Perspectives*. London and New York: Routledge, pp. ix–xv.

———— (2010b), 'Vector, Flow, Zone: Towards a History of Cinematic Translation', in eds Nataša Ďurovičová and Kathleen Newman, *World Cinemas, Transnational Perspectives*. London and New York: Routledge, pp. 90–120.

Ezra, Elizabeth, and Terry Rowden (2006), 'General Introduction: What is Transnational Cinema?', in *Transnational Cinema: A Film Reader*. Abingdon and New York: Routledge, pp. 1–14.

Fanon, Frantz (2004), *The Wretched of the Earth*. Trans. Richard Philcox. New York: Grove Press.

———— (2008), *Black Skin, White Masks*. London: Pluto.

First Look Studios (2008), 'Takashi Miike's *Sukiyaki Western Django*: Production Notes." 7 September. Available online: www.scifijapan.com/articles/2008/09/07/takashi-miikes-sukiyaki-western-django-production-notes/. Accessed 1 July 2016.

Fisher, Austin (2011), *Radical Frontiers in the Spaghetti Western: Politics, Violence and Popular Italian Cinema*. London and New York: IB Tauris.

———— (2013), 'A Cult Called Django: On The Controversial Tail of A Transnational Bandito', *Cine-Excess* (1). Available online www.cine-excess.co.uk/a-cult-called-django.html

Fisher, Austin, and Iain Robert Smith (2016), 'Transnational Cinemas: A Critical Roundtable', *Frames Cinema Journal* 9. Available online: http://framescinemajournal.com/article/transnational-cinemas-a-critical-roundtable/. Accessed 10 July 2016.

Follows, Stephen (2013), '49 Interesting Facts about the UK Film Industry'. Available online: https://stephenfollows.com/49-interesting-facts-uk-film-industry/. Accessed 3 June 2016.

———— (2015), 'The Scale of Hollywood Remakes and Reboots'. Available online: https://stephenfollows.com/hollywood-remakes-and-reboots/. Accessed 15 June 2016.

Forgacs, David (2007), 'Italians in Algiers', *Interventions* 9(3): pp. 305–364.

Foucault, Michel (1979), 'What is an Author?', *Screen* 20(1): pp. 13–29.

Frayling, Christopher (2006), *Spaghetti Westerns: Cowboys and Europeans from Karl May to Sergio Leone*. London and New York: IB Tauris.

Freire-Medeiros, Bianca (2014), *Touring Poverty*. London and New York: Routledge.

Fu, Poshek, and David Desser (2000), 'Introduction', in *The Cinema of Hong Kong: History, Arts, Identity*. Cambridge: Cambridge University Press, pp. 1–11.

Galt, Rosalind (2011), *Pretty: Film and the Decorative Image*. New York: Columbia University Press.

Gedalof, Irene (2011), 'Finding Home in *Bend It Like Beckham* and *Last Resort*', *Camera Obscura* 26(1): pp. 131–157.

Gerow, Aaron (2002), 'The Empty Return: Circularity and Repetition in Recent Japanese Horror Films', *Minikomi: Informationen des Akademischen Arbeitkreis Japan N.* (64): pp. 19–24.

Gilroy, Paul (2007), 'Shooting Crabs in a Barrel', *Screen* 48(2): pp. 233–235.

Grewal, Inderpal, and Caren Kaplan (1994), *Scattered Hegemonies: Postmodernity and Transnational Feminist Practices*. Minneapolis: University of Minnesota Press.

Gueneli, Berna (2014), 'The Sound of Fatih Akin's Cinema: Polyphony and the Aesthetics of Heterogeneity in *The Edge of Heaven*', *German Studies Review* 37(2): pp. 337–356.

Hall, Stuart (1996), 'When was the Post-colonial? Thinking at the Limit', in eds Iain Chambers and Linda Curti, *The Post-colonial Question: Common Skies, Divided Horizons*. London and New York: Routledge, pp. 242–260.

Haltof, Marek (2004), *The Cinema of Krzysztof Kieślowski: Variations on Destiny and Chance*. London & New York: Wallflower.

Hansen, Miriam (1999), 'The Mass Production of the Senses: Classical Cinema as Vernacular Modernism', *Modernism/modernity* 6(2): pp. 59–77. Available online: https://muse.jhu.edu/article/23266. Accessed 21 June 2016.

Harrison, Nicholas (2007), 'An Interview with Saadi Yacef', *Interventions* 9(3): pp. 405–413.

Henniker, Charlie (2013), 'Pink Rupees or Gay Icons? Accounting for the Camp Appropriation of Male Bollywood Stars', in eds Russell Meeuf and Raphael Raphael, *Transnational Stardom: International Celebrity in Film and Popular Culture*. New York: Palgrave Macmillan, pp. 207–227.

Herbert, Daniel (2010), 'Circulations: Technology and Discourse in *The Ring*', in eds Carolyn Jess-Cooke and Constantine Verevis, *Second Takes: Critical Approaches to the Film Sequel*. Albany: State University of New York Press, pp. 153–170.

Hess, John, and Patricia R. Zimmerman (2006), 'Transnational Documentaries: A Manifesto', in eds Elizabeth Ezra and Terry Rowden, *Transnational Cinema: The Film Reader*. London and New York: Routledge, pp. 97–108.

Higbee, Will (2007), 'Beyond the (Trans)national: Towards a Cinema of Transvergence in Postcolonial and Diasporic Francophone Cinema(s)', *Studies in French Cinema* 7(2): pp. 79–91.

Higbee, Will, and Song Hwee Lim (2010), 'Concepts of Transnational Cinema: Towards a Critical Transnationalism in Film Studies', *Transnational Cinemas* 1(1): pp. 7–21.

Higson, Andrew (2002), 'The Concept of National Cinema', in ed. Catherine Fowler, *The European Cinema Reader*. London: Routledge, pp. 132–142.

———(2006), 'The Limiting Imagination of National Cinema', in eds Elizabeth Ezra and Terry Rowden *Transnational Cinema: A Film Reader*. Abingdon and New York: Routledge, pp. 15–25.

———(2011), *Film England: Culturally English Filmmaking Since the 1990s*. London and New York: IB Tauris.

Hill, John (1992), 'The Issue of National Cinema and British Film Production', in ed. Duncan Petrie, *New Questions of British Cinema*. London: BFI, pp. 10–21.

——— (1994), 'The Future of European Cinema? The Economics and Culture of Pan-European Strategies', in eds John Hill, Martin McLoone and Paul Hainsworth, *Border Crossing: Film in Ireland, Britain and Europe*. Belfast: Institute of Irish Studies, pp. 53–80.

Hills, Matt (2005), 'Ringing the Changes: Cult Distinctions and Cultural Differences in US Fans' Readings of Japanese Horror Cinema', in ed. Jay McRoy, *Japanese Horror Cinema*. Edinburgh: Edinburgh University Press, pp. 161–174.

Hjort, Mette (2010), 'On the Plurality of Cinematic Transnationalism', in eds Nataša Ďurovičová and Kathleen Newman, *World Cinemas, Transnational Perspectives*. London and New York: Routledge, pp. 12–33.

Hudson, Dale (2006), '"Just Play Yourself, "Maggie Cheung"": *Irma Vep*, Rethinking Transnational Stardom and Unthinking National Cinemas', *Screen* 47(2): pp. 213–232.

Hunt, Leon (2003), *Kung Fu Cult Masters: From Bruce Lee to Crouching Tiger*. London and New York: Wallflower.

——— (2008), 'Asiaphilia, Asianisation and the Gatekeeper Auteur: Quentin Tarantino and Luc Besson', in eds Leon Hunt and Leung Wing-Fai, *East Asian Cinemas: Exploring Transnational Connections on Film*. London: IB Tauris, pp. 220–236.

——— (2011), 'The Good, The Bad and the Culturally Inauthentic: The Strange Case of the "Asian Western"', *Asian Cinema* 22(1): pp. 99–109.

Hutcheon, Linda (2006), *A Theory of Adaptation*. New York and London: Routledge.

Inuhiko, Yomota (2007), 'The Menace from the South Seas: Honda Ishirō's *Godzilla* (1954)', in eds Alastair Phillips and Julian Stringer, *Japanese Cinema: Texts and Contexts*. London and New York: Routledge, pp. 102–111.

Iordanova, Dina (2010), 'Rise of the Fringe: Global Cinema's Long Tail', in eds Dina Iordanova, David Martin-Jones and Belén Vidal, *Cinema at the Periphery*. Detroit: Wayne State University Press, pp. 23–45.

Iordanova, Dina, David Martin-Jones, and Belén Vidal (2010), 'Introduction: A Peripheral View of World Cinema', in *Cinema at the Periphery*. Detroit: Wayne State University Press, pp. 1–19.

Iwabuchi, Koichi (2002), *Recentering Globalization: Popular Culture and Japanese Transnationalism*. Durham and London: Duke University Press.

Iyer, Pico (1989), *Video Night in Kathmandu: And Other Reports from the Not-so-Far East*. New York: Vintage Departures.

Jameson, Frederic (1991), *Postmodernism, or the Cultural Logic of Late Modernism*. London: Verso.

Johnson, Randal (2005), 'TV Globo, the MPA, and Contemporary Brazilian Cinema', in eds Lisa Shaw and Stephanie Dennison, *Latin American Cinema: Essays on Modernity, Gender and National Identity*. Jefferson and London: McFarland, pp. 11–38.

Jones, Huw David (2016), 'The Cultural and Economic Implications of UK/European Co-production', *Transnational Cinemas* 7(1): pp. 1–20.

Kim, Soyoung (2005), 'Genre as Contact Zone: Hong Kong Action and Korean *Hwalkuk*', in eds Meaghan Morris, Leung Li Siu and Stephen Ching-kiu Chan, *Hong Kong Connections: Transnational Imagination in Action Cinema*. Durham and London: Duke University Press, pp. 97–110.

Kitses, Jim (1969), *Horizons West: Anthony Mann, Budd Boetticher, Sam Peckinpah: Studies of Authorship within the Western*. Bloomington: Indiana University Press.

Klein, Christina (2004), '*Crouching Tiger, Hidden Dragon*: A Diasporic Reading', *Cinema Journal* 43(4): pp. 18–42.

—— (2007), '*Kung Fu Hustle*: Transnational Production and the Global Chinese-language Film', *Journal of Chinese Cinemas* 1(3): pp. 189–208.

Kountz, Samantha (2015), 'The Other Side of the Wall: Technology and Borders in *Sleep Dealer*', *International Journal of Humanities and Cultural Studies* 1(4): pp. 287–299.

Krings, Matthias, and Onookome Okome (2013), 'Nollywood and it Diaspora: An Introduction', in *Global Nollywood: The Transnational Dimensions of an African Video Film Industry*. Bloomingtom and Indianapolis: Indiana University Press, pp. 1–21.

Kuhn, Annette, and Guy Westwell (2012), *A Dictionary of Film Studies*. Oxford: Oxford University Press.

Lau, Jenny Kwok Wah (2007), "*Hero*: China's response to Hollywood globalization', *Jump Cut: A Review of Contemporary Media* 49. Available online: www.ejumpcut.org/archive/jc49.2007/Lau-Hero/index.html. Accessed 7 June 2016.

Lázaro-Reboll, Antonio (2007), 'The Transnational Reception of *El espinazo del diablo* (Guillermo del Toro 2001)', *Hispanic Research Journal* 8(1): pp. 39–51.

Lee, Vivian P. Y. (2011), 'Introduction: Mapping East Asia's Cinemascape', in *East Asian Cinemas: Regional Flows and Global Transformations*. London: Palgrave Macmillan, pp. 1–12.

—— (2015), 'Staging the "Wild Wild East": Decoding the Western in East Asian Films', in eds Marek Paryz and John R. Leo, *The Post-2000 Film Western: Contexts, Transnationality, Hybridity*. London and New York: Palgrave Macmillan, pp. 147–164.

Lim, Bliss Cua (2009), *Translating Time: Cinema, the Fantastic, and Temporal Critique*. Durham: Duke University Press.

Lin, Feng (2011), 'Glocalizing stardom: Internet Publicity and the Construction of Chow Yun-fat's Transnational Stardom', *Transnational Cinemas* 2(1): pp. 73–91.

Livingstone, Sonia (2013), 'Challenges to Comparative Research in a Globalizing Media Landscape', in eds Frank Esser and Thomas Hanitzsch, *The Handbook of Comparative Communication Research*. New York: Routledge, pp. 415–429.

Lobato, Ramon (2012), *Shadow Economies of Cinema: Mapping Informal Film Distribution*. London: British Film Institute.

Lobato, Ramon, and Mark David Ryan (2011), 'Rethinking Genre Studies through Distribution Analysis: Issues in International Horror Movie Circuits', *New Review of Film and Television Studies* 9(2): pp. 188–203.

Lu, Sheldon Hsiao-peng (1997), *Transnational Chinese Cinemas: Identity, Nationhood, Gender*. Honolulu: University of Hawai'i Press.

Lusted, David (2014), *The Western*. London and New York: Routledge.

Maciel, David R. (1990), *El Norte: The U.S.-Mexican Border in Contemporary Cinema*. San Diego: Institute for Regional Studies of the Californias.

Manuel, George, and Michael Posluns (1974), *The Fourth World: An Indian Reality*. New York: Free Press.

Manzoor, Sarfraz (2011), 'British-Asian Cinema: the Sequel', *The Guardian*. 17 February. Available online: www.theguardian.com/film/2011/feb/17/future-of-british-asian-cinema. Accessed 22 April 2016.

Marchetti, Gina (2006), *From Tian'anmen to Times Square: Transnational China and the Chinese Diaspora on Global Screens, 1989–1997*. Philadelphia: Temple University Press.

Marciniak, Katarzyna, and Bruce Bennett (2016), 'Introduction: Teaching Transnational Cinema: Politics and Pedagogy', in *Teaching Transnational Cinema: Politics and Pedagogy*. New York and London: Routledge, pp. 1–35.

Marciniak, Katarzyna, Anikó Imre, and Áine O'Healy (2007), 'Introduction: Mapping Transnational Feminist Media Studies', in *Transnational Feminism in Film and Media*. New York and Basingstoke: Palgrave Macmillan, pp. 1–18.

Marks, Laura U. (2000), *Skin of the Film: Intercultural Cinema, Embodiment and the Senses*. Durham: Duke University Press.

Martin, Daniel (2009), 'Japan's *Blair Witch*: Restraint, Maturity, and Generic Canons in the British Critical Reception of *Ring*', *Cinema Journal* 48(3): pp. 35–51.

Martin-Jones, David (2006), *Deleuze, Cinema and National Identity: Narrative Time in National Contexts*. Edinburgh: Edinburgh University Press.

Mathijs, Ernest, and Xavier Mendik (2008), 'Editorial Introduction: What is Cult Film?', in *The Cult Film Reader*. Maidenhead: Open University Press, pp. 1–11.

Mazdon, Lucy (2000), *Encore Hollywood: Remaking French Cinema*. London: British Film Institute.

McDonald, Keith, and Roger Clark (2014), *Guillermo del Toro: Film as Alchemic Art*. New York and London: Bloomsbury.

Meeuf, Russell, and Raphael Raphael (2013), 'Introduction', in *Transnational Stardom: International Celebrity in Film and Popular Culture*. New York: Palgrave Macmillan, pp. 1–16.

Mizsei-Ward, Rachel (2011), 'Film Review of *The Karate Kid* (1984) and *The Karate Kid* (2010)', *Scope: An Online Journal of Film and Television Studies* (20). Available online: www.academia.edu/16067657/Film_Review_of_The_Karate_Kid_1984_and_The_Karate_Kid_2010_. Accessed 7 June 2016.

Monar, Francisco R. (2014), '*Sin nombre*, *Norteado*, and the Contours of Genre and La Frontera', *Frames Cinema Journal* (6). Available online: http://framescinemajournal.com/article/sin-nombre-norteado-and-the-contours-of-genre-and-la-frontera/. Accessed 7 July 2016.

Morris, Meaghan (2004), 'Transnational Imagination in Action Cinema: Hong Kong and the Making of a Global Popular Culture', *Inter-Asia Cultural Studies* 5(2): pp. 181–199.

—— (2005), 'Introduction: Hong Kong Connections', in eds Meaghan Morris, Siu-Leung Li and Stephen Ching-Kiu Chan, *Hong Kong Connections: Transnational Imagination in Action Cinema*. Durham and London: Duke University Press, pp. 1–18.

Naficy, Hamid (2001), *An Accented Cinema: Exilic and Diasporic Filmmaking*. Oxford: Princeton University Press.

—— (2003), 'Phobic Spaces and Liminal Panics: Independent Transnational Film Genre', in eds Ella Shohat and Robert Stam, *Multiculturalism, Postcoloniality, and Transnational Media*. New Brunswick: Rutgers University Press, pp. 203–226.

—— (2012), *A Social History of Iranian Cinema, Vol. 4: The Globalizing Era, 1984–2010*. Durham: Duke University Press.

Nagib, Lúcia (2004), 'Talking Bullets: The Language of Violence in *City of God*', *Third Text* 18(3): pp. 239–250.

—— (2006), 'Towards a Positive Definition of World Cinema', in eds Stephanie Dennison and Song Hwee Lim, *Remapping World Cinema: Identity, Culture and Politics in Film*. London and New York: Wallflower, pp. 30–37.

Nagib, Lúcia, Chris Perriam, and Rajinder Dudrah (2012), *Theorizing World Cinema*. London and New York: IB Tauris.

Newman, Kathleen (2010), 'Notes on Transnational Film Theory: Decentered Subjectivity, Decentered Capitalism', in eds Nataša Ďurovičová and Kathleen Newman, *World Cinemas, Transnational Perspectives*. London and New York: Routledge, pp. 3–11.

Noriega, Chon (1987), '*Godzilla* and the Japanese Nightmare: When "Them!" Is U.S.', *Cinema Journal* 27(1): pp. 63–77.

Nornes, Abé Mark (2007), *Cinema Babel: Translating Global Cinema*. Minneapolis and London: University of Minnesota Press.

Oliete-Aldea, Elena, Beatriz Oria, and Juan A. Tarancón (2016), 'Introduction: Questions of Transnationalism and Genre', in *Global Genres, Local Films: The Transnational Dimension of Spanish Cinema*. New York and London: Bloomsbury, pp. 1–15.

Ong, Aihwa (1999), *Flexible Citizenship: The Cultural Logics of Transnationality*. Durham and London: Duke University Press.

O'Regan, Tom (1999), 'Cultural Exchange' in eds Toby Miller and Robert Stam, *A Companion to Film Theory*. Oxford: Blackwell, pp. 262–294.

Pang, Laikwan (2004), 'Mediating the Ethics of Technology: Hollywood and Media Piracy', *Culture, Theory and Critique* 45(1): pp. 19–32.

Peberdy, Donna (2014), 'All the World's a Stage: Global Players and Transnational Film Performance', *Transnational Cinemas* 5(2): pp. 95–97.

Perneczky, Nikolaus (2014), 'Continual Re-enchantment: Tunde Kelani's Village Films and the Spectres of Early African Cinema', *Frames Cinema Journal* (6). Available online: http://framescinemajournal.com/article/continual-re-enchantment-tunde-kelan-is-village-films-and-the-spectres-of-early-african-cinema/. Accessed 23 June 2016.

Prasch, Thomas (2013), 'Aquaterrorists and Cybraceros: The Dystopian Borderlands of Alex Rivera's *Sleep Dealer* (2008)', in eds Jakub Kazecki, Karen A. Ritzenhoff and Cynthia J. Miller, *Border Visions: Identity and Diaspora in Film*. Lanham: Scarecrow, pp. 43–58.

Prashad, Vijay (2001), *Everybody was Kung Fu Fighting: Afro-Asian Connections and the Myth of Cultural Purity*. Boston: Beacon.

Raussert, Wilfred (2011), 'Inter-American Border DIscourses, Heterotopia, and Translocal Communities in Courtney Hunt's *Frozen River*', *NORTEAMÉRICA* 6(1): pp. 15–33.

Rawle, Steven (2009), 'From The Black Society to The Isle: Miike Takashi and Kim Ki-Duk at the intersection of Asia Extreme', *Journal of Japanese and Korean Cinema* 1(2): pp. 167–184.

—— (2011), 'Transnational, Transgeneric, Transgressive: Tracing Miike Takashi's Yakuza Cyborgs to Sukiyaki Westerns', *Asian Cinema* 22(1): pp. 83–98.

—— (2014), 'The Ultimate Super-Happy-Zombie-Romance-Murder-Mystery-Family-Comedy-Karaoke-Disaster-Movie-Part-Animated-Remake-All-Singing-All-Dancing-Musical-Spectacular-Extravaganza: Miike Takashi's *The Happiness of the Katakuris* as "cult" hybrid', in eds Leon Hunt, Sharon Lockyer and Milly Williamson, *Screening the Undead: Vampires and Zombies in Film and Television*. London: IB Tauris, pp. 208–232.

Richards, Jeffrey (1997), *Films and British National Identity: From Dickens to Dad's Army*. Manchester: Manchester University Press.

Rings, Guido (2011), 'Questions of Identity: Cultural Encounters in Gurinder Chadha's *Bend it Like Beckham*', *Journal of Popular Film & Television* 39(3): pp. 114–123.

Rocha, Glauber (1995), 'An Esthetic of Hunger', in eds Randal Johnson and Robert Stam, *Brazilian Cinema*. New York: Columbia University Press, pp. 68–71.

Rose, Steve (2013), 'Why Hollywood Doesn't Get South Korean Cinema', *The Guardian*, 29 November. Available online: www.theguardian.com/film/2013/nov/29/old-boyremake-south-korea-cinema. Accessed 19 February 2016.

Rosen, Philip (2006), 'History, Textuality, Nation: Kracauer, Burch and Some of the Problems in the Study of National Cinema', in eds Valentina Vitali and Paul Willemen, *Theorising National Cinema*. London: BFI, pp. 17–28.

Ruberto, Laura E., and Kristi M. Wilson, eds (2007), *Italian Neorealism and Global Cinema*. Detroit: Wayne State University Press.

Saeys, Arne (2013), 'Imag(in)ed Diversity: Migration in European Cinema', in eds Brian Michael Goss and Christopher Chávez, *Identity: Beyond Tradition and McWorld Neoliberalism*. Newcastle upon Tyne: Cambridge Scholars Press, pp. 27–45.

Said, Edward W. (2003), *Orientalism*. London: Penguin.

Schilling, Mark (2007), 'Sukiyaki Western Django: Spaghetti Western Served up in Japan', *The Japan Times Online*, 14 September. Available online: www.japantimes.co.jp/culture/20007/09/14/films/film-reviews/sukiyaki-western-django. Accessed 1 July 2016.

Sconce, Jeffrey (1995), '"Trashing" the Academy: Taste, Excess, and an Emerging Politics of Cinematic Style', *Screen* 36(4): pp. 371–393.

Shaw, Deborah (2013), 'Deconstructing and Reconstructing "Transnational Cinema"', in ed. Stephanie Dennison, *Contemporary Hispanic Cinema: Interrogating Transnationalism in Spanish and Latin American film*. Woodbridge: Tamesis, pp. 47–66.

Shaw, Deborah, and Armida De La Garza (2010), 'Introducing Transnational Cinemas', *Transnational Cinemas* 1(1): pp. 3–6.

Shaw, Miranda (2005), 'The Brazilian *Goodfellas*: *City of God* as a Gangster Film', in ed. Else Veira, *City of God in Several Voices*. Nottingham: Critical, Cultural and Communications, pp. 58–69.

Shiel, Mark (2006), *Italian Neorealism: Rebuilding the Cinematic City*. New York: Columbia University Press.

Shin, Chi-Yun (2008), 'Art of Branding: Tartan "Asia Extreme" Films', *Jump Cut: A Review of Contemporary Media* 50. Available online: www.ejumpcut.org/archive/jc50.2008/TartanDist/. Accessed 30 August 2017.

—— (2012), '"Excessive" Remake: From *The Quiet Family* to *The Happiness of the Katakuris*', *Transnational Cinemas* 3(1): pp. 67–79.

Shingler, Martin (2014), 'Aishwarya Rai Bachchan: from Miss World to World star', *Transnational Cinemas* 5(2): pp. 98–110.

Shohat, Ella (2003), 'Post-Third-Worldist Culture: Gender, Nation, and the Cinema', in eds Anthony R. Guneratne and Wimal Dissanayake, *Rethinking Third Cinema*. New York and London: Routledge, pp. 51–78.

Shohat, Ella, and Robert Stam (1994), *Unthinking Eurocentrism: Multiculturalism and the Media*. London and New York: Routledge.

Smith, Iain Robert (2013), '"You're Really a Miniature Bond": Weng Weng and the Transnational Dimension of Cult Film Stardom', in eds Kate Egan and Sarah Thomas, *Cult Film Stardom: Offbeat Attractions and Processes of Cultification*. London: Palgrave Macmillan, pp. 226–239.

—— (2017), *The Hollywood Meme: Transnational Adaptations in World Cinema*. Edinburgh: Edinburgh University Press.

Solanas, Fernando, and Octavio Getino (1985), 'Towards a Third Cinema', in eds Bill Nichols, *Movies and Methods*, vol. 2. Berkeley: University of California Press, pp. 44–64.

Spence, Alex (2016), '*Star Wars*: Disney got £31 million from UK taxman for *Force Awakens*', *Politico*. Available online: www.politico.eu/blogs/spence-on-media/2016/03/star-wars-disney-got-31-million-from-uk-taxman-for-force-awakens/. Accessed 30 August 2017.

Spicer, Andrew (2001), *Typical Men: The Representation of Masculinity in Popular British Culture*. London and New York: IB Tauris.

Spivak, Gayatri Chakravorty (1988), 'Can the Subaltern Speak?', in eds Cary Nelson and Lawrence Grossberg, *Marxism and the Interpretation of Culture*. Chicago and Urbana: University of Illinois Press, pp. 271–313.

Staiger, Janet (2003), 'Hybrid or Inbred: The Purity Hypothesis and Hollywood Genre History', in ed. Barry Keith Grant, *Film Genre Reader III*. Austin: University of Texas Press, pp. 185–199.

Stam, Robert (2003a), 'Beyond Third Cinema: The Aesthetics of Hybridity', in eds Anthony R. Guneratne and Wimal Dissanayake, *Rethinking Third Cinema*. New York and London: Routledge, pp. 31–50.

—— (2003b), 'Fanon, Algeria, and the Cinema: The Politics of Identification', in eds Ella Shohat and Robert Stam, *Multiculturalism, Postcoloniality, and Transnational Media*. New Brunswick and London: Rutgers University Press, pp. 18–43.

Stam, Robert, and João Luiz Vieira (1990), 'Parody and Marginality: The Case of Brazilian Cinema', in eds Manuel Alvarado and John O. Thompson, *The Media Reader*. London: British Film Institute, pp. 82–104.

Stam, Robert, and Louise Spence (1983), 'Colonialism, Racism and Representation: An Introduction', *Screen* 24(2): pp. 2–20.

Stringer, Julian (2007), 'The Original and the Copy: Nakata Hideo's *Ring* (1998)', in eds Alastair Phillips and Julian Stringer, *Japanese Cinema: Texts and Contexts*. London and New York: Routledge, pp. 296–307.

Tartaglione, Nancy (2016), '*Crouching Tiger, Hidden Dragon: Sword of Destiny* Tops $32M In China As Netflix Begins International Rollout', *Deadline Hollywood*, 26 February. Available online: http://deadline.com/2016/02/crouching-tiger-hidden-dragon-sword-of-destiny-sequel-china-box-office-netflix-1201709675/. Accessed 7 June 2016.

The Numbers (2016), 'Box Office History for James Bond Movies'. Available online: www.the-numbers.com/movies/franchise/James-Bond#tab=summary. Accessed 2 June 2016.

Truffaut, François (1976), 'A Certain Tendency of the French Cinema', in ed. Bill Nichols, *Movies and Methods,* vol. 1. Berkeley: University of California Press, pp. 224–237.

Tsutsui, William (2004), *Godzilla on My Mind: Fifty Years of the King of Monsters*. New York: Palgrave Macmillan.

—— (2014), 'For Godzilla and Country: How a Japanese Monster Became an American Icon', *Foreign Affairs*, 28 March. Available online: www.foreign affairs.com/articles/141472/william-m-tsutsui/for-godzilla-and-country. Accessed 4 December 2015.

Ugor, Paul (2013), 'Nollywood and Postcolonial Predicaments: Transnationalism, Gender, and the Commoditization of Desire in *Glamour Girls'*, in eds Matthias Krings and Onookome Okome, *Global Nollywood: The Transnational Dimensions of an African Video Film Industry*. Bloomington and Indianapolis: Indiana University Press, pp. 158–175.

Vann, Michael G. (2002), 'The Colonial Casbah on the Silver Screen: Using *Pepe le Moko* and *The Battle of Algiers* to Teach Colonialism, Race, and Globalization in French History', *Radical History Review* 83(1): pp. 186–193.

Varndell, Daniel (2014), *Hollywood Remakes, Deleuze and The Grandfather Paradox*. London: Palgrave Macmillan.

Verevis, Constantine (2004), 'Remaking Film', *Film Studies* 4: pp. 87–103.

—— (2006), *Film Remakes*. Edinburgh: Edinburgh University Press.

Vieira, Else R. P. (2007), '*Cidade de Deus*: Challenges to Hollywood, Steps to *The Constant Gardener*', in eds Deborah Shaw, *Contemporary Latin American Cinema: Breaking into the Global Market*. Lanham: Rowman & Littlefield, pp. 51–66.

Vieira, Joao Luiz. (1995), 'From *High Noon* to *Jaws*: Carnival and Parody in Brazilian Cinema', in eds Robert Stam and Randal Johnson, *Brazilian Cinema*. New York: Columbia University Press, pp. 256–269.

Vitali, Valentina, and Paul Willemen (2006), 'Introduction', in *Theorising National Cinema*. London: BFI, pp. 1–14.

Wada-Marciano, Mitsuyo (2009), 'J-horror: New Media's Impact on Contemporary Japanese Horror Cinema', in eds Jinhee Choi and Mitsuyo Wada-Marciano, *Horror to the Extreme: Changing Boundaries in Asian Cinema*. Aberdeen, Hong Kong: Hong Kong University Press, pp. 15–37.

Wang, Yiman (2013), *Remaking Chinese Cinema: Through the Prism of Shanghai, Hong Kong, and Hollywood*. Hong Kong: Hong Kong University Press.

Ward, Glenn (2014), '"There Is No Such Thing": Del Toro's Metafictional Monster Rally', in eds Ann Davies, Deborah Shaw and Dolores Tierney, *The Transnational Fantasies of Guillermo del Toro*. New York: Palgrave Macmillan, pp. 11–28.

Warshow, Robert (2001), 'Movie Chronicle: The Westerner', in *The Immediate Experience: Movies, Comics, Theatre & Other Aspects of Popular Culture*. Cambridge and London: Harvard University Press, pp. 105–124.

Watt, Michael (2000), '"Do You Speak Christian?" Dubbing and the Manipulation of the Cinematic Experience', *Bright Lights Film Journal*, 1 July. Available online: http://brightlightsfilm.com/speak-christian-dubbing-manipulation-cinematicexperience/#.V3JLoDWg9l0. Accessed 28 June 2016.

Wheatley, Catherine (2011), *Cache (Hidden)*. London: BFI.

White, Bill (2008), '"Sukiyaki Western Django" is too Absurd and Predictable to be Any Fun to Watch', *Seattle Post-Intelligencer*, 2 October. Available online: www.seattlepi.com/movies/381526_suzuki03q.html. Accessed 1 July 2016.

Willemen, Paul (2006), 'The National Revisited', in eds Valentina Vitali and Paul Willemen, *Theorising National Cinema*. London: BFI, pp. 29–43.

Wilson, Emma (2009), *Atom Egoyan*. Urbana and Chicago: University of Illinois Press.

Wright, Will (1975), *Sixguns and Society: A Structural Study of the Western*. Berkeley: University of California Press.

Xu, Gary G. (2007), *Sinascape: Contemporary Chinese Cinema*. Lanham and Plymouth: Rowman & Littlefield.

—— (2008), 'Remaking East Asia, Outsourcing Hollywood', in eds Leon Hunt and Leung Wing-fai, *East Asian Cinemas: Exploring Transnational Connections on Film*. London and New York: IB Tauris, pp. 191–202.

Yecies, Brian M. (2007), 'Parleying Culture against Trade: Hollywood's Affairs with Korea's Screen Quotas', *Korea Observer* 38(1): pp. 1–32.

Yu, Sabrina Qiong (2012), *Jet Li: Chinese Masculinity and Transnational Film Stardom*. Edinburgh: Edinburgh University Press.

Zaniello, Tom (2007), *The Cinema of Globalization: A Guide to Films About the New Economic Order*. Ithaca and London: Cornell University Press.

Zavattini, Cesare (2000), 'Some Ideas on the Cinema', in ed. Aristides Gazetas, *An Introduction to World Cinema*. Jefferson and London: McFarland, pp. 143–150.

Zhang, Yingjin (1998), 'Transnational Cinema: Mainland China, Hong Kong and Taiwan', in eds Yingjin Zhang and Zhiwei Xiao, *Encyclopedia of Chinese Film*. London and New York: Routledge, pp. 63–65.

—— (2006), 'Comparative Film Studies, Transnational Film Studies: Interdisciplinarity, Crossmediality, and Transcultural Visuality in Chinese Cinema', *Journal of Chinese Cinemas* 1(1): pp. 27–40.

——— (2011), 'National Cinema as Translocal Practice', in eds Song Hwee Lim and Julian Ward, *The Chinese Cinema Book*. London: British Film Institute/Palgrave Macmillan, pp. 17–25.

Zulian, Paula (2013), '"*City of God – 10 Years Later*" Co-Director on Where the Stars of the Brazilian Hit Are Today (Q&A)', *Hollywood Reporter*, 12 October. Available online: www.hollywoodreporter.com/news/city-god-10-years-director-648069. Accessed 21 January 2016.

Index